MW00776011

DAVID THOMPSON
Skywalker

David Thompson
with Sean Stormes
and Marshall Terrill

Sports Publishing L.L.C.
www.SportsPublishingLLC.com

© 2003 David Thompson, Sean Stormes and Marshall Terrill
All Rights Reserved.

Director of production: Susan M. Moyer
Project manager: Greg Hickman
Developmental editor: Erin Linden-Levy
Copy editor: Cynthia L. McNew
Dust jacket design: Kerri Baker

ISBN: 1-58261-652-3

Printed in the United States.

SPORTS PUBLISHING L.L.C.
www.SportsPublishingLLC.com

ACKNOWLEDGMENTS

The authors wish to thank, in alphabetical order, the following people for their various contributions to this book: Larry Berman, Eddie Biedenbach, Charlie Board, Crystal Carpenter, Tom Castleman, Steve Cernich, Rick Clemens, Pete Ehrmann, Arthur Hundhausen, Stan Korczak, Greg Korn, Meagan Krause, Doug Murren, Ed Peeler, Jerry Phillips, Terry Pluto, Norm Sloan, Carolyn Terrill, Mike Terrill, Zoe Terrill, Robert Walker and Bill Walton.

CONTENTS

FOREWORD BY BILL WALTON

The Day the Earth Stood Still

How do you write a foreword for a book about someone who ruined your life?

March 23, 1974...One of the bleakest days in the history of Western Civilization...North Carolina State 80, UCLA 77...Double overtime.

Playing for Coach John Wooden was a dream come true for all of us at UCLA in the early 1970s. Not so much for the basketball—although that was pretty good—but rather for the daily lessons of life that we, as young college students, learned from this master teacher. He reminded us every day to do our best and to not beat ourselves, because that would be the worst kind of defeat that we would ever suffer and that we would never get over it. We thought Coach Wooden was nuts—a walking antique, totally out of touch with the modern world with all his silly little maxims. It wasn't until, as college seniors, we suffered the kind of major adversity that he alone expected that we started to think even for a nanosecond that he might have the slightest clue as to what was going on.

I have relived that fateful spring day in Greensboro, North Carolina for the last 29 years, turning it all over time and time again, trying to figure out how things could possibly go so wrong. After all the successes at UCLA—the flawless execution, the team game, the style, the records, the domination—to have it all come crashing down so hard...My heart, soul and psyche have been tortured for almost three decades now with the devastating knowledge that we, the mighty Bruins from UCLA, lost a championship-level NCAA Tournament game after leading by 11 points late in the second half. We had suffered a painful flameout in the second overtime after being up by seven points with just scant seconds remaining. To have this all happening in an era that predated the shot clock and three-point line in college basketball only pours salt on the festering wound. During all of the lonely years, desolation and the abject misery that comes with falling flat on your face with everything on the line and the whole world watching, I have been able to put salve on my eternal wounds with the somewhat comforting rationalization that we really blew it that day:

If we only could have just one more shot at the infidels from North Carolina State so that we could finally put to rest all of our demons and restore proper order to the universe. I now realize, after all the tears, sleepless nights, sadness, and inner turmoil, how wrong I have been for all this time. We lost that horrendous day not because we beat ourselves; we lost to a better player and ultimately a better person.

David Thompson was the single greatest college player whom I ever played against. He would easily have been one of the greatest professionals to have ever played had he not torn up that magnificent body that carried his dreams. David Thompson is a unique gem who represents the best of what our world has to offer. Hailing from the most humble of backgrounds, he made a life for himself through an activity that he loved and mastered, only to have it all taken away by a few awkward landings. But then, more importantly, he built a new and, eventually, better life by picking himself up off the scrap heap of failure, defeat and despair—discarded by those who used him for their own selfish ends—and made the world a saner, more compassionate place because of the quality of his soul.

As great a player as David Thompson was—and there were none better in his day—he has become a better man. If you have any appreciation of how terrific David was when he walked out onto that basketball court, you know that is hard to do.

How can you recognize, honor and respect the talents of someone whose career was like a comet—flaming through our universe, so bright, so hot, so mercurial, but ultimately touching us for such a brief moment? How can you evaluate how special this man who could fly was when he predated ESPN, cable television, *USA Today* and even VCRs, the whole time playing in an era when it was against the rules to throw it down?

As a player, David Thompson was Michael Jordan, Kobe Bryant, Tracy McGrady and LeBron James rolled into one. There has never been anyone like him, no one who could do the things that he did so routinely. So petite—tiny actually—yet conquering a world dominated by giants.

David Thompson was barely 6'3", but he epitomized so many of John Wooden's maxims that we, for so long, considered ludicrous…

"Be quick, but don't hurry." David Thompson was as quick as a hummingbird, but never out of control.

"Failing to prepare is preparing to fail." The lifetime of commitment always so evident in his game, but sadly overlooked because of the unparalleled physical gifts that made his accomplishments seem so effortless.

"Happiness begins when selfishness ends." He was the consummate team player, who was all about winning while making his less talented teammates the stars of his show.

"It's not how big you are; it's how big you play." So small, so delicate, so fragile, but David was a true giant, dwarfing other mere mortals.

"It's not how high you jump; it's where you are and when you jump that matters." They called him "Skywalker," but David Thompson personified Wooden's basic tenant—basketball is not a game of size and strength, but rather a game of skill, timing and positioning.

David Thompson's game predated the era of hype and self-promotion. He was so good that he didn't need it.

David was such a special player. Every time he walked on the court he had to play against someone bigger, stronger and more powerful than he was. He has the smallest of hands. He cannot palm the ball, but he was as prolific a dunker as the game has ever seen. He had to cup or cradle the ball to throw it down, making his devastating jams all the more remarkable. Words cannot describe or legitimize the physical gifts that David Thompson had. You had to personally witness the amazing flights of fancy…even then you were somewhat skeptical that this was some sort of animation or special effect.

Combined with David's incomparable and incomprehensible abilities to soar ever higher for balls that were totally out of reach for everybody else was his sense of anticipation. David was always the first to the ball in spite of the fact that he had further to go. His game and his body were visually perfect—as pure and clean as crystal. More importantly, though, David had a real basketball game: a masterful shooting touch with virtually unlimited range; exquisite ball-handling skills—the ball an extension of his creative and expansive mind; and extremely long arms that complemented his phenomenal work ethic and translated into him becoming an outstanding defender. But even his rare combination of power, skill and finesse cannot come remotely close to revealing the real core of David Thompson. More than anything, it was David's heart, soul and mind that made him as fine a player and person as has ever played this game.

It was always a privilege to play against David Thompson. He personified class and dignity. He brought such raging energy and passion to everything that he did. And he always had fun. David Thompson presented to me the greatest of challenges. David Thompson never stopped attacking, never stopped coming at you. Some opponents would settle for the easy play, often pulling back if they weren't sure they could get it done in the face of adversity. David Thompson was relentlessly determined and convinced that he was going to put it in your face every time. The epic battles, contested high in the stratosphere, were what we lived for, even though he usually won. And I was a player who absolutely had to win…

And then the injuries… First the knee, followed shortly thereafter by the shoulder. It was a different world in those days. News traveled slowly and was often sketchy, but it was as if somebody took *my* life away—David Thompson was my motivation. He drove me to heights that I never could have reached by myself. I lived to play against this master of the universe. I saw how the devastating pain and the resultant limitations changed his life. I saw the glow of the brightest star go dark. We were all shortchanged. It ruined me and made the world a lesser place. Imagine what it did to him…

David Thompson's injuries changed the course of history, but they have become the best part of his story. The tale is now longer of one of the greatest ball players to ever grace the game—so perfect in so many ways that he was a first-ballot Hall of Famer. The real saga now is of a man who was cruelly denied his dreams, yet fought on to play in the bigger game of life. The life story of David Thompson is really "The Greatest Story Ever Told." Life is easy when you're hot…David's story is: What do you do when the ball bounces the other way?

I regularly think back to the spring of 1974…Nixon, Vietnam, Watergate, the end of UCLA's run to glory—all signs of the death of hope. I have said many times that I wish I could have that one week to live over—that week leading up to and including March 23, 1974. Missed opportunities are the bane of my existence. We had the chance to do something special at UCLA in those days, but the errant shots, the missed rebounds, the careless turnovers, the minute-by-minute preparation…Oh, to have one more crack at it…

In the three years that I played varsity basketball for John Wooden, he *never* mentioned the other team and certainly no individual opponent—preferring to focus on what we needed to do. The *one* exception was David Thompson, in the hours leading up to that fateful day. Maybe Coach should have said a bit more. It took a rare jewel like David Thompson to wreck what we had. In retrospect today, as much as I would like to have it to do over, I am no longer convinced that it would have made any difference. David Thompson was that good. He was so good, he could have played for UCLA…

PROLOGUE

The good Lord only gives us one life to live, one life to maximize. I have learned the hard way that this one precious chance is not to be taken lightly. Though I have been successful for the majority of my life, I have also tasted bitter, personal defeat. And that is why I decided to finally share my life story—because there is so much to be learned from hard work, achieving success, temptation, failure, resiliency, perseverance, love of family, and love of God.

There are other important reasons I welcomed this endeavor. As I approach my 50th birthday, I feel a stronger need for reflection and the comfort it can provide. I also have a better understanding and appreciation today of my place in basketball history. With so many great memories, I felt it would be selfish to keep them all to myself.

Because I have apparently touched other people's lives, I thought this book would give me a unique opportunity to tell you who has touched *my own life* so profoundly. My family, former coaches and teammates, and a strong faith in God have all played compelling roles in the life story of David Thompson. I want you to have the pleasure of knowing each of these people who have so profoundly influenced and guided my life.

Opening the doors to my life did not happen without strong reservation. I feared that the darker moments in my life might overshadow my accomplishments and the important work I do today. But I realized that everyone has obstacles to overcome—that everyone has baggage—and that what is most important is how you deal with it, and what you *learn* from it. I have learned some of life's greatest lessons from my mistakes, and that has helped me become the man I am today.

Please understand that mine is not another story about a ghetto kid who escaped the inner city only to find fame, fortune and, ultimately, despair. The fact is, I was raised in the country—in a small town in rural North Carolina at the foot of the Appalachian Mountains—by a loving, Christian family. We didn't have much money, but my parents worked hard and sacrificed for me and my 10 brothers and sisters. The values they taught me served me well. I am very proud of the fact, for example, that I stayed all four years in college while the trend was to go to the pros early via the "Hardship Rule."

I was one of the first players to play the game "above the rim," which was how I acquired the nickname "Skywalker." My game appeared spectacular, because I blended sound fundamental skills with eye-popping athleticism—including a 42-inch vertical leap. To soar like that today is common, but in the early 1970s, it was—*revolutionary.* It became the stuff of legend that I could pluck a quarter from the top of a backboard and leave change.

I am thankful for so much. In my sophomore year at North Carolina State we went 27-0, but could not participate in the NCAA Tournament because of previous recruiting violations involving me. The next year we won the national championship, ending UCLA's seven-year stranglehold on the title. I was a two-time College Player of the Year, and we became the only ACC team to finish undefeated in the conference two consecutive years. It was a wondrous time for me, both athletically and personally. Consider, too, that the "Alley-Oop" play was invented by me and my good friend, Monte Towe.

My first season as a professional was surreal. The No. 1 pick in the NBA draft had always signed with an NBA team—until me. I chose to play for the Denver Nuggets of the upstart American Basketball Association, and many experts cite this watershed event as the catalyst for the NBA/ABA merger that occurred the following year. I was the MVP of the All-Star Game, Rookie of the Year, first team All-Pro, and battled Julius "Dr. J" Erving and the eventual champion New York Nets in a memorable six-game final. I experienced all this and was only 21 years old. I played over 100 games that year, and the resulting physical and mental exhaustion led me to the worst decision of my life—experimenting with cocaine. It would become my poison, ruining my dreams and almost ruining my life.

Following the league merger, my NBA career started right where my incredible rookie season had left off. I was once again voted a first-team All-Star and led the Nuggets into the playoffs. Then in 1978, heading into the last game of the season, I was within a few percentage points of the league individual scoring title. I came through with a 73-point effort against the Detroit Pistons. It was an afternoon game, and that night George "The Iceman" Gervin of the San Antonio Spurs responded with 63 points against the New Orleans Jazz to edge me out for the crown. The 73 points is still the third highest single-game point total in the history of the NBA.

My basketball talents brought me fame and money. In 1978, I signed a contract for $4 million, spread over five years. This made me the highest-paid player in the history of the game. But I eventually discovered that neither fame nor money could deliver true happiness. My bouts with drugs and alcohol hastened my exit from the game I loved, but my long road back to sobriety taught me how to be a better husband, a better father, a better friend—a better man.

Today, as I attempt to positively influence people, young and old, with the work I do, I often recount my basketball exploits, but I make sure to let people know that the values I learned from my parents are still the most effective blueprint for success and happiness I have ever known. I have been sober for 15 years now, and my purpose in life is clear to me.

I was renowned for my leaping ability, and now I hope my story is able to lift you up to new heights. I may not have been the greatest player in the history of the game, but I have become a better person as a result.

David Thompson
May 2003

CHAPTER 1

OUT IN THE COUNTRY

I t all started in North Carolina. To be more specific, in the foothills of the Appalachian Mountains. Cleveland County, to get even more fussy about it.

Or, as a writer once put it so succinctly, "Nine miles from Shelby, and three miles from nowhere."

At the time, it was nowhere.

My hometown was a rural area primarily composed of pastures, woods, land and cotton and soybeans. The land was also inhabited by cows and other farm animals. This lush, green, beautiful country served as the backdrop of my youth.

Even today I have family who live off that same rural tobacco road I once called home. And it was my family that would serve as the common thread in a roller-coaster life filled with the highest of highs and the lowest of lows.

On July 13, 1954, David O'Neal Thompson entered the world with an assist from doctors at Boiling Springs General Hospital. I was the baby— the 11th and final child of Vellie and Ida Thompson, the two best parents a person could have ever been blessed with. How two people could have raised 11 children with such meager resources has always astounded me, yet they provided us with a life that was decent, full and virtuous. They loved us children deeply and never complained about the daunting task it must have been to raise a house full of kids on an income that barely surpassed minimum wage.

Life was never boring with 13 people under one roof, that's for sure. Sara, my oldest sister, left the house when I was fairly young. My oldest brother was Furman, and then came Johnny, who passed away in 1991. Irene, Mary, Margaret, Joyce, Sara, Etta Mae (who also passed away a few years ago), and Pecora rounded out the girls. Vellie Jr., the fourth youngest—and seven years older than me—played an important role in my life during my formative years. I was also close to my sister Pecora, because she was only one grade ahead of me in school.

The Thompson clan resided in a pale yellow modest cinderblock house at the end of a dirt road a quarter-mile off Highway 150. The house used to be an old roadside café, but my father's brawn, sweat and tears transformed it into a typical country home. Though it would never be confused with the Taj Mahal, it was home and where I comfortably lived out my youth.

Across the road from our house was a pasture with cows and other animals, and behind our property was a flowing creek that was our swimming hole.

Pure country.

Inside the house, mounted high up in the corner of the living room, was our only television. It was on that old black and white set that I would religiously watch the *ACC Basketball Game of the Week* every Saturday. They say that the only sure things in life are death and taxes, but something else you could count on back then was that every Saturday afternoon during college basketball season young David Thompson would be glued to the TV, watching the North Carolina Tar Heels. Charlie Scott, who played for the Tar Heels, became my boyhood idol.

Some weekends I would also tune in to watch Duke or the Wolfpack of North Carolina State—the team that would ultimately become my alma mater. Also, I clearly remember watching Wake Forest when Billy Packer played and Eddie Biedenbach of NC State in the early 1960s.

Packer had a teammate named Dave Wiederman, and my brother Vellie Jr. nicknamed me after him.

Packer and Weiderman were exciting to watch, but when Charlie Scott came on the scene a few years later, everybody else faded to the background. I was drawn to Scott for two reasons. He was the first African-American player at North Carolina, a real pioneer at the time. And man, he was something to watch, a college All-American whose style of ball I patterned my game after. Scott could run, jump and shoot. He had such grace and great moves and, more important, was a clutch performer under pressure. He was a guy whom I really looked up to, and in a wonderful twist of fate, years later Charlie became a pro teammate of mine.

Of course, when I watched him and other players on our little TV, I was seeing my face on their bodies. Children who are raised in the country tend to have greater imaginations than children raised in the suburbs or inner city. There wasn't much else to do out in the country.

The other luxury in our home was a console stereo that played gospel music day and night. My mother would hum along while she cooked breakfast for us every morning over a wood-burning stove. Saint that she was, she got herself up at dawn just to ensure we had something to eat before heading off to school. She would awake while the air was still chilly, brave the journey outside to gather the wood, and get the kindling started in the stove. Whether homemade bread with molasses and sugar, or fatback bacon and scrambled eggs, we always had something to fill our demanding bellies. She'd bake cakes and other treats after we left. Considering all of her other household chores, this must have been rough on her, but you would never have guessed it from her always sunny disposition. Back then, I just thought that was the way it was, but you really only appreciate things like that as you get older and reflect. My mother was truly amazing. Her love and care more than compensated for the material things we lacked.

As you might have guessed by now, one of the latter was indoor plumbing. We drew our water from a well, and used an outhouse down by the creek.

We only had three bedrooms, and they were appointed according to sex. My parents occupied one, and the three boys who were still home at the time (me and my older brothers Johnny and Vellie Jr.) shared a room. Our five at-home sisters shared the other room. As for personal space, there was always the outhouse.

Crowded and rundown though it was, our house was always home, sweet home. My parents made it that way by virtue of the love and affection they bestowed upon each of us. They were truly exceptional and extraordinary people.

My father was an honest, no-nonsense, hard-working man. Born and raised on the outskirts of Chesney, South Carolina, he became self-made without the benefit of a complete formal education. Though he did not go beyond the sixth grade, he gained his real knowledge and wisdom from within the pages of the Bible. He was often found with his head buried in the Good Book and based most of his life decisions on what he had read. It served him well.

Some of my earliest memories are of accompanying him on trips to different army bases. It was Dad's job to pick up supplies for the Army Surplus store that employed him in Boiling Springs. It was an adventure for me to travel to military installations like Fort Bragg, Polk Air Force Base, and Cherry Point. Mostly, I just wanted to be near my father and bask in his love and attention. With 10 other siblings competing for his attention, it was a rare opportunity to have him all to myself. He worked such long hours that there wasn't a lot of time to spend with him after he came home in the evening. Usually exhausted, he would watch some television and fall into bed. That was his routine almost every night.

On our trips together I often helped him load and unload the truck while we passed the time with idle ordinary conversation. It was the kind of talk that takes place between fathers and sons that can last for hours without seeming important or substantial at the time. And yet somehow those were some of the most meaningful and significant discussions of my life.

Occasionally we stayed overnight in hotels, though they certainly wouldn't hold a candle to the Ritz Carlton or even your basic Holiday Inn. Mostly, they were rundown rooming-type places. But we did get to eat bologna sandwiches and binge on all kinds of junk food, and to a wide-eyed seven-year-old kid from the country, that was fine dining at its best!

Bologna was meat, and back home we didn't have much meat to eat—except for the occasional chicken we'd butcher ourselves. If my mother needed a chicken, we'd just go out to the yard and grab one. That's how you did it back then. Mother took the chicken and held it real tight until the head just disconnected from the body. The body would flop around awhile, and when it stopped, Mother picked up it up by the feet and put it in boiling water for a few seconds. That took all the fight out of it. Mother still had to pluck the feathers, and what she couldn't pluck off, she singed off over an open fire. Then she carefully washed the chicken, removed all the innards, cut it up and fried or baked the meat. It might have been a painful process—especially for the chicken—but the result for us was always delicious and fresh.

Mother was especially close to my maternal grandmother, Etta Gentry. We called her Mama Etta, and she lived only a few miles away in a house that sat on a fairly large lot. My grandfather was Papa John Quincy Gentry, and he and Mama Etta could sure serve up quite a feast. Everybody pitched in to help buy the pigs and hogs they kept, and would also help slaughter and smoke the animals. The shoulders would be gathered and made into sausage. The less said about that process, the better. Suffice it to say that the chickens probably considered themselves lucky. That was always a large annual event where our whole family would gather for joyous times.

Though my father was a relatively quiet man—not one to always wear his thoughts or emotions on his sleeve—I knew he loved me. When I was just a boy, he often referred to me as his "prize." In return, my affection and adoration of him were deep and unsurpassed. I can safely say that my work ethic—and much of the man I am today—is directly attributable to Vellie Thompson. For instance, he treated people of all colors equally, a trait that I still emulate today. It must not have been easy to be that way in the Deep South during that time of great racial division, but he was a fair man even in the face of great provocation and adversity.

My father spent 19 years at that Army Surplus store, and right before he would have qualified for his pension, the owner fired him so he wouldn't have to pay him one. These were the days before the Civil Rights Act or the EEOC took employers to task, and the man just let him go after 19 years of faithful service. Everybody in our family was upset and disappointed, especially my brothers and sisters.

Being the kind of man he was, my father chose to turn the other cheek and never said much about it. Don't get me wrong—he was very perturbed at the time, but he just wasn't vocal about the situation. His feeling was that the man had provided him with a job for 19 years, and he chose to focus on that bright side of the picture.

Instead of going around bemoaning the fact that he was cheated out of his retirement, Vellie Thompson marched right down to the Fiber Industries plant in Shelby and secured a job as a janitor. *That's* the kind of man my father was. He knew he couldn't change what had been, but he sure could affect what *would be*. In my life I have never met a more practical man. He never said much, but when he talked, I listened. My father once said, "No use in shouting, because all that will do is strain your heart." He talked softly, but carried a big stick.

As you'd expect, my father was very well respected in the community. Honest to a fault, he was also kind to everyone. Though reserved, he loomed large at home and in the consciousness of everyone who knew him.

Faith in God may have had a lot to do with his disposition. A deacon in the Maple Springs Baptist Church, my father was a deeply religious man. He was a chairman of the deacon board and, with some of my cousins, had founded the church. They actually built the original church by hand because they had experience as bricklayers. Though it was small in size, it was powerful in its purpose.

When your father is a deacon, you spend a lot of time in church. Wednesday nights and all day on Sunday we were in attendance at that little church. I started out at Sunday school, then moved on to services, and choir in the afternoon. After that, I went back for a church service at night. We would also go visit other churches in the afternoon, so it was definitely an all-day event.

I sang in that church as a small boy. My family put me up in front of all those people when I was only five years old. I would sing, "Yes, Jesus Loves Me," and the people in the congregation would give me quarters. It might not have been the second coming of Marvin Gaye, but the Motown crooner and I were both getting paid handsomely for our singing chops. While ol' Marvin spent his money on wine, women and song, I took my stash of quarters and spent it on two-for-one cent cookies at Doc Henderson's Country Store, or on a six-cent soda at Hambricks, another general store in town.

My passion for singing brought me joy, and I continued with it throughout my church years by performing in the choir. I was even in my high school chorus. In fact, my cousin—professional coach Alvin Gentry—sang in the church choir with me. To this day, music is a great release for me and something I know I could not live without. It has a great healing power.

Of course, as I got older, being a singer and a top area basketball player had its drawbacks. While singing at other churches, there would occasionally be some opposing players sitting in the pews. And they invariably tried everything they could think of to mess me up. They would try to make me laugh by making funny faces and silly gestures. Sometimes they would get to me—breaking me up or making me sing off key—

but most of the time I was able to ignore them. I like to think I returned the favor by taking it out on them on the basketball court.

We all played basketball together at the church after services, and sometimes we played off the court. There was a baptismal pool out in the creek behind the church. The grapevine that swung out over the creek provided us with the perfect launching pad to go skinny-dipping. In between services, we disappeared and ended up naked in the creek. "Up a creek" is where we ended when my parents discovered us, laughing it up, splashing each other, and swinging in the breeze. Of course, I had to ask the Lord for forgiveness. The Lord was more merciful than my parents, who communicated their displeasure with a belt or a switch—whichever was closest.

Actually, Mother's whippings weren't so bad. It was my father who could light up my backside with his powerful strokes. They did what they had to do to keep us in line, and using the belt from time to time was definitely in accordance with the Bible's teachings about sparing the rod and spoiling the child.

Despite life's pesky setbacks, I couldn't complain. We often took trips with the church and even ventured to Six Flags in Atlanta one year. That was a major event, because we experienced very few family vacations because of the expense. Other than the working trips I took with my father, we rarely ventured out beyond a 40-mile radius from our home.

Mother was entirely different from my father. She was very outgoing and funny, always teasing everyone in the house. She always had something going on, like singing in the church choir, and keeping the entire house on the straight and narrow like a train engine pulls the other railcars along. Mother was a witty and intelligent woman, though she, too, did not graduate from high school. She attended high school and did well, but did not graduate. Back then, young people were expected to help out their families, and while school was valued, work was necessary to keep food on the table and help to make ends meet. In our case, my parents broke the cycle by having the wisdom and foresight to see that education was the key to having a better life.

I don't recall my parents ever discussing with us how they met or courted each other. I believe they hailed from the same area of South Carolina, and my father was approximately two years older than my mother. I do know this: The bond that my parents shared was stronger than Pittsburgh steel. They taught me that marriage meant forever, in sickness and in health, and that lesson would serve me well later in life. They were each other's best friends and always found time to spend together, regardless of how many children and obligations they had. Church and family were their common bonds.

Basketball was a common bond between me and Vellie Jr., and out back, beyond our house, we cleared off an area that would become my personal "Court of Dreams." What started out as a grassy meadow was quickly reduced to red dirt because of the countless hours we pounded the ball out there. Even in the rain, when the makeshift court ran thick with burgundy mud, we played. I was five and had fallen in love with the game of basketball. With wooden backboards, steel rims, and homemade nets, it felt like Madison Square Garden to me.

The hoops were 10 feet high, so if you couldn't reach them with the ball, you sat your sorry butt on the sidelines. Sure, it was tailor-made for the big guys, but I did what I had to do in order to stay in the game. Thankfully, being tall for my age at five allowed me to put the ball through the hoop without much difficulty.

The contests were highly competitive, and I was usually playing with older boys who were excellent players. Many of my cousins would come down and play. We'd run full-court games all day long and never tire. That was a common, recurring theme in my development as a basketball player—competing against senior players, which helped me progress faster than other kids my age. In the beginning, I was the youngest and many times they wouldn't let me play. But since I owned the basketball (a Christmas gift from my mother), they usually had no choice. I had the control, and that's how I got into the games. That cheap rubber ball was my free pass to furthering my hoops education.

Often when my father would arrive home from work, he would park the car so that I could turn on the headlights and play throughout the night. Sometimes I played a little too long, and in the morning when my father tried to start his car the battery would be dead. Then he pulled a switch from the tree to give his boy another butt-whupping for making him late to work. The sacrifices I made for the love of the game.

It was Vellie Jr. who really taught me how to play. I attended all of his high school games and studied his every move on the court. I really looked up to him during those formative years; he was, more than anybody, the single most influential person in my development as a player.

And it was out on that court, in the middle of a country field, that I began to dream of what I could be. I just couldn't get enough of the game. We even played ball in our house, which went over about as big as skinny-dipping during church time. Vellie Jr. used to make his own nets, which he hung from rims made out of old springs. He also made nets for our outdoor court out of thick, long nylon cord my father would bring home from the Army Surplus store. He had to because traditional nets wouldn't last long with as much stress as we put on them.

My basketball education went to a new level when I was 10. That's when I began playing in competitive pickup games at Gardner-Webb College in Boiling Springs, just a few miles from my home. Vellie Jr. took me everywhere he played, and Gardner-Webb was a favorite venue because of the level of competition there. He would bring me along and match me up against older players, such as future pro players like Artis Gilmore, forward John Drew, and guards Larry Brown and Bob Verga. Going up against those guys, I couldn't help but get better. As I became older and better, Vellie would seek out greater challenges for me.

Holly Oak Park in Shelby was another basketball hotbed, and I was able to compete there with some other outstanding players.

Not only did I have pretty good basic skills, but I discovered I could literally jump out of the gym. People think that my jumping ability was a God-given talent that came naturally to me. That is the furthest thing from the truth. I worked on my jumping all the time. All the guys who played high school ball wore ankle weights, so I started wearing them, too. I'd wear them even when I was just practicing jump shots. By the time I was in the eighth grade, I was 5'7" and could dunk the ball.

I also took full advantage of the Gardner-Webb Field House weight room and did leg extensions and toe raises. They also had a rebounding machine that reached twelve and a half feet. I would practice on that thing all the time. By the tenth grade I was rebounding all the way to the top. Nobody else on the team was doing that, so not only was I pretty impressed, but the coaches were, too.

But perhaps what really built my jumping ability and agility was the fact that I grew up near a graveyard. Almost every night after I worked out, my buddy didn't want to drive me all the way home, and so he dropped me off at the entrance of a graveyard that cut through to my house. Because it was dark and spooky, I took off through the graveyard, jumping over and dodging the headstones. I'm not recommending it to your young hoopsters, but try it some inky night and see if you don't leap like a singed cat.

Growing up in the country was a great way to experience childhood, develop strong family values and forge relationships that have lasted a lifetime. It's the foundation of my youth, and I wouldn't change any part of it. School was another integral part of my youth. I know that my parents had high academic expectations for us because they did not graduate from high school, and my dad was relegated to working manual labor jobs. What parents don't want a better life for their children? In fact, Vellie Jr. was the valedictorian of his senior class and went on to college. He was extremely intelligent and ended up being my tutor. When he helped me with my homework, he hammered home the point that if I wanted to go to college and play basketball, I would have to have good grades all the way through high school. I took that advice to heart in a very serious way and performed well all through my academic career.

I journeyed off to school at the age of five because I could already read and write, and I was big for my age. Mother thought I could handle it both emotionally and academically. Green Bethel in Boiling Springs was an all-black school, and I went there up to the eighth grade. We rode the bus into town every day. Desegregation had not yet become a reality, so the school encompassed K-12. I enjoyed school and did well above average in all of my studies.

Part of the fabric of growing up in the 1960s was racial tension, not that I ever dwelled on it. Though we lived out in the country and didn't experience it as much as someone who lived in the inner city, I knew what racism was. There were a few incidents that I remember. There were times when ignorant people would throw bottles at me and hurl racial epithets while my brother and I walked down the street—that sort of thing. I also recall rocks and other objects being thrown at the house in the middle of the night, causing both physical and emotional damage.

Because of the cultural landscape back then, this sort of thing was, for the most part, an accepted part of life. Even most black people got used to it and accepted it. My father always taught me to treat people the way you want to be treated. Growing up in the church, we didn't hold any prejudices against anybody. For the life of me, I never understood why people would do something like that to someone they didn't even know, who had not done anything to provoke them. It just didn't make sense to me.

It wasn't until the ninth grade, in 1967, that I was able to fully experience interaction with both white and black people under one roof. Crest High School in Shelby opened its doors for the first time that year.

For the next four years I grew more as an individual, and a basketball player, than ever before. Education would be my ticket to a better life, but that round leather ball opened doors anywhere I wanted to go.

CHAPTER 2

RIDING THE CREST

To say I was fired up about entering Crest High School would be a gross understatement.

New surroundings, new challenges, new people—both black and white—and the chance to play *organized basketball* for the first time was a dream come true.

With approximately 1,000 kids in school, this was uncharted territory for me. The school was about 70 percent white and 30 percent black, and it was the first year of integration in our area. While integration was a big issue all over the Deep South and the cause of widespread panic for many, it was no big deal to me. My parents had instilled the proper values in me and taught me to judge people by how they individually treat you, not based on the color of their skin. Heck, I just wanted to do well academically and play ball.

Luckily, basketball season was upon us in no time flat. I thought I was going to just burst at the seams if I couldn't get out on that new hardwood court, put on a Crest Chargers uniform and show what I could do. Because of all the hard work my brother Vellie Jr. put me through—teaching me the fundamentals, taking me to basketball camps, pitting me against older kids to rapidly advance my game—I was ready to take on the world and had the attitude to back it up.

Basketball was also my ticket into a new world and a way for me to make friends quickly. Some of the best friends I've ever had played with me on that junior varsity team at Crest High. Guys like Carl Clayton, Larry Hawkins, and Doug Surratt, a buddy I had actually grown up with since the first grade. Though we competed like every practice was Game 7 of the NBA Finals, we were especially close, which made it all the more fun.

The adjustment to organized ball was easy for me because I was noticeably ahead of my teammates in terms of development and ability. Physically I stood 6'0", weighed 165 pounds, and could already jump through the roof. The year before, in eighth grade, a group of us were at the elementary school in Boiling Springs playing in a pickup game. That was the first time I dunked. Hey, I used to practice dunking volleyballs on my hoop at home, but doing it in a gym against competition is a completely different story.

I don't mind telling you that a lot of chins hit the floor when I made that first dunk. Word got around pretty fast. There were a lot of players on the varsity who couldn't dunk, and here was this skinny eighth grader showing them up in a big way and already developing an impressive reputation.

But I knew the game was much more than slamming and jamming. Besides, you couldn't dunk in games at the time because of the Lew Alcindor rule. Big Lew—known as Kareem-Abdul Jabbar today—was the dominating 7'2" center for UCLA in the late '60s, so the NCAA rules committee outlawed the dunk. And that was passed down to the high school level as well. As luck would have it, the dunk was not reinstated until two years *after* I left college. Go figure.

It was thrilling for me to learn team offense and defense from our coach, Hubert McGinnis. We would practice for about an hour and a half after school, sharing the gym with the girls' team. They practiced on one side, while we used the other.

Basketball to me wasn't just a sport—it was a way of life. I considered every single drill a personal challenge to prove that I was the best. While practice was a drag to many of the players, it was something I genuinely looked forward to, unlike many players of today. I just loved the game so much, I would have played any time, anywhere. Give me a ball and a hoop and I was just as happy as Einstein with a new theorem.

My dream was alive and well—to one day play in the storied ACC. *Just like Charlie Scott.* So both my work ethic and discipline were in high gear, with my talent not far behind.

We played teams from schools in the surrounding three counties, all within a 30-mile radius. Some of the schools were R. S. Central, East

Rutherford, Cherryville, Kings Mountain, Burns, and Chase. Because basketball was king in North Carolina, the competition was fierce and every team presented a genuine threat.

We started off well, and soon winning became the norm. The satisfaction of being part of a real team, and helping that team to succeed, felt unbelievably good. Obviously the coaches thought that I had done well, too, because in December of 1967, during Christmas break, Ed Peeler, the varsity head coach, asked me to join his squad. I was deeply honored, of course, but it was a tough and gut-wrenching decision for me. I was only a freshman and in my first real year of organized basketball. My friends were so important to me, and I felt as though I would be letting them down if I agreed to being called up. I knew I could play with the older kids and probably contribute greatly to the team. But loyalty won out, and I remained a member of our esteemed junior varsity. Coach Peeler understood and never held it against me. In fact, I think I may have earned his respect even more.

We had a winning record that year, and I averaged 17 points and about 10 rebounds per game. The losses were emotionally painful, so I tried to do everything I could to keep them to a minimum. I played to win every time out on the court, but as I would find out during my sophomore season, it takes a strong *team* to win consistently.

I grew very little between my freshman and sophomore years, to 6'1" and 175 pounds. I felt so much more prepared heading into tenth grade with a year of seasoning under my belt. Coach Peeler did not have a very good core group to begin with, so I was counted on heavily to deliver the goods from the small forward spot. That's when I learned that one good player cannot carry a whole team on his back. Great players like Wilt Chamberlain, Michael Jordan, Oscar Robertson, Earl Monroe and Jerry West never won a title until surrounded by a competent, solid *team*.

Playing for Coach Peeler was an absolute joy. He was a good coach who had a lot of excellent players come through his program. He was a sound, fundamental coach who taught me how to play the game the way it was supposed to be played: unselfish, team first, and very disciplined in the offensive and defensive structures. Though a mild-mannered man, Coach Peeler could get under your hide if needed. He was always very positive, and I always stacked up my future coaches against him because his style was so appealing and productive.

Coach Peeler ran a North Carolina-style offense because he was a good friend of Dean Smith's, and that suited me just fine. It was a system predicated upon passing—usually a 2-3 or 2-1-2, passing to the wings and setting screens on the opposite man. We ran a lot of the same sets that the Tar Heels did. On defense, we played very tough and overplayed a lot—also like Smith's teams. It was an approach that brought Coach Peeler much success, although in my first year of varsity play we just didn't have the horses. We were in a rebuilding mode, and the other schools were simply loaded.

I realized something very important about myself as a sophomore: The better the competition I faced, the better I became on the floor. The opposition forced me to play at a higher level, and as a result I grew as a player. My game improved immensely once I put on a varsity uniform, but even as skilled as I was becoming, I could not single-handedly prevent us from losing. And the losing I took very personally. Personal statistics never meant much to me. Winning did. So as we struggled, I became more and more determined to not only improve my game, but to become a better team player as well. Just for the record, though, I finished third in the conference in scoring with 18 points per game, grabbed 9.4 rebounds per game, and made All-Conference at the forward spot.

That was the only losing year I experienced through high school, college, and the first five years of my pro career. One losing season in 13 years is not bad, and I attribute a lot of that to my "never say die" attitude.

With an 18 points-per-game average as a 14-year-old sophomore, the name David Thompson began to circulate throughout the region. It was during this time that the first letters began arriving from various universities and colleges. They initially came from the East Coast—schools like South Carolina, Virginia, North Carolina, North Carolina State, and even as far as Tennessee. I played at camps with guys like South Carolina's All-American Tom Owens, and they would tell their coaches there was a kid in Boiling Springs who could really play ball and who was worth their while to pursue.

Naturally, the recruitment letters that really sent me flying were from schools in the ACC, which to me was the elite conference. Their interest only made me more determined to take my game to the next level.

One way I found to accomplish that was through track and field. Coach Peeler prodded us to participate in track during the off season as a way to stay in shape. Well, the workouts definitely helped me keep my edge, but like everything else, I wanted to *win*.

My track coach was one of our assistant basketball coaches, Jim Hutchins. Hutchins graduated from North Carolina, so he was constantly reminding me of where I should go to college when the time came.

My favorite track events were those in which I could utilize my superior jumping ability, including the high jump (my best effort was 6'3"), the broad jump (22'8"), and triple jump (45'6"). I was fast, too, so the mile relay was another preferred event.

My senior year, teammate Jerry Hunt and I even made it to the state finals in the jumping events. I placed first in the triple and long jump. Not bad for a high school basketball player messing around with track "just to stay in shape."

During the summer between my sophomore and junior years, I would go to Coach Peeler's house after church and pick up the key to the gym. Gathering as many good players as possible—even those from opposing schools—we'd engage in some great pickup games at Crest. Coach Peeler trusted me, and that's something else I'll never forget. I am proud to say that Coach Peeler is still a dear friend of mine today.

Something else happened that summer that was a bit more significant. I sprouted three whole inches and added some extra pounds that got me up to 185. Everything was coming together nicely.

When I was a junior, my Crest Chargers went 23 games with only a handful of losses. Kings Mountain, another area powerhouse, knocked us out of the conference tournament finals when we missed a couple of free throws at the end of the game. In the state tournament, Kings Mountain lost to Avery County High School in Newland, with my future North Carolina State teammate Tom Burleson at center for Avery. Burleson was a 7'2" legend (he would grow another two inches while at NC State) in North Carolina by then, and carried with him a mammoth average: 32 points and 27 rebounds per game.

I played against a lot of excellent players that year. Otis Cole went on to play at Florida State, and Bessemer City High School had Tony Byers. Byers would become All-Conference at Wake Forest. Forrest Toms played at Middle Tennessee State. Another guy I have to mention is George Adams, a senior at a rival high school when I was just a freshman. That guy could just flat-out *play*. He played pickup ball at Gardner-Webb with us and was a regular at all the camps.

A local product who played college ball at Gardner-Webb, Adams went on to play three seasons in the American Basketball Association for the San Diego franchise. I was disappointed to see him get cut prior to the start of the 1975-76 season, which was my rookie season in the ABA. I was looking forward to competing against him and showing him how much I'd developed as a player.

As a result of me leading the conference in scoring with 26.8 points per game, the volume of recruiting letters picked up considerably, and the postmarks on the envelopes weren't just from the Mid-South anymore. It was all very flattering to me, and at times a little overwhelming.

Then everything came tumbling down at the pinnacle of the 1969-70 season. Expectations were high in my senior year because we had an experienced group of players, and we responded with a 31-game winning streak. Averaging 90 points per game, we did not lose a single contest all year heading into the 3A Western North Carolina Association's state championship game, where we faced a tough Salisbury Boyden High at Catawba College.

They were the defending champs, an experienced, cohesive squad with a loyal, raucous cadre of hometown fans who traveled the circuit with them. Boyden's only chance was to keep point production down by holding the ball as much as possible. It worked well for them. We fell behind early and never recovered.

As it seems with all great games, there is a story within the story. My teammate at the other forward spot, Jerry Hunt, was in his first year with the varsity. He had played solid all year long, but against Boyden he was called for a technical foul early in the game for supposed rough play. Boyden High was a big and very physical team and just took it to us.

They played a box-and-one on me and slowed the ball down to a snail's pace. Boyden matched up well with us. They also had outstanding guards who could handle the ball. One of them was Sheldon Shipman, and he ran the four corners just like Phil Ford at North Carolina. He must have just dribbled around for more than half the game. Shipman dribbled so much that he looked like a high school version of Marques Haynes during one of his Globetrotter routines.

We were defeated 41-40, and emotionally I was absolutely crushed. Thirty-one wins in a row isn't much consolation when you lose the last game of the season for the state championship. Not even the fact that we'd made Kings Mountain pay the piper for ousting us from the playoffs the previous year, in a game in which I went on a 51-point tear, seemed like such a big deal now. That was the most points I ever scored in a high school game, by the way.

Averaging 29.2 points per game in my senior year, and with a four-year school record of 54-15 at Crest, my mailbox was bulging every day with letters from college coaches. More than a hundred coaches wrote to me, asking me to come visit them, but I instinctively knew I was going to stay close to home.

By that time, our family had moved from the house on the dirt road to a stone, almost prehistoric-looking structure that my older brother affectionately nicknamed "Bedrock," after the stone-age architecture in the wildly popular cartoon, *The Flintstones*.

Some fairly recognizable names came out to Bedrock to chat with my parents. Esteemed coaches such as Dean Smith of North Carolina, Frank McGuire of South Carolina, Bucky Waters of Duke, and, of course, Norm Sloan of North Carolina State all made the pilgrimage to the Thompson household to try to court favor with me and my folks.

I remember Coach Sloan bringing his wife Joan to our humble abode in Shelby. It was an experience, Coach likes to say, that he'll never forget.

"It was an education for Joan and me," Sloan recalled. "The flooring boards were literally on dirt, and the walls were open studding—two-by-fours and crossbeams."

My parents were there as well, and Joan tried to find some common ground with my mother, Ida. Joan asked where she worked, and my mother told her a hosiery mill.

"Oh, I should get a job there," Joan smiled. "My two daughters just go through hose left and right."

The comment warranted a raised eyebrow from my mother, who knew this dainty little woman wouldn't last a day in the mill.

"Oh, honey," my mother said. "You couldn't handle it. The work's too hard for you."

The only common ground we found that day was basketball and college, and where I should be doing both.

The coaches always tried to impress upon my father and me the good education I would receive at their schools, along with the opportunity to play in one of the best programs in the country. Getting a starting spot my freshman year wasn't the issue it is today, because freshmen back then were ineligible to play on the varsity. However, we still pressed hard to ensure that I would be a starter on the varsity when my sophomore year rolled around.

It was a tough decision, especially after Dean Smith showed up at our door. When you're born and bred in North Carolina, and grow up with a basketball in your hand, it's almost expected that you'll only have eyes for the University of North Carolina, with its great roundball tradition and hallowed basketball program.

Back then, black folks from North Carolina did not grow up with dreams of attending NC State. Ed Leftwich, the school's first black player, wasn't a very happy member of the Wolfpack and left after his junior year.

Besides, I had a personal relationship with Dean Smith, as I had attended one of his basketball camps as a kid. He was always very polite and respectful, and I thought the world of him. Coach Smith even came and spoke at my high school sports banquet my senior year to try to win me over.

Later in the process, the Tar Heels relaxed their full-court press and sent assistant coaches John Lotz and Bill Chamberlain in Smith's place. I think by then Dean assumed I was a lock for his program and figured he no longer needed to come around to personally seal the deal. Through that small window of opportunity soon walked a wolf.

Eddie Biedenbach was an excellent player at North Carolina State from 1965-67 and was an assistant to head coach Norm Sloan in 1970. Eddie was the most persistent individual I had ever met and was as tenacious as a recruiter as when he played guard for the Wolfpack. He was also a knowledgeable basketball man. I think he lived at the local Shelby Holiday Inn, off I-74, for about a month, because he was at every practice, every game, and even attended some of my track events. Nobody had to point out that Eddie and Coach Sloan wanted me very badly.

Today, it is no surprise to me that Eddie is a highly successful coach at UNC-Asheville, with a lengthy and prosperous career in the college coaching ranks. Whenever coaches came to our house, they usually spoke to my father and me. They would also catch a Crest basketball game just to evaluate my skills and abilities. Occasionally I would also speak to them at the Holiday Inn, while dining on my favorite meal—a thick, juicy steak, a whopping baked potato with all the fixings, and topped off with apple pie a la mode. I had the same thing every time. It sure beat bologna sandwiches.

Biedenbach not only put in the time, but he also put a bug in my ear that still resonates today. "David, do you want to go to North Carolina and follow in the footsteps of Charlie Scott," he said, "or do you want to go to North Carolina State and forge your own identity?"

I had never heard anything so profound that spoke so directly to my soul. Charlie Scott was my hero, but I needed to make a name for *myself*. Eddie was basically saying that if I went to North Carolina, I would always be measured against the great Tar Heel players of the past. At NC State, it would be the chance to make my own mark. Besides, Tom Burleson had chosen NC State the year before, and I knew that Coach Sloan was building something special in Raleigh. It was an irresistible situation. But that doesn't mean I still didn't suffer pangs of guilt and indecision before I went public with my choice.

Though the Big Four ACC schools—North Carolina, Duke, NC State and Wake Forest—were always the front-runners, I also had a soft spot in my heart for little Gardner-Webb. The school had given so much to me as a youth that it was especially hard to say no to them. Considering that the school was located only two miles from my home, and that Coach Eddie Holbrook and I went way back together, you can see why it was an attractive option. But the sound of the Wolfpack just kept howling louder and louder in my head.

When the media were notified that I would attend NC State, there wasn't the circus-like atmosphere there is today, but it was fairly big news around the Tar Heel State and especially in my hometown of Shelby. Some mail from the townspeople was delivered to me after the announcement, and they didn't exactly wish me bon voyage. A lot of people really wanted me to attend Gardner-Webb, and they felt betrayed by my decision. But at least I wasn't doing something really treasonous, like playing ball for an out-of-state school, and after a while everything quieted down.

A funny story went around about Coach Sloan's response to the news that I was joining the Wolfpack. Sloan was on the golf course at the time, enjoying a leisurely day of fun and sun. As I would later find out playing under him, the coach was easily excitable, which in this case made him a menace to his fellow duffers and everyone else in the vicinity. For upon learning of my decision, Coach Sloan reportedly threw the golf club in his hands so high into the air that it probably registered on radar screens at every airport on the Eastern Seaboard. Then, without waiting for it to come down, he headed toward the clubhouse to begin making plans for the next season. It sure is nice to be wanted.

I don't know about that golf club, but I sure came crashing down with a bang thanks to a series of totally innocuous incidents that eventually came to haunt me and my new school.

As most people know, NC State was put on probation by the NCAA during my sophomore campaign of 1972-73. And even though we went 27-0 that year—*an undefeated season*—we were denied the chance to participate in the NCAA Tournament. Why, you ask? Well, even now it's hard for me to fathom, as ridiculous as that might sound.

When I graduated from high school, my parents threw me a nice big party. It was also a going-away party, since I was bound for Raleigh. Because my family didn't have much money, an elderly friend, who was the vice president of a mill in Shelby, bought me a suit jacket and a pair of pants as a graduation present. He had received an invitation and thought it was proper etiquette to bring a gift. And the fact was that I didn't have many nice clothes for college. Our friend was approximately 70 years old and was just being nice. Later on, he invited Ed Peeler and me to Charlotte for the ACC Tournament. He provided transportation to and from the game, and tickets.

I didn't know that the man was an alumnus of Duke University and still represented the school. And if I had, it never would have dawned on me that there was any connection between that and his generosity. Maybe if he'd given me a Cadillac, I'd have raised an eyebrow. But a simple suit coat? Anyway, somebody less naïve than me apparently whispered something to somebody close to the NCAA, and in its infinite wisdom the overseer of college sports deemed the gift and the trip a recruiting violation. The only person more shocked than me about it was the gift giver himself. *Never once* were basketball or my collegiate career discussed with this man.

The NCAA approached me regarding this incident at the beginning of my freshman year at NC State. They reached me through the school and eventually via Coach Sloan. I could tell they had been snooping around all summer, behaving like the *National Enquirer,* trying to dig up something sensational on me.

Lord knows there were plenty of juicy rumors going around about my familiy and me. According to one of them, some NC State boosters had actually paved the road to our home, contracting with Daniels Construction Company, which employed my father, to do the bulldozing. Well, the road was in fact put in, but my father himself paid $125 a month to have the work done over a period of a year.

Another rumor involving NC State was that they built the Thompson family a $35,000 home. The NCAA's visit to our home promptly shot down that allegation.

Other rumors had it that one school had offered me a Cadillac, while another offered my father a job with a handsome salary. It was even claimed that I was seen driving around in Dean Smith's Cadillac, and that he told me I could keep the luxury vehicle if I came to UNC.

Even tiny Gardner-Webb was ludicrously accused of offering me huge sums of cash to lure me there. So many rumors, so little truth.

Coach Sloan advised me to be straightforward and just tell the NCAA investigator the truth. He expected, at most, a slap on the wrist.

My interview lasted just a few hours. The man started out very nice, but then began asking a lot of leading questions. The tone of his voice became more serious with each passing minute. I just tried to be truthful, as my parents had always taught me, and told him everything I knew.

Then all of a sudden another lightning bolt struck—in the form of NCAA infractions. The first one occurred the summer before my freshman year. My two close friends and high school teammates, Jerry and Larry Hunt, were working a basketball camp at NC State. They stayed in the dorm in the evenings, and one night I slept there. The NCAA was notified by an "unknown" source, and they eventually deemed my overnight stay another violation. Their reasoning was that the school provided me with housing before I was actually registered as a student there, even though I had already signed with the school. The NCAA found NC State guilty of not charging me $8 a week for using the dorm room.

Still another time that same summer, after I had signed with the Wolfpack, I played in some pickup games in Carmichael Gym, the practice facility on campus. Eddie Biedenbach, the NC State assistant coach, also participated in a few of the pickup games when an extra man was needed to make the teams even. Tipped off again, the NCAA ruled that "a coach cannot 'try out' players before school starts, even if that player has already signed with the school."

Excuse me, but…try out? Let's see. *I was one of the top players in the country and had already signed with NC State.* Why in the world would the team be "trying me out?" What was the reasoning behind that decision?

Another violation was deemed to have occurred when Charlie Bryant, a former assistant for NC State, gave me a ride to and from NC State on a school-paid visit. Bryant, who at the time was in the banking business and lived in nearby Gastonia, gave me a ride to the campus. But because Charlie had been in the coaching business, the NCAA called his actions those of a "scout," which were illegal under its rules.

Later I heard two possible explanations for the hubbub. Who knows if they're accurate? One was that a North Carolina football player was in the gym the day we were playing ball, told his coach about it, and he, in turn, ratted me out to the NCAA. The other was that someone from Gardner-Webb, not happy with my decision to play elsewhere, had gotten wind of my stay at NC State and the pickup games and then blown the whistle on me.

Whatever. The point is that it was all ticky-tacky stuff that somehow was built up into a major bump in my college career.

Unfair? Yes. Insurmountable? Of course not. I had overcome obstacles all my young life, so I just took it all in stride. I was a lot like my dad that way. There was nothing I could do about it, so I just tried to make the best of it. Unfortunately, those really trivial incidents ended up changing the history of college basketball forever.

It's almost funny when you consider that throughout my basketball life, I seemed to have had a knack for being in the wrong place at the wrong time—always with undesirable results.

Having to leave home for the first time and go off to school was nerve-wracking because my family was so close-knit; but my parents put me at ease by telling me, "If you get up there and you don't like it, you can always come home." I was filled with second thoughts, wondering if I had made the right move. I could easily have gone to Gardner-Webb and played it safe. It was my dad who made everything right with his final words of encouragement. He said, "You just go up there, son, and you'll do *great*." If he believed in me like that, it was good enough for me.

Even though I was filled with anxiety, I couldn't wait to get to Raleigh.

All of this drama, and I had just turned 17.

CHAPTER 3

RUNNING WITH THE PACK

A good friend of mine named Eddie Pipkin pulled up to my house in his car and honked the horn. Freshmen at NC State were not allowed to have cars, so Eddie was kind enough to play chauffeur for me. My old GTO stayed parked at home as I said my goodbyes, and down the tobacco road we went.

It was about a four-hour drive from Shelby to Raleigh in 1971, but it seemed like half a world away to this 17-year-old. The Interstate 85 bypass had not yet been built, so we had to drive through about 50 other towns, cities and municipalities until we finally reached our destination. I was starting to wonder if we would ever get there. And when we did, it was almost surreal.

Late summer at NC State was magical. The day I arrived on campus, there was an excitement in the air, an atmosphere full of hope and new beginnings. Every morning the Memorial Bell Tower greeted me as I stepped on campus. The 115-foot tower was erected in memory of NC State alumni who perished in World War I. It gave me a noble feeling of being a full-fledged college student.

Though I had seen Reynolds Coliseum—home of the basketball Wolfpack—on my recruiting visit, there was something special about standing in front of the arena now that I was an official member of the team. Located centrally on campus, the $2.3 million building is named for William Neal Reynolds, one of five brothers who developed the R. J. Reynolds Tobacco Company in Winston-Salem. Alumnus David Clark conceived the idea in 1940 when a farmers' market, with 5,000 people in attendance, was being held outdoors and a rainstorm stranded all of them. I always noticed that some of the doors to the Coliseum were absolutely huge, and rumor had it that Clark wanted them large enough so that elephants could pass through just in case there was a circus in town. I didn't doubt it.

I felt a real sense of history and awe staring at its magnificence, and then a powerful thought crossed my mind. This was going to be *my house.* Maybe David Clark had conceived the Coliseum, but David *Thompson* was going to *own* it. In the not-so-distant future, 12,400 screaming, delirious fans were in for something special, and I would play a big part. I could definitely sense great things were going to happen when we stepped out on the floor.

There was an omen that I have never mentioned to anyone before. Guess what the name was of the building that served as the Wolfpack's home basketball floor until Reynolds Coliseum opened? That's right— Thompson Gymnasium. It's a theater now, but something told me this was a promising sign of good things to come.

I loved everything about NC State: the 1911 Building, Mary Yarbrough Court, the Court of the Carolinas, the trees that enveloped the campus. It was an eye-poppin' sight for this impressionable country kid.

While I couldn't wait to begin my college basketball career, there were so many other things I wanted to experience. The State campus was home to more than 15,000 bustling students. Boiling Springs had maybe 1,000 people, and that was only when relatives came to visit. It was a bit overwhelming at first, but I must admit to enjoying every minute of it.

It was a much more culturally diverse setting than I was ever exposed to. There were many adjustments to be made, such as being away from home and family for the first time, understanding different types of people and handling much more free time than I was accustomed to. Not to mention competing against more highly talented basketball players than I was used to playing with and rising to a higher academic standard. But I felt that I was up to all of those challenges. It was also a lot of fun—almost *too* much fun.

In high school, I would go to school from morning to mid-afternoon, finishing at three o'clock. From there, it was basketball or track practice for a few hours. I'd usually get home around six, eat dinner, do homework, and go to bed by 10:00 p.m. In college, some days I had maybe two classes to attend, and then the rest of the day was mine. That left a lot of free time to incorporate fun into my new schedule.

Academically, the adjustment wasn't all that bad, because there was more time to prepare for my classes.

I didn't have a tutor, but we did have a study hall that we were required to take part in, and I was very conscientious about using my time wisely. Enrolled in the school's liberal arts program, I was required to take courses that all freshmen had to take, including science, math, and a foreign language. Some of those classes were especially tough, like accounting and physics. With a little brains and a lot of sweat, somehow I got by. My GPA wasn't great, but it wasn't bad, either, hovering around 2.8. I took great pride in the fact that my eligibility was never in jeopardy, and I never got into any academic difficulty like so many athletes you hear about today. Atlantic Coast Conference schools were known for their strong academic standards, so there was comfort in knowing I could do the work.

One thing really stands out about my first six months as a college student. Every night I set my alarm clock for 7:00 a.m. to make sure I wouldn't miss my eight o'clock class. And every day for the first six months the same song would wake me up—Rod Stewart's classic rock anthem "Maggie May." He must have made a fortune on that song!

Every single morning I'd hear the lyrics, "Wake up, Maggie, I think I've got something to say to you. It's late September and I really should be back at school…" It was like a scene from the movie *Groundhog Day*, in which the same scenario repeats itself over and over again. I was actually a little shocked the first morning that song wasn't playing when my alarm went off.

During one of my first days on campus, I attended freshmen orientation with some of my new teammates. Being very excited to be surrounded by such great talent, I couldn't wait to meet the guy who would be our starting point guard—the ball-handling whiz kid I had heard so much about who would be feeding me the rock for the next four years.

I noticed Joe Cafferky, a starting junior guard on the varsity, walking in with some little kid. I asked some of the guys who the midget was with Cafferky, the one with the cutoff jeans who looked about 13 years old. His little brother, perhaps?

"Oh, that's Monte Towe," they all said. "He's a freshman, too, and your new point guard." My jaw hit the ground like a sledgehammer.

"Are you kidding me? That little dude *can't* be our starting point guard. He looks like he hasn't even reached puberty."

While I had heard all about Monte Towe and his long list of accomplishments on the hardwood, I hadn't ever seen him in person. He was the last player to sign on with the team. Monte was like an afterthought in the beginning, but turned out to be the key figure the year we won the national championship. He was probably the greatest floor leader I ever had the pleasure of playing with.

All the guys got together that day to play some pickup games. I'd be on one team, and Tom Burleson would be on the other, just to keep it fair. Monte would play on Tom's team one game, and then on mine the next. The funny thing was, whichever team Monte played on, that was the team that always won. He didn't just control, he *dominated* the entire flow of the game. It didn't take me long to figure out that Monte Towe was a *winner*, and it was right then that I knew our team was going to be something special.

In addition to his leadership skills, Monte was simply the best ball handler I had ever seen or played with. He could pass unbelievably well and could hit the J from the outside with regularity. You wouldn't think a guy who was all of 5'7" on his tiptoes could be that skilled, and, more importantly, that effective. But Monte was all of that, and more. We struck up a friendship almost immediately, and it's a friendship that's still going strong today.

People have assumed that because Monte and I have always been very close we started rooming together as freshmen. But we didn't actually room together until the summer after our freshman year. I roomed with another black guy on the team, Carl Lile, the first half of my freshman year. Carl was a 5'10", 165-pound sophomore guard from Indianapolis. I thought Carl was a pretty good player and a great athlete. But Carl didn't get a lot of playing time and averaged only 1.4 points per game. I was sad to see him go when he transferred out at Christmas break. I genuinely liked him.

I was then paired with Biff Nichols, a teammate of mine on the freshman squad. Biff had a rare, unique quality—a "gift"—that endeared him to every member of the freshmen team. It was something that none of us, even with all of our remarkable basketball skills, could match. It was a truly amazing thing, a beautiful sight to behold.

Biff had a car.

There was only one way to get around the freshman rule prohibiting the use of personal vehicles, and Biff took advantage of it. He was from Raleigh and lived in town. That gave him the right to drive his old Mercedes-Benz wherever and whenever he wanted to. We latched onto Biff the way barnacles latch on to the hull of a ship. He was public transportation at its finest, and we went everywhere with him. Biff was a great guy and another class act, and he eventually married Coach Sloan's daughter, Leslie.

So this begs the question, "Who, then, was Monte Towe rooming with our freshman year?" Did you ever read the old comic strip, "Mutt and Jeff?" Well, I don't know whose idea it was, but Monte was put with Big Tommy Burleson—all 7'4" of him. Funny thing was, Tommy had a seven-foot bed, which took up most of the room.

In fact, I've thought for years that it was kind of cool that we had the tallest player in the country, the shortest player, and the player who could jump the highest—all on one team. Amazing.

Back to the reason why Monte signed very late to play for the Wolfpack. Coach Sloan knew he was in need of an outstanding point guard, so he turned to one of the nation's hotbeds for talent and where he himself had grown-up: the basketball-crazy state of Indiana. Coach Sloan had a very good friend and basketball source who still lived in Indiana and asked him if would do a little scouting for him.

Dick Dickey was a former teammate of Coach Sloan's at State from back in the 1940s. They were such good friends that Dickey was best man at Coach Sloan's wedding. Coach Sloan asked Dickey to scout a specific player about whom the coach had been hearing good things. But when Dickey called back to submit his report, he strongly recommended that Coach Sloan take a serious look at another player who was on the opposing team that day—a diminutive point guard named Monte Towe.

"*How* diminutive?" Sloan asked Dickey.

"About five feet, seven inches," came the reply.

Coach Sloan was quite adamant that a 5'7" guard could not play in the ACC—the toughest basketball conference in the country, in case Dickey had forgotten. Dickey then very pointedly reminded him that Sloan had not listened to him back in 1967, when he suggested that John Mengelt be offered a scholarship to play at NC State. Mengelt went on to a great college career at Auburn and then a productive 10-year career in the NBA. To make matters worse, Mengelt himself later told Coach Sloan that he would have played at State in a heartbeat—if only he had been asked.

That very same year, 1967, Dickey recommended another star Midwestern player to Sloan—Rich Yunkus. Once again, Sloan took a pass. Yunkus went on to score 2,232 points with a three-year varsity average of 26.6 for Georgia Tech. Maybe it was time, Dickey suggested, for Sloan to listen to him for a change.

Which is what happened. Coach Sloan sent Eddie Biedenbach to sign Monte Towe from little Converse, Indiana, to be his point guard of the future. Biedenbach could not believe that Coach Sloan would sign Towe without seeing him play—especially at 5'7".

"Eddie, we passed on Mengelt and Yunkus," Coach Sloan told Biedenbach. "I'm not making that mistake again. Let's get him signed." That's why Monte signed so late. But as that old saying goes, "Better late than never."

As we began to prepare for the upcoming season, there was a lot of talk about the NCAA repealing its freshman ineligibility rule. But it did not happen soon enough, so we began training for the freshman schedule.

One of the first things the school did was put me on a program that had a strong emphasis on weight training. The thrice-weekly workouts on the Nautilus machines were grueling, but resulted in a firmer, stronger body for me. We also did three and a half miles a day of cross-country running that did wonders for our stamina and endurance.

One personal routine I did mothball while in college was wearing ankle weights to help my leaping ability. Most of the time I just did toe raises, and the university also had machines that would help me improve my vertical leap.

It was at this time that I made the *Guinness Book of World Records* for my hops. I believe Eddie Biedenbach contacted the Guinness people because he couldn't believe how high I had been getting up and thought it was worth documenting for posterity. Eddie denies it to this day, but I still think it was him.

The Guinness people came to our gym, pasted pieces of tape on the walls at various heights, and asked me to jump as high as I could from a standstill. Not very scientific, but it did the trick. I mustered all of my energy and shot straight up like a Saturn rocket, as high as my legs would take me.

It wasn't as earth-shaking as eating a hundred goldfish in 60 seconds, maybe, but the Guinness folks were impressed enough to put me in their book with a new world standing vertical jump of 42 inches. That record stood until it was broken sometime in the 1980s. But that little entry in the *Guinness Book of World Records* brought me world recognition and helped to build the legend of David Thompson.

Along with Monte and me, there was another freshman player who would become a real force over the next four years. Timothy Paul Stoddard was a 6'7" strongman from East Chicago, Indiana, who not only excelled at basketball, but also baseball—the sport that he would, one day, play professionally.

Tim played on one of the greatest high school basketball teams of all time that included Junior Bridgeman and Pete Trgovich, the same two guys who visited NC State with me during our senior years. Bridgeman would go on to star at Louisville and enjoy an excellent 12-year NBA career primarily with the Milwaukee Bucks as a forward, while Trgovich, a playmaking guard, played an integral part on the UCLA national championship teams of 1972-73 and 1974-75. Trgovich was chosen by the Detroit Pistons in the third round of the 1975 NBA draft and in the fourth round of the 1975 ABA draft by the San Diego Conquistadors, but he didn't play professionally. Stoddard obviously had played with some real talent, but more importantly, understood how important a role player could be to a winning team.

This book would not be complete without one Tim Stoddard baseball story. I saw him pitch against Clemson one year in the ACC Tournament, and it was one of the most dominating performances I ever witnessed on the diamond. State had to win two games against Clemson to advance in the tournament. First, Stoddard pitched the Wolfpack to an opening-game win, and then he threw four innings of relief in the second game to clinch that victory. No wonder he spent 13 years in major-league baseball as a very effective relief pitcher, throwing in 485 games and playing in two World Series (1979 and '83)—winning a championship with the Baltimore Orioles in 1983.

Tim played center for us that first year, but moved to power forward opposite me the next two years because of Burleson's presence in the middle. Tim was one of the smartest players on the team, a great passer and rebounder, and was very physical. In fact, he was an enforcer. He possessed great knowledge of the game and could play many positions. Our steady rock, Tim would do *anything* to help us win.

Mark Moeller, a 6'3" guard from Canfield, Ohio, and Leo Campbell, a 6'6" forward, rounded out our starting five. Both Mark and Leo stayed all four years, but Leo only played through our sophomore year though he was still on scholarship. Mark was one of the first players off the bench the next three years.

Our freshman coach was Art Musselman, who doubled as an assistant to Coach Sloan on the varsity. The bond between the coaches went back to when Musselman was a star player for Sloan at The Citadel in the late 1950s. A mild-mannered man, Musselman could see that we were quite talented and often just let us play our own game.

Though we were playing pickup games daily during open gym, basketball practice did not officially begin until October 15. With Sloan looking on, Musselman began putting us through the various drills and sets that we would be using for the upcoming season. Both coaches obviously liked what they saw.

We got off to a great start once the season began. I was averaging nearly 50 points per game after the first four contests, and *Sports Illustrated* put me in its "Faces in the Crowd" section in the front of the magazine. I knew we had played a handful of creampuffs, but the national recognition was nice.

We went 15-1 for the year, losing to North Carolina at Chapel Hill in the first of two clashes against them that year. It was a close game until Stoddard, Campbell and yours truly fouled out. The freshmen Tar Heels fielded a highly talented lineup with five high school All-Americans, including Donald Washington, Ed Stahl and Ray Harrison.

We played them again in Raleigh later in the year and won by 20 points. My hunger for payback resulted in 49 points before I fouled out with 10 minutes left in the game—four more than the entire Tar Heel squad. At one point, I connected on 13 straight field goals. I had wanted to make a statement punctuated with an exclamation point. An English major couldn't have done it better.

Revenge was very sweet, especially when it came to beating North Carolina.

Things could have been very different, though, that freshman year. *Very different.* There was an interesting series of events in January of 1972 that could have changed our entire story. The NCAA had again been considering allowing freshmen to play on the varsity, and Coach Sloan lobbied vehemently in favor of the change because he knew exactly how positively that would affect his varsity team.

But the other schools all knew, also, and so voted to let freshman play varsity ball—*starting the following season.* There was no golf club flinging—at least the celebratory kind—that day.

When the season was over, my numbers read like this: 35.6 points and 13.6 rebounds per game, with a high game of 54 points against Isothermal Community College (and I only played three-fourths of the game).

There was one minor setback. I twisted my knee near the end of the year performing some minor drills in practice. Even with rest and standard treatment the pain didn't go away. I never complained and continued to participate in spring track.

That was one of the reasons that I turned down an invitation to try out for the 1972 U.S. Olympic basketball team. My knee still hurt, and I needed some time off after the long season. Besides, I didn't really know anyone else trying out except Burleson, and I wasn't nuts about the well-known plan to use me, at least initially, as an alternative. That year's U.S. team ended up losing to the U.S.S.R. in the infamous and forever debatable "double inbounds" gold medal game. Though I've wondered if I could have made a difference, I never have regretted my decision to pass on the Olympics that year.

Coach Sloan's varsity squad had done fairly well, too. They finished 16-10 overall and 6-6 in the ACC conference. That was a measurable improvement over the previous season, when they went 13-14 and only 5-9 in the ACC (there were 14 conference games per season then). The season ended for good when Duke (14-12) took it to the Wolfpack, 73-60, eliminating them in the first round of the ACC Tournament.

While Coach Sloan was naturally disappointed, he could not help but envision what the next season would bring. Burleson had averaged 21.3 PPG and 14.0 RPG. Tommy had lived up to everyone's enormous expectations of him. With Monte Towe, Tim Stoddard, and myself joining him the next year, the sky was truly the limit.

And no man deserved success more than Coach Norman Sloan.

Originally from Huntington, Indiana, "Whitey" (his nickname as a youth) was the product of a proud and strict father who taught him never to accept anyone's charity, to always look out for himself, and to stand up for what he believed in—even if it meant hardship. Coach Sloan's father talked the talk, but also walked the walk. In the midst of the Great Depression, the Sloan family went without meat on Thanksgiving, refusing any type of handout. It was a harsh but memorable lesson for young Norm.

When Sloan visited North Carolina State as a hot basketball prospect, it was because head coach Everett Case was a native Hoosier and always kept tabs on the young phenoms back in his home state. Though Sloan only saw Case twice on the trip, Case sold him on NC State by guaranteeing him the opportunity to get an education that would allow him to put food on the table, clothes on his family's back and a roof over their head.

That was enough for Sloan. He studied textiles for two years and decided he would become a coach when he graduated.

Back then it was an easier road if you coached both basketball and football. Knowing this, Sloan quit basketball after his sophomore year to play football, much to Case's chagrin. But it did accomplish his objective. Sloan was offered a job as assistant football coach at Presbyterian College, a small school in Clinton, South Carolina. One of the other assistants was a guy named Bo Schembechler, who would one day lead the Michigan Wolverines to national prominence as a constant powerhouse in college football. The tiny college also asked Sloan to head up its basketball program.

While he enjoyed his tenure at Presbyterian College, Sloan left for an assistant's job in 1955-56 at Memphis State under Dr. Eugene Lambert. Soon thereafter, though, he went back to South Carolina to discuss head basketball coaching positions with both The Citadel, in Charleston, and Clemson University. Clemson was the job that interested him; Sloan interviewed at The Citadel just because the job was open.

What he didn't figure on was taking such a shine to The Citadel's athletic director. When he ended up accepting the reins at The Citadel, Sloan's wife, Joan, was about as happy as you'd expect someone to be upon hearing that her husband had taken a job that would pay 30 percent less ($5,200 a year) than the job he was leaving. After two days of serious discussion, Sloan decided to go back to Charleston and tell the AD at The Citadel that he could not accept the job after all.

But before that happened, the values passed down by his father asserted themselves, and Sloan knew he could not go back on his word. As for Mrs. Sloan, the scrimping she had to do to make ends meet in Charleston may have made up for her own unexpected new role in the athletic department at The Citadel. It was a tradition that before every game at the Field House an instrumental version of "The Star-Spangled Banner" be played. As a welcoming gesture to the Sloans, General Mark Clark allowed Joan Sloan to sing the National Anthem before one game. She did such a boffo job that her rendition became a new tradition at all home games—even after Norm became head basketball coach at Florida in 1960.

When Sloan took over the basketball program at Florida, he quickly realized that this was a *football* school. He replaced John Mauer, who had a beautiful office next to that of Ray Graves, the head football coach. Sloan assumed he would be moving into Mauer's office, but he was in for a rude awakening. Mauer was staying on as an assistant football coach. He was also keeping his desirable office—the very one Sloan envisioned himself in.

Sloan thus found out quickly that an assistant football coach at Florida had a lot more status than the head basketball coach. Sloan's office ended up being a real fixer-upper, the old football position meeting room—with the classroom chairs still in it.

Then there was "The Case of the Missing Season Tickets." Since Gatorland was football country, season tickets had never been approved for basketball. Sloan took that battle all the way to the chairman of the athletic board, and season tickets for basketball were finally approved after a well-fought and lengthy battle.

As it turned out, a grand total of four season tickets were sold to one person that first year. It was an inauspicious beginning for the new coach and his program.

But Sloan forged ahead, and by the time he exited for NC State in 1966—replacing the departing Press Maravich ("Pistol" Pete's dad), who was LSU bound—he was ready for a new challenge, having made the Florida program successful and popular.

Coach Sloan brought outstanding players to North Carolina State with him, such as Vann Williford, Ed Leftwich and Tom Burleson. He worked tirelessly to make State not only competitive, but an elite team in an elite conference.

Prior to my arrival, his greatest success was in the 1969-70 season, his fourth year at the helm of the Wolfpack. Coach Sloan's team went 23-7 that year and 9-5 in the conference. As they headed toward the ACC Tournament, the mighty South Carolina Gamecocks lurked in the distance. Frank McGuire's South Carolina team was the cream of the ACC crop that year, going 14-0 in the conference and 25-3 overall. As I would find out later, going undefeated in the powerful ACC was a daunting task. South Carolina was loaded with great players, including super guard John Roche, 6'10" Tom Riker, 6'10" Tom Owens, guard Bobby Cremins and 6'8" John Ribcock. They outrebounded their ACC opponents by an average of 13 per game and outscored them by 18 points per game.

Sloan knew what he was up against, and he was prepared for all-out mental and physical warfare on the court.

That was an era where only the conference winners went to the NCAA Tournament. In the first round of the ACC Tournament, South Carolina won a yawner over Clemson, 34-33, in a game where the deliberately slow pace would've drawn protests from a snail. State dumped Maryland rather easily, 67-57. During the game, Sloan could be heard constantly yelling at Terrapins head coach Lefty Driesell, telling him to "shut up!" Outbursts like that were responsible for the nickname affixed on Sloan by media: "Stormin' Norman."

The semifinals saw the Gamecocks destroy Wake Forest 79-63 and Sloan's boys squeak by Virginia, 67-66, on a late follow-up shot by Rick Anheuser. That set up a battle of the league's two best teams, and South Carolina—ranked in the top five nationally—was the overwhelming favorite.

But the Wolfpack would not go down without a fight.

SC star guard John Roche's ankle was sprained, significantly reducing his mobility. McGuire decided to play a 2-1-2 zone to make it a little easier on Roche, but it had the unintended effect of negating the Gamecocks' tremendous advantage underneath the boards. The zone defense also slowed the tempo of the game down. The first half ended with South Carolina on top, 24-17.

State was in foul trouble early in the second half, so Sloan ordered his team to slow the ball down every time South Carolina went into its zone defense. He needed to shorten the game.

Momentum suddenly shifted with South Carolina ahead by 11. McGuire ordered his team out of the zone, but Williford slipped in underneath for an easy basket. State then stole the inbounds pass and scored again. With Rick Anheuser grabbing rebounds and Williford red hot, State tied the game at the end of regulation play at 35-35.

The first overtime also ended in a tie as Roche missed a game-winning shot. In the second OT, Ed Leftwich stole the ball from Cremins and went the distance for an easy layup and the lead. The Wolfpack never looked back. Anheuser added two foul shots to make the final score 42-39. In 10 minutes of overtime, the State "D" had come up big.

North Carolina State had pulled off one of the year's most stunning upsets, and Vann Williford was named the tournament's MVP. State was off to the NCAAs to take on St. Bonaventure in the first round. They lost, but the Wolfpack's season was one for the ages.

I could tell that Coach Sloan was a man of conviction, and that was very appealing to me. He desperately wanted to win, and so did I. I was going to do everything I could do to make sure he experienced a lot of winning and maybe even a national championship. He deserved it.

As I looked forward to my sophomore year, a national championship for the Wolfpack seemed like a distinct possibility. But the bomb about to be dropped on us by the NCAA would reduce that dream to mere baying at the moon.

CHAPTER 4

RUNNING THE TABLE

Even though North Carolina summers are known for their blistering combination of unrelenting heat and humidity, I must say I was feeling quite cool and relaxed in the summer of 1972. I had become more comfortable in my new surroundings and the college lifestyle, and I missed Boiling Springs less and less. My teammates had become my new family and we were inseparable.

But all of the grand, teenage experiences that were part of college life were suddenly disrupted in October 1972 by the approaching loud, menacing footsteps of the National College Association of Athletics. What should have been the ordinary beginning of fall basketball practice became something so bizarre and foreign as to be utterly incomprehensible.

Without warning, the anticipated "slap on the wrist" from my freshman year investigation by the NCAA instead became a two-by-four across the skull. It was the NCAA's decision that the North Carolina State men's basketball program would be put on probation for the entire 1972-73 season and would not be eligible to participate in that season's NCAA Championship Tournament.

My heart ached as the excitement about what could have been was extinguished like a campfire doused in water. How could such minor infractions have resulted in such an extreme penalty?

My teammates, coaches and I struggled with this for many a long hour, and then, finally, the answers came. But before I share with you how we overcame such frustrating adversity to record one of the greatest seasons in college basketball history, I will describe a tale of jealousy and deceit that has never been shared in print until now.

There was no question that the University of North Carolina coveted me as a player. In fact, it was taken for granted in some quarters that I would sign and become a Tar Heel for four years. Visions of multiple national championships, and the dethroning of the vaunted UCLA dynasty, surely danced in their heads. Over time, UNC came to the belief that it was it their God-given right to claim every blue-chip athlete who hailed from the state, and the UNC muckety-mucks and important alumni were so suffused with their own righteousness and pride that they couldn't even conceive that a player might not opt to go to their institution of higher education.

When I chose NC State, the Carolina Blue hoops leadership was not only stunned, but also stung. And when they didn't get what they wanted, they decided to at least get even.

In the summer of 1971, when I attended early orientation at NC State, my high school teammates and friends Jerry and Larry Hunt were working at a weeklong basketball camp. Naturally they extended an invitation because they were my friends, and I stayed with them *one night* in their dorm room.

At that camp were various players and personnel from numerous colleges, including all the schools that I had turned down. Which of these people notified the NCAA of my stay with the Hunt brothers is not a matter of record, but the cosmic finger points directly at the representatives of North Carolina.

Here's why.

Not many weeks later when I actually arrived at NC State to attend school, I played in a few pickup games during the late orientation phase of registration. Many great players from the region would come to the school for the opportunity to play in these games because of the irresistible lure of the high level of talent and competition. For example, I distinctly remember the great Bob McAdoo playing in some of those games.

A University of North Carolina football player by the name of Bill Brafford was there as well, and supposedly he took word of my presence in the gym back to Chapel Hill.

Our ace recruiter and assistant coach, Eddie Biedenbach, also played in a few of those games, and that was another ostensible infraction by us because a coach could not play with his players. The school was accused of "trying me out during the off season." Biedenbach was furious and did some investigating of his own, and that's how Bill Bolton was identified as the informer.

But wait, it gets better.

Bill Guthridge, the longtime UNC assistant coach to Dean Smith who eventually succeeded him as head coach for three years, had friends in all the right places. The fact is that Guthridge had played and coached at Kansas State University for 10 years (1958-67). You devout basketball historians will remember that NCAA headquarters, then located in Kansas City, Missouri, was only a short two-hour trip from the Kansas State-Manhattan campus.

That may seem innocent enough, but Guthridge's college roommate for a time was a man I'll call "Mr. X"—who was the very same individual responsible for bringing the ton of bricks down on the NC State program.

Are you sitting down?

Mr. X happened to be the man who performed the investigation on me and North Carolina State for the NCAA.

Coincidence? Not hardly.

Biedenbach had a friend at the Raleigh airport who would call him whenever Mr. X came to town to do his NCAA gumshoeing. But before he'd get around to us, Mr. X would drive his rented car to the UNC campus to see his good buddy Bill Guthridge. When they were finished catching up on old times and reciting their alma mater, Mr. X would mosey on over to Raleigh to pay us a visit.

You get the picture.

When everything is added up, it makes for a strong case that the Tar Heels acted like a bunch of heels. Not that they'll ever admit it.

"We at Carolina solemnly swear we did not report North Carolina State," Dean Smith told a reporter for *The News and Observer* in Charlotte. "I'm tired of being blamed for turning them in. I hear it everywhere, on the streets, everywhere. It is the most widely rumored thing I've heard in North Carolina."

However, Smith did tell the reporter that the NCAA possessed an aerial photo of a truck paving the driveway at my parents' home in Shelby and added that the truck reportedly belonged to an NC State alumnus.

Aerial photograph? Did UNC have a spy plane at its disposal to provide them with an overview of my parents' property? What, no wiretap transcripts, too? The whole thing was a big joke.

It is important to note that the rumors had become so rampant in college basketball circles regarding NC State's supposed infractions that the NCAA probably felt compelled to issue a severe penalty, lest it be accused of not being harsh enough.

In any case, Coach Sloan was not about to let the situation prevent us from realizing our full potential and destiny.

After the initial shock and despair dissipated, Coach Sloan reminded us that we were still *the major force* in college basketball to be reckoned with. There might not be any pot of gold at the end of our season, in the form of an opportunity to knock UCLA off its high horse in the NCAA Tournament, but that didn't mean we still couldn't show the entire country who the real kings of the collegiate court were.

Our job now, Coach said, was to make a boldly indelible, profound, season-long statement that would make UCLA's or any other team's claim to the title of best team in the land as dubious as Mr. X's ethics. We needed to play every game as if the national championship were on the line.

We needed to not lose. Period.

And toward that end, we unveiled *The Secret Weapon*...

During practice one day, Monte and I noticed something peculiar that that we began seeing with regularity—defenders would always overplay me. While I usually found a way to get open, it occurred to me that the result of overplaying me was that an open cut to the back-door area was usually available.

So one time I went back-door, and Monty threw me a pass like it was going to sail right out of the gym. I jumped as high as I could, caught the ball at its apex, and all in one motion, laid it into the basket.

Coach Sloan saw everything unfold, rubbed his chin and said, "Hmmmm. That looks like a play we should use!" He was not only a great coach, but a *smart* man, too.

The press dubbed our new play the "Alley-oop." The original "Alley-oop" was a character in a 1930s comic strip who was so tough that, in the words of a 1960s pop song, "he don't eat nothing but bearcat stew..." I'm not sure if the nickname for our new play came from that or from a football play popularized by the San Francisco 49ers in the 1950s and '60s. 49er quarterback great Y. A. Tittle would loft high, arching passes to standout receiver R. C. Owens in the end zone, and Owens consistently out-leaped defenders to snag the ball for touchdowns.

Another possibility comes from a French phrase, "allez-oop," which was said when hoisting a baby in the air.

We must have run the Alley-oop over a hundred times during my sophomore year and countless times thereafter. When I was a senior playing against Buffalo State, we ran the play 10 or 11 times and I scored 57 points—my all-time college high game. Buffalo State played a zone, and I would repeatedly sneak in the through the back door, catch Monte's high arching passes, and score, score, score. I thought they'd catch on after a while, but much to my surprise and delight, they did not.

Generally speaking, if my defender didn't go out to the top to guard me, I'd pull up and take jump shots and score that way. That's when they'd start to overplay me—after I popped in a few long jumpers. When I had possession of the ball, I had several options: feed it to Burleson on the inside, kick it out to the wing, drive to the basket, get the return alley-oop pass and *voila*—two points for NC State. It was even easier when I didn't have the ball. Monte was our point guard, and whenever the defense overplayed me, he would throw the perfectly timed pass and I would go back-door and drop it in the hoop like dropping apples into a basket.

We constantly refined the Alley-oop, and it became a thing of beauty. If imitation is the sincerest form of flattery, then we are certainly flattered. It's safe to say that the Alley-oop became one of the most exciting plays in all of sports. Who could deny the awe engendered while watching Michael Jordan, Julius Erving or Dominique Wilkins complete the Alley-oop? And today, with young stars like Vince Carter, Kevin Garnett and Kobe Bryant all throwing down the Back Door Beauty, it's still bringing fans right out of their chairs. We were glad to make such a contribution to the great game of basketball.

The only difference between the Alley-oop then and now is that now you can slam it home. I missed the dunk being allowed back into college basketball by one year, as the rule against it was repealed in the 1975-76 season. I also missed the freshman eligibility rule change by one year (freshmen were allowed to play varsity ball during my sophomore season). Bad timing just seemed to follow me around like a lost puppy dog. And just like a puppy dog, it was hard to get rid of and usually stank.

One thing that didn't stink was the 1972-73 Wolfpack squad. We were loaded with superior talent.

Rick Holdt and Joe Cafferky were senior co-captains. Rick was a
6'5", 207-pound forward from Paramus, New Jersey, who averaged more
than 10 points and four rebounds per game during his three varsity years
at NC State. Joe was a 6'2", 170-pound guard from Havertown, Pennsylvania, who averaged approximately 11 points per game his two years. As
the lone starting seniors on a relatively young team, their leadership was
unquestionably needed and valuable.

Tommy Burleson was such a dominant force in the middle at 7'4",
225 pounds, that he commanded attention from the defense at all times.
Big Tom was the leading returning scorer from the 1971-72 team (16-
10), with 21.3 points per game, but he knew that we wouldn't have to
depend on his scoring so much now that there was more offensive firepower available. The scoring as a team could now be more evenly distrib-
uted. Moreover, Tom knew that his 12 to 14 boards each game were even
more necessary for us to accomplish our lofty goal of perfection.

At point guard, Monte started opposite Cafferky, and I was at one
forward spot with Rick Holdt at the other. Tim Stoddard came off the
bench for me or Holdt, and collectively that made for as imposing a first
string as there was in all the land.

As for me, *Sports Illustrated* quoted Purdue head coach Fred Schaus
as saying, "David Thompson is one of the top ten players in the country
today—pro or college." The magazine also cited key figures in the ACC
who believed that I was the best player *ever* in the history of the conference—before I had even played a varsity game. Coach Sloan agreed, telling *SI*, "He is the best I have ever seen. There is something about the way
he moves and acts that says 'great.' He'll be recognized soon as one of the
best who ever played the game. Because of him it is justifiable to say we'll
have one of the best teams in the country this year."

No pressure there on the new sophomore!

Anticipation was high as we approached our first game. We wanted
to go right out and establish ourselves as one of the top teams in the ACC
and in the country. Maryland was ranked No. 3 in an Associated Press
preseason poll, and they also just happened to be in our conference. We
were ranked No. 8, which was all the motivation a team could ask for.

My varsity debut came against a seemingly insignificant opponent.
Though Appalachian State was only in their first year of Division 1 basketball, they were coached by one of the all-time greats, Press Maravich.

Press, of course, was the father of Hall of Fame guard "Pistol" Pete Maravich and coached him at LSU from 1967-70. And though most people know Pete as the most prolific scorer in college basketball history, what many people don't know is what a creative offensive genius Press Maravich was— a coach simply ahead of his time.

Additionally, it was Press Maravich whom Norman Sloan succeeded in 1966 as head basketball coach at NC State. Therefore, the game had its own built in mini-drama—however short-lived.

The memories I have of that first varsity game are vivid. It was a beautiful, crisp November evening, a great night for a basketball game in Reynolds Coliseum. The home crowd, a veritable sea of Wolfpack red, was roaring its support with unbridled enthusiasm. We did not disappoint them.

Unfortunately for Appalachian State, the game was not even remotely close. In fact it was an all-out, old-fashioned *rout*. The Wolfpack took it right to Press Maravich's team, and the result wasn't pretty for the visitors.

We were up 18-2 before they knew what hit them, courtesy of our full-court defensive pressure. It took them forever just to get the ball across halfcourt. You learn to take out a lesser team like that early in the game with the full-court press, and we did that right from the opening tipoff. In fact, we only allowed our opponent 17 second-half points.

The final score was 130-53. Poor Appalachian State would take beatings like that all year long as they adjusted to Division 1 play. Somehow it didn't seem fitting to a great coach like Press Maravich.

I ended up with 33 points—20 in the second half—and 13 rebounds. When asked about me after the game, Coach Maravich said, "He can shoot, he can rebound. He's got all the moves and all the tools to be an All-American." That meant a lot to me coming from such an esteemed coach, and after only my first varsity game.

Our guards, Monte Towe and Joe Cafferky, just tore them to shreds. They each scored 10 points, and Joe handed out nine assists. But it was their smothering defense that was the real key to victory. Rick Holdt added 16, and two of our key reserves—Greg Hawkins and Mark Moeller— chipped in 18 and 13 points, respectively. Our bench played most of the second half, as they would in our first four games.

Our opponents were of the cream-puff variety. After Appalachian State came Atlantic Christian, Georgia Southern, and then South Florida. The final scores were 110-40, 144-100, and 125-88. I averaged 33.4 points per game.

During that early run, *Sports Illustrated* reporter Curry Kirkpatrick called us the "Ken-L-Ration" team, because our opponents, he said, were a bunch of dogs. Coach Sloan wasted no time turning that negative into a positive. After each game he gave one player the "Ken-L-Ration Award," recognizing the "top dog" for his performance. Many times I was seen as the team's greyhound who always finished strong in the stretch.

The sniping didn't keeping us from moving up two spots in the Associated Press rankings. Now we were ranked sixth nationally. There was something else that came as a nice surprise my sophomore year. Whereas my parents came up only a few times to see me play during my freshman year, they were now making the long drive from Boiling Springs quite frequently. They would come up on a weeknight, watch the game, say hello and goodbye, then make the four-hour drive back home—and still have the energy to work that next day. I appreciated their support so much. To have family in the crowd regularly cheering me on gave me a great sense of comfort and, I believe, made me play better.

The Wolfpack moved onward. Tougher competition soon arrived in the form of the ACC "Big Four" Tournament in mid-December.

Basketball is so big in North Carolina that even football is dwarfed, and the biggest excitement in state hoops surrounds the Big Four—North Carolina, NC State, Duke and Wake Forest.

Sheer proximity alone would be enough to stir rivalry on such proud Southern campuses, but at least in basketball, members of the quartet had for years also shared one common attribute—*excellence*. Consider that as of 1972, a Big Four team had won 17 of the 19 ACC championships.

The Big Four Tournament was only in its third year at that point, yet the fans had embraced it like an only child. It was just cause for un-abashed hysteria. And that year's edition had several added dimensions. Duke was improving at a rapid rate, and Wake Forest—though rebuild-ing under placid coach Carl Tacy—was now a legitimate threat. Of course, the real draw was the anticipated finals matchup between North Carolina and the Wolfpack. Experts were quoted as saying that the dominant Dean Smith era might be interrupted by an NC State team favored with one, possibly two superstars.

One might wonder, though, why the ACC would have wanted such an early-season battle of its premier teams, given the regular-season schedule and the end-of-season ACC Tournament. In addition, there was the dis-tinct possibility of a postseason tournament such as the NIT, which could well have included more than one of the Big Four. By the end of the season, the Big Four would be just a little tired of seeing each other. Consider, too, that we would collectively hurt ourselves in the national polls if we routinely knocked each other off during the regular season—which occurred often.

The answer should be obvious—*money*. Each of the four schools became approximately $45,000 richer after the tournament. The crowds in the 15,362-seat Greensboro Coliseum were always at or near capacity, and tickets went for a premium price: $7 apiece. Expenses for the participating schools were kept at a minimum since travel was not an issue—we were all very close to Greensboro. Therefore, the Big Four Tournament was one of the most financially rewarding in the nation.

Duke coach Bucky Waters had his own pet name for the premature shootout: "The Budget Bowl."

Something else interesting about the tournament was that the games did not count in the ACC standings. But while the games may not have counted there, the two-day competition gave rabid fans ample ammunition and bragging rights around the water cooler Monday morning.

On opening night, the two well-hyped powerhouses were nearly reduced to also-rans. We did not play well and were fortunate to escape with an 88-83 win over an inspired Wake Forest team. I had spurts of good play, but was generally inconsistent. I did account for 29 points and brought the wild crowd out of its seats with some showy shot blocking on defense. Burleson got in foul trouble early and was therefore not much of a factor—which definitely contributed to our problems and the close final score.

UNC had its hands full with Duke before prevailing 91-86. But even with our respective lackluster performances in the opening round, both teams were able to provide the fans with the final they so desperately wanted. And that one game represented many things to our team.

There were multiple players now on the Tar Heel varsity who had handed us our only loss as freshmen. But even more galvanizing was the burning desire to take out the team we suspected was behind our clobbering by the NCAA. We didn't need any more inspiration than that.

The 14,886 screaming lunatics in the Coliseum exhibited exemplary patience as the consolation game went to Duke 80-67. Even now, I distinctly remember the rumbling, ear-splitting applause emanating from the stands the moment the North Carolina and NC State teams emerged from the dressing rooms. I'm not saying the frenzied atmosphere affected us, but both teams continued their dismal play from the previous evening. Errant passes, missed shots, frayed tempers and traveling violations marked the first half.

The two teams that had averaged a combined 219 points per game up to that point now combined for just 55 in the opening 20 minutes. UNC summoned enough focus to gain a 29-26 lead. Bobby Jones managed to slip by our defense to get open under the basket a few times and led the Tar Heels with 12. I had six points, and Burleson contributed four.

Everything changed in the second half as both teams began to hit their strides. North Carolina was breaking fast, passing effectively, and pressing intently on defense. We started shooting well from the outside and capitalizing on Burleson's height on the inside. I hit two shots quickly and passed for another two points. Tommy and I ruthlessly harassed the Tar Heel inside shooters.

But neither of us would be the hero this day. The credit for reviving Wolfpack basketball in the state of North Carolina would go to the smallest man on the floor—dynamo Monte Towe. Monte's marvelous ball handling thoroughly frustrated and demoralized the dogged Carolina press.

With 9:01 to play and the score tied at 49, Monte picked up his fourth personal foul. Coach Sloan was going to sit him down, but Monte rushed over to the bench and pleaded his case to remain in the game. Coach Sloan relented, a tribute to his own savvy as well as Monte's fervor.

Monte was a marked man back on the court, but he controlled the ball like a yo-yo, to the total frustration of the Tar Heel guards. It was quite a sight to see all of those high-profile former high school All-Americans chase a guy all over the court who looked like he was barely in junior high. Monte delivered crisp, accurate passes when he wasn't doing his Marques Haynes impression, and he moved us into the lead almost single-handedly.

The final five points were scored on free throws. Monte made two, and I hit three. Six-foot, ten-inch North Carolina center Ed Stahl performed well with 16 points and 11 rebounds, as did forward Bobby Jones, who had 18 points and eight boards. Luckily for us, we were able to pull out the win, 68-61. Though I did not shoot particularly well from the field, going seven for 16, I still led all scorers with 19 points—good enough for tournament MVP honors. Burleson came alive in the second half and finished with 15 points and 13 rebounds. It might not have counted in the ACC standings, but you sure couldn't tell that from the faces of the Tar Heel players.

With subsequent wins against Davidson (103-90), Georgia (97-83), Virginia (68-61), Duke (94-87) and Lehigh (115-53), we were still undefeated at 11-0. It was January of 1973 and time to find out if we really belonged in the penthouse with the nation's elite teams. So far, the view was pretty nice.

Maryland was now ranked second in the country, and they were just waiting for us to do battle at their place—the intimidating Cole Field House.

Most sports fans remember January 14, 1973, as Super Bowl Sunday. The 16-0 Miami Dolphins, en route to the only perfect season in NFL history, were actually the underdogs heading into Super Bowl VII against the Washington Redskins, affectionately remembered as the "Over-the-Hill Gang."

NC State, like the Dolphins, was also undefeated and gunning for a perfect season. And also like the Dolphins, we felt we were the better team before the game was even played. Maybe both teams felt as though they weren't getting the respect they deserved, but at least Maryland was still in the running for the official national title.

That day the Dolphins and the Wolfpack both made believers out of the skeptics.

That game was one of many epic duels I would have in my career against Maryland coach Lefty Driesell's mighty Terrapins. Maryland was thoroughly loaded with great players, a testament to Driesell's drive to make the Terrapins the "UCLA of the East."

Driesell had landed one of the greatest high school players ever, 6'11" Tom McMillen from Mansfield, Pennsylvania. Talented as a ballplayer (a 1972 Olympian, NCAA All-American, and NBA journeyman), McMillen was just as impressive as a student (he was pre-med and eventually valedictorian, a Rhodes Scholar and U.S. Congressman). He always gave us fits.

Freshman point guard John Lucas, a future NBA star, made the Terps get up and go, and 6'9" junior forward Len Elmore was a rebounding machine (his rebounding records at Maryland may never be broken). Jim O'Brien was a tough 6'7" senior forward who averaged 16.6 points per game that year, and 6'4" senior Bob Bodell was the other guard opposite Lucas.

It was always fun playing against Maryland, because, unlike other coaches, Driesell let his team *play* with us. As we became a premier team over the next three years, many teams would try to slow the ball down against us and put the paying customers asleep. Playing against Maryland was enjoyable because they didn't fear us, and we didn't fear them. They ran with us, and what battles we waged.

The first Maryland game was one of the first nationally televised ACC college basketball games, and the drama and expected level of play were too much for network TV to pass up. The cameras added an additional aura of importance to this red-hot matchup.

The score was close throughout the first half, but we emerged after the first 20 minutes with a nine-point lead, 53-44. But then McMillen, Lucas and Elmore kicked into high gear, and almost before we knew it we were all knotted up at 85 apiece near the end of the game. No surprise there. After all, this was the No. 2 team in the land that we were battling. Their pride was on the line.

But so was our perfect season. With 10 seconds left in the game, Burleson had the ball at the hash mark on the right side of the court, just outside the lane. I was at the top of the key, and the defense was really overplaying me in an effort to keep me away from the ball. Tommy launched an off-balance jumper with about three seconds left on the clock, and as soon as I saw the ball leave his hands, I went directly to the basket behind the defense. My thought was that if he missed, I would be there to grab the rebound and try to score.

As the ball bounced off the cylinder, I met it at exactly the right time, well above the rim, and dropped it in for the winning basket as time ran out. Final: NC State 87, Maryland 85.

One reporter described the end of the play like this: "Thompson seemed to fall from the sky as he seized Burleson's errant shot and dropped in the winning goal."

Those Terrapins were awfully tough, and it was a blow to them to lose on their own turf. McMillen had riddled us with 29 points on 12-22 shooting and snared 14 rebounds. Elmore and Lucas combined for 33 points, with Elmore pulling down 11 boards and Lucas dishing out eight assists. I'm sure they looked forward to the rematch at Reynolds Coliseum in a few weeks.

As for the Wolfpack, Joe Cafferky had a very productive game handing out nine assists. Tommy ended up with 20 points, and I led all scorers with 37. We were moving through the ACC like a wrecking ball and replaced Maryland as the No. 2-ranked team in the country; the Terrapins dropped to third.

One of the things that helped us in many of our close games that season was a book Coach Sloan had given us at the beginning of the year. He was big on reading, and this book in particular, *Psycho Cybernetics: The Power of Positive Thinking*, was intended to help us become mentally tough. I thought that was pretty innovative for a coach to do, and I know it helped me.

We next traveled to Clemson to take on the Tigers and won, 86-76. I led the way with 24 points and 11 rebounds, while Big Tom scored 15 and snagged 10 boards. Rick Holdt had an excellent game with 14 points and seven rebounds.

Next up on our extended road trip was Furman, in Greensboro. We ran away with that one, 98-73, as Tim Stoddard had his first of many big games with 12 points and 12 caroms. I threw in 27 and grabbed 12 rebounds.

The time had arrived for the greatly anticipated rematch with Maryland on January 31, 1973. But this time war would be waged on *our* home court.

Once again, the teams were evenly matched through the first half. At intermission the score was tied 42-42. We felt we were playing at our peak—a finely tuned cohesive unit—but couldn't shake off the highly talented Maryland crew. Tom McMillen continued to torment us, and John Lucas had them running.

Somehow, we took it to another level in the second half, outscoring the Terrapins 47-36 in the second stanza to walk away with an impressive 89-78 victory.

A primary reason for our victory was that we won the battle of the boards 43-36, with me nabbing 11, Burleson getting 10, and Stoddard seizing seven in only 13 minutes before fouling out. Our senior co-captains, Cafferky and Holdt, went a combined 9-10 from the field to contribute 18 points. They just shot the lights out.

For Maryland, McMillen was stellar once again, shooting 10-16 and garnering 25 points and snaring six rebounds. Jim O'Brien had 18 and six rebounds, and Lucas chipped in with 14 points.

We had officially established dominance in the ACC with an astonishing 15-0 record. We stayed ranked No. 2, while Maryland dropped to ninth in the polls. You-know-who from the West Coast was still ranked No. 1.

Our confidence kept building as the winning streak took on a life of its own. We were playing so well together, like we could read each other's minds. And even though there were some tough, close calls along the way, we always found a way to win. It was truly the power of positive thinking, just like Coach Sloan had taught us.

Some games Tommy Burleson might take over, or Tim Stoddard, or Monte Towe might make a big play to bust things open. This was not a one-man team. For example, in one game, key reserve Mark Moeller came off the bench and hit some big shots for us. Joe Cafferky came up big many times, too. Somebody would always step up to the plate in any given game.

We thought we could beat anyone, including John Wooden's UCLA Bruins. We pressed forward, knowing we would never get the chance, but used their status as top dog to motivate us.

Virginia came to visit on February 3, and Cavalier senior guard Barry Parkhill took it right to us, pouring in 26 points. He gave us quite a scare. Fortunately, we narrowly escaped with a 64-59 win. I scored 18 and secured nine rebounds.

We won another nail-biter at home two days later against North Carolina, 76-73, making it two in a row over our bitter rivals. We were now 17-0 and counting.

In Charlotte, for the annual North/South doubleheader, I chipped in 30 points and grabbed 13 boards as we disposed of Clemson 68-61.

In the championship game of the tournament versus Georgia Tech the next night, I nailed 12 of 13 free throws on the way to 36 points and a decisive 118-94 NC State victory. I was really feeling it on the court that day because I was shooting well, going 12-18 from the field. I also contributed nine rebounds. Burleson was on fire too, netting 24 points in addition to pulling down 15 rebounds.

On February 13, East Carolina fell 105-70 as my shooting hand stayed hot. I had 33 points, going 13-15 from the field, and was 7-8 from the line. Burleson was dominating as usual, tallying 19 points while cleaning the glass with 17 rebounds.

Wake Forest (81-59), Duke (74-50), and UNC-Charlotte (100-64) were our next victims, and we were on top of the world at 23-0. Tommy and I combined for 129 points and 70 rebounds in the three victories.

We traveled to Chapel Hill on February 27 to face the Tar Heels of North Carolina one last time. The excitement and tension were palpable inside the arena, and UNC would have loved nothing more than to end our winning streak on their home floor. But it was not to be.

With senior guard George Karl—now a head coach in the NBA—leading the way with 21 points, and Mitch Kupchak and Ed Stahl tossing in 30 more, the Heels kept it close. They made a respectable run at us in the second half, but we finally pulled out an 82-78 win, and how sweet it was.

Our last regular season ACC game was against Wake Forest at home on March 3. We were still ranked second in the country behind Bill Walton and UCLA, and we were 24-0.

The hometown crowd went berserk as Burleson turned in an unbelievable performance of 27 points and 19 rebounds in just 33 minutes. The Demon Deacons had no answer for the 7'4" All-American, and we knew that no team had an answer for our 25-0 Wolfpack.

Something bothered me, though, and it became clear as the ACC Tournament loomed on the horizon: No matter how perfect our record was, it wasn't going to be good enough.

CHAPTER 5

CHAMPIONSHIP TIMES TWO

O ne prevailing thought crossed my mind as we headed into the ACC Tournament: All our wins would mean *nothing* if we lost at the end. I took it upon myself to ensure we would be successful and let every basketball fan in the world know who was, without a doubt, No. 1.

We had a first-round bye in the tournament due to our undefeated record in the conference. In the semifinals in Greensboro, on March 9, 1973, we dumped a scrappy Virginia team 63-51. This time we were sure to keep Barry Parkhill in check; he only shot 6-18 from the field and ended up with just 12 points.

We had a very balanced offensive attack that game, with Burleson, Monte Towe, Joe Cafferky and myself (37 points) all scoring in double figures. We were 26-0, with one game left to make our dream a reality.

Only tenth-ranked Maryland stood in our way, and they were getting a little tired of us getting all the glory in the ACC.

Playing in my first ACC championship game was a dream come true for me. I had fantasized about this many times as a kid—making the game-winning shot, knifing through the defense on the way to the hoop, hearing the roar of the crowd—and now I was here.

That's when the reality of our probation really sank in. No matter if Maryland won or lost the game, *they* were going to the NCAA Tournament, not us. We could finish with an unblemished record including three wins over the Terrapins, but it would still be them heading off to NCAA Tournament play by virtue of making it to the ACC championship game, while we fulfilled our probation. It just didn't seem fair.

Given the way my timing was off all year, it figured that I saved the last game to register my lowest scoring output.

The 1973 ACC championship game took place on March 10, at the Greensboro Coliseum. Both teams were prepared to wage battle, but Maryland would have to take the floor without star forward Len Elmore. Elmore had hurt his foot, and as much as he wanted to play, could not.

It was another close contest right from the opening tip, and once again Tom McMillen was having his way with us. McMillen knew that he would be counted on even more than usual with Elmore sitting on the sidelines. Knowing they would miss Elmore's relentless board crashing, the Terrapins slowed the tempo considerably. That meant far less opportunities for us—and me—to score.

We were deadlocked at the half, 32-32. We had been averaging over 90 points per game, so the slowdown tactic was working for Maryland.

NC State only shot five free throws in the entire game, but the two I made in the closing minutes helped seal the win, 76-74, and the ACC championship for the Wolfpack. Because of the slackened pace at which Maryland had forced us to play, I could only manage 12 shots and hit just four. My 10 points were my lowest point production of the year.

Burleson played well again, though, going 7-13 from the field for 14 points. Partially benefiting from Elmore's absence, Tom also hauled down 14 very important rebounds.

For his efforts against Maryland and Virginia, Big Tom was awarded the Everett Case award given to the MVP of the tournament, and justifiably so.

McMillen tallied 24 points for Maryland on 12-20 shooting and grabbed eight rebounds. John Lucas had a superb overall game with 21 points on 10-20 shooting, with seven assists and five rebounds. The Terps were tough, but we just out-persevered them.

Maryland would eventually lose to Providence, 103-89, in the NCAA regional finals. The Friars, in turn, would succumb in the Final Four to an excellent Memphis State team coached by Gene Bartow and featuring 6'9" star center Larry Kenon. Providence's Marvin Barnes went down in the first half with a dislocated kneecap, and though he returned late in the game, it was too little, too late for Providence. The final score was 98-85, Memphis State.

In the other semifinal game, Bobby Knight—in only his second year as head coach of Indiana—and his valiant Hoosiers fell to the reigning kings of college basketball, the UCLA Bruins, by a score of 70-59. Indiana had pulled to within two at 57-55 with only 5:51 remaining, but it wasn't enough as the Bruins sped to victory.

UCLA went on to win the NCAA championship for the seventh consecutive year, as Memphis State fell 87-66 in the title game and became the Bruins' 75th consecutive victim in the process.

Bill Walton turned in *the* greatest performance in championship game history by scoring a record 44 points with an otherworldly shooting display. Big Red went 21-22 from the field, and chipped in 10 rebounds just for good measure.

Of course, I believe things would have been different had 6'11" Walton faced 7'4" Burleson, but we will never know. What we did know was that the No. 2 team in the nation did not have a crack at the No. 1 Bruins, and that was a crying shame. Maybe we hadn't won 75 in a row as UCLA had, but 27 straight wins sure gave us the confidence that we could hold our own against the mighty Bruins. We had averaged 95 points per contest against excellent competition, so we knew we could play with them.

Our dream year had come to a close, and we had accomplished our goal of not losing a single game. Going through the ACC undefeated, beating both North Carolina and Maryland three times apiece when those teams were ranked in the Top 10 at one time or another, was nothing short of miraculous.

Burleson was named All-ACC, leading the conference in rebounding with 12 boards per game while averaging 17.9 points. The ACC named me MVP and Player of the Year, mainly because I led the conference in scoring with a 24.7 average. Personally, I was especially proud of my 56.9 field goal percentage and 8.2 rebounds a game. Players who are 6'4" don't usually have that kind of accuracy, and many of my shots were from long distance.

Other honors were bestowed upon me as well. At 18 years of age, I was the youngest player ever to be unanimously named First Team All-American. There were three seniors on the team—forward Ron Behagen from Minnesota and guards Ed Ratleff from Long Beach State and Doug Collins from Illinois State. The list also included one junior, the great Bill Walton from UCLA. I was the lone sophomore and was very proud to have been so honored.

The debate has raged for years as to which Wolfpack team was better, the 27-0 team of 1972-73, or the 30-1 national championship team of 1973-74. Here is my honest opinion: the 1972-73 team had a greater per-game margin of victory spread than the succeeding team, but in 1973-74, we added Phil Spence and Mo Rivers to the roster. That chemistry and the fact that we were a year older counted for a lot, so I'll let you be the judge.

What still hurts me and my teammates most about the 1972-73 team is that they are rarely discussed, especially when compared to the 1973-74 national championship team. We accomplished so much—perfection, in fact—playing in the most formidable conference in the country, and yet that team is barely given a nod by basketball historians.

Our team was stout, and I would pit it against any team from any era. We were that good.

When the season was over, I underwent minor knee surgery in April. I had played the whole year with torn cartilage in my knee, since I hurt it performing routine drills right before the season started. I never really had full motion in that leg, and sometimes it would catch. It was nothing major.

As the North Carolina spring quietly slipped into summer, I patiently awaited a phone call from Coach Sloan. USA Basketball was holding tryouts for the World University Games, and Coach Sloan had been tabbed as an assistant coach.

The games were being held in Moscow, Russia, in August, and that sounded like something I wanted to be a part of, especially after the debacle of the 1972 Olympic games. I wanted to personally avenge that painful 51-50 loss to the Russians in Munich the previous summer, and I knew this would be my only chance. And how sweet it would be to do it on their home turf.

I remember a funny story Tommy Burleson told me at the beginning of the season. While playing on the 1972 Olympic team in Munich, Germany, Tom had pulled star guard Doug Collins from Illinois State to the side to tell him that there was a kid (me!) on the NC State freshman team who was more gifted than everybody on the Olympic team. Collins howled with laughter and told Tom to stop smoking so much wacky North Carolina tobacco. Others found out about Burleson's statement, too, and ridiculed poor Tom. After I became a pro, Collins conceded that Burleson had been right after all. It was a humbling experience, and I appreciated Doug's kind words.

Even more humbling was the phone call telling me to report to Buffalo, New York, with 40 other players to try out for the World University Games. The tryouts were actually held at Niagara Falls, and it didn't take the coaching staff long to pare the roster down to the 12 players who would make the journey to Russia.

World University Games head coach Ed Badger would someday coach the Chicago Bulls in the NBA, but then he was at Wilbur Wright College in Chicago. Actually, Badger and Sloan oversaw the team equally. That worked out well for all of us since both men had so many good qualities. What I liked most about Coach Badger was that he would let us play a wide-open, unbridled style of ball—the same kind of ball that I thought the Olympic team should have been allowed to play in the 1972 games. That's why we put so many points on the board.

Of course, the best part of playing in the World University Games was that I got to *dunk*. Talk about a kid in a candy store!

Because of international rules, we were also able to knock the ball off the rim whenever we wanted. It was just such a different experience, from the shape of the widening lane, to playing against older and more experienced players from various countries, to playing in front of hostile foreign crowds. Remember, this was smack dab in the middle of the Cold War, and the games took on a much greater meaning than a mere sporting event.

I pulled out a map, and as I suspected, Moscow really was a long way from Boiling Springs. I couldn't believe my good fortune.

Our team was said to be one of the worst that USA Basketball had ever assembled. We were young and inexperienced, with a plethora of underclassmen, but our personal feeling was that we were immensely talented and would prove a lot of people wrong. Being the underdog can provide great emotional value

I felt comfortable embarking on such an exciting international journey knowing that I had friends on the team. Not only was Coach Sloan there, but so was Tom Burleson. It was only natural that Coach Sloan would pick his star center for the trip. There were other players whom I would come to respect and enjoy spending time with.

Quinn Buckner had just led Indiana into the Final Four as a 17-year-old freshman guard. His initials were "QB," and that fit him perfectly, for he was the quarterback of the team. Quinn was my roommate on the long trip, and we became tight. Next to Monte Towe, Quinn Buckner was the greatest point guard I ever played with. They called his coach, Bobby Knight, "The General." But personally, I believe that title belonged to Quinn. He commanded respect on the floor and directed us with pinpoint precision that belied his youth.

Quinn and I were co-captains of the squad. Though we were both viewed as leaders on the court, Quinn was more vocal, while I preferred to let my play do the talking.

Two stars from Providence College, forward Marvin Barnes and guard Kevin Stacom, also found a spot on the roster. Kevin was one of the few white guys I knew who had an authentic Afro, and, man, he played like a brother, too!

Marvin was 6'9", could shoot, handle the ball, and could flat-out run. He was a very athletic guy, a great rebounder, and just possessed unbelievable natural talent. It was a shame to see him waste his talents and self-destruct a few years after he turned pro. But Marvin played like a man on a mission in Moscow. Sometimes he would start at center, and other times it was Burleson. But no matter where Marvin played, he dominated the opposition with ease.

Marvin and I used to challenge one another at the end of practice to see who could dunk on the other the most. We'd get a running start and try to dunk while the defender would try to jump up and block his shot. When I think about it now, it does seem kind of dangerous. I mean, we could have broken a limb very easily. I usually dunked on Marvin more than he dunked on me (sorry Marvin, but you know it's true!). Marvin was a very outgoing and fun-loving guy, so we had many laughs about those dunking wars.

Alvan Adams, who hailed from the University of Oklahoma, played one of the forward positions and was counted on as a good passer and shooter. He matured into a good pro center, winning the NBA Rookie of the Year in 1975 with the Phoenix Suns, and enjoyed a very successful professional career.

A big, strong center from North Carolina, 6'9" Mitch Kupchak was a sweetheart of a guy with a rugged style of play, which is exactly what we needed against some of the teams who fielded older, more physical players. Mitch, who tipped the scales at 230 pounds, was especially effective around the basket, an impressive skill considering he was just entering his sophomore season.

Wally Walker, a 6'6" forward, was an excellent perimeter player from the University of Virginia. He was already an acquaintance of mine from the ACC, and it was also good to have him there. He had just come off an outstanding freshman season at UVA that saw him average almost 14 points and seven rebounds per game. Wally embraced the team concept, was very smart and could shoot the lights out of the gym.

Gus Bailey, the veteran of the team at 22, was also our "stopper." He was the best, most tenacious defensive player we had. Gus was 6'5", rangy, and a starting guard. He played college ball at the University of Texas-El Paso, and was just an excellent, all-around player and great teammate.

Tulsa University supplied Willie Biles, a 6'3" substitute guard. Willie didn't get too much court time, but he played an important role for us just the same. Then there was Melvin Weldon from Mercer County Junior College in New Jersey. Melvin was a young, 6'1" point guard who started frequently and meshed well with Buckner and Stacom.

Finally, there was Maurice Lucas. Maurice, at 6'9" and 215 pounds, was a very strong player from Al McGuire's Marquette Warriors. Raised in the Steel City, Pittsburgh, Pennsylvania, Maurice was one tough customer. He and the 6'9", 225-pound Barnes roomed together, and they made an imposing pair. You've probably heard the term used to describe Maurice before, and let me tell you he was 100 percent the literal definition of the word "enforcer." Maurice started for us at forward and was a valuable contributor.

Before we reached Moscow, we warmed up for two weeks against a few European teams en route. I distinctly remember playing in Warsaw, Poland, and squaring off against another team in Czechoslovakia. We were winning easily, but knew that the Russians would be much more formidable.

It was a fantastic scene when we finally arrived in Moscow. I never envisioned myself going to Russia as a kid, seeing the Kremlin, Red Square, and all the other historical buildings the city had to offer. We stayed at the University of Moscow, one of the largest universities in the world, and, if you can imagine, all under one roof. The place was just a monster and it would've been easy to get lost, but for the fact that everywhere we went we were followed by "chaperones." Security was very strict due to the violence experienced at the 1972 Olympic Games in Munich. Everywhere we traveled on the city's impressive subway system, our escorts were never far behind.

The cultural stuff was great, but basketball burned in our souls. The United States had brought home silver medals twice in the last three years—

in the 1970 World University Games, and in the 1972 Olympics (although technically they refused the latter medal and didn't bring anything home except a bad memory). There was no way we were going to let that happen again.

We played the games right there at the University of Moscow, and they all took place between August 16-24.

The first one was against Great Britain, and we smashed them 123-74. Barnes tossed in 24 points and Burleson added 14 rebounds. Sweden was next, and we simply annihilated them 120-31. Burleson accounted for 24 points and 21 rebounds.

Burleson stayed hot the following night as the carnage continued, and we destroyed Portugal 140-34. Tom went for 24 points and 14 rebounds in that one.

Matched in quarterfinals pool-play against France, Czechoslovakia and Great Britain, we were already 1-0 in quarterfinals play without even playing a game by virtue of the team's preliminary-round win over Great Britain, which carried over into the quarterfinals standings.

We easily handled France, 137-43, behind 27 points from Barnes, and then faced 4-0 Czechoslovakia. We weren't sure what to expect from the Czechs, but it didn't matter. It was the same old story as we cruised to a convincing 110-59 victory. Barnes again was the main man with 19 points and 19 rebounds.

It was around this time that opposing teams starting asking us for our autographs, just like opposing players would ask the original 1992 U.S. Olympic Dream Team with Larry Bird, Magic Johnson and Michael Jordan. It felt a little strange, but given that this was also a diplomatic mission, we obliged.

In the next round, I exploded for 34 points against a decent Cuban team. Though we won the game handily, 98-76, the contest was not without incident.

The Cubans were looking to take it to us, so when we jumped out to a huge lead, as we had done against of all of our opponents, they reacted very negatively. We could sense their anger and frustration building up, and soon they began to play some odd combination of football and basketball, and it got very rough out there.

The Cubans tried to put pressure on us, taking an early lead but also picking up a bunch of fouls in the process. We had pulled ahead at the end of the first half.

Near the end of the game, violence erupted when Tommy Burleson and Cuban player Juan Domenco fell to the floor diving for a loose ball. While they mixed it up, another skirmish broke out when an unidentified Cuban player kicked Kupchak in the midsection when he wasn't looking. Kupchak went down, but he came up swinging. A bench-clearing brawl from both sides erupted. Chaos ensued, and it was darn near an international incident there in the Red Army gym.

Just when I thought I had seen it all, Cuban head coach Ernesto Diaz charged across the court at our head coach, Ed Badger. Then Diaz and Cuban players Domenco and Franklin Standardt picked up chairs and began swinging wildly at any American on their radar.

Standart managed to knock down Duane Woltzen, our assistant team manager, with his chair, and another Cuban kicked Woltzen in the groin. Woltzen needed medical treatment before getting back on his feet.

Diaz caught up with Badger and kicked him in the stomach, actually leaving two footprints on the front of his nicely starched white shirt.

Things really came to a head when one of the Cuban players ran over to the scorer's table, grabbed the timer's pistol and aimed it at one of our players. At that point, police swarmed in along with Games officials and wrestled the gun away from the maniac. A bottle was thrown by a rowdy Cuban spectator. Wally Walker fell on a piece of broken glass and suffered a cut on his right hand, requiring three stitches.

The police began chasing the Cuban players around and finally surrounded them near their own bench. They forced the other Cuban competitors out of the gym.

Like in an old John Wayne movie, Quinn Buckner and I were out on the floor back to back, ready to take on anyone looking for action. But we were merely bit players next to the Duke himself, Maurice Lucas. The Enforcer more than lived up to his name by single-handedly taking on the Cuban weightlifters and boxers who spilled out of the stands. What a mismatch—he fended off every single one of them. "I now know what it felt like at the Alamo," Badger said to a reporter after the incident.

It was a very scary moment, to say the least.

After order was finally restored, we actually played the last 90 seconds of the game. We scrupulously let them score their last two baskets unopposed and didn't try on our end, either. No sense in pissing anybody off needlessly.

Now if we could get past a formidable and talented 7-0 Brazil squad, it would be showdown time with the Russians.

I figured prominently in the Brazil game, scoring 17 points as Lucas pulled down 17 rebounds. Still, we barely slipped by the Brazilians, 66-60. They were an excellent team all right, but the game was not as close as the score indicated. They were a mature bunch who played a slow-tempo type of game and moved the ball around very well.

It was time to show the Russians how basketball was meant to be played.

The Russians were an older, burly bunch of guys, and their squad contained six of the players who had ended America's 36-year Olympic dominance of the sport in Munich. They were unbeaten, too, and we knew we were in for an old-fashioned dust-up. There was a partisan crowd of 14,800 in the arena, which really pumped me up.

We started quickly and built a strong lead early in the game. I had some good dunks over their seven-foot center, and had around 20 points at the half, by which we were ahead by 18 points.

I finished with 24 points and 10 rebounds, and despite a valiant effort by the Russians to come back in the second half, we won 75-67 to bring the gold medal back where it belonged. It was the United States' first gold medal in these games since 1967.

Because of our team's dominance early in games, the whole roster got to play equally. The starters knew they would not be playing the majority of the game, and so tried to score as much as they could early on. That's how we built those huge, early leads so consistently. It was actually the fear that we would not be playing for very long, not because we were superior.

We finished 9-0 in the tournament. The Soviet Union took silver, of course, and Brazil got the bronze after dispatching Canada in a nail-biter of a consolation game, 80-79.

We all became very close, being on the road so long together, soaking up the education of being in Russia and other countries, and sharing so many experiences that can leave such a lasting impression on young men's minds.

The World University Games put some of the other guys and me on the map because they were televised worldwide. If you look at who went on to have productive careers in the NBA from our team versus the 1972

Olympic team—with the exception of Bobby Jones and Doug Collins—I think you would agree that ours was the more talented.

I was awarded the MVP trophy for averaging 21 points over the course of nine games. You wouldn't believe the award they gave me. It was like some kind of steel airplane that looked more like military hardware than a basketball trophy. Was it because I flew so high on the court, or were the Russians trying to enlist me as a double agent?

"Well, this looks pretty unique," I commented on my new acquisition. "I don't think anybody back home will have a trophy like this!" I think I still have it around the house somewhere, gathering more dust than intelligence.

I was also voted "Lifesaver of the Month" by Lifesavers Candy for my performance in the Games. The sponsors flew me to New York, honored me with a luncheon at the Waldorf-Astoria Hotel, and donated $10,000 to the charity of my choice. I was glad to be able to give back to my community by turning the check over to the Boys and Girls Club of Shelby, North Carolina.

As the summer wound down, it was nice to reflect that I had helped reestablish America's dominance in world basketball. Now it was time to draw a bead on the 800-pound gorilla of collegiate hoops—seven-time national champion UCLA.

CHAPTER 6

THE LONG JOURNEY TO REDEMPTION

The pressure on us to repeat as ACC champions in 1973-74 was so intense that the alternative would have been cataclysmic. There was a crucial reason why we had to accomplish that feat.

Think about this for a moment: We had completed one of the greatest college basketball seasons ever played. *Twenty-seven and 0!* We thumped every team in the always-tough ACC, even with North Carolina and Maryland ranked in the top 15 all year.

Winning the ACC Tournament meant that we should have been able to enjoy all the spoils of war, chief among them advancement to the NCAA Tournament and the chance to prove our mettle against the nation's other supreme teams, mainly UCLA.

But of course the NCAA probation kept us at home, so all we had to look forward to was next season.

Now next season was here, but with a merciless twist.

North Carolina State University was scheduled to host the NCAA East Regional Final at the end of my junior season. It was an NCAA rule that when a school hosted a tournament regional final, it could *not* participate in the NIT—normally regarded as a consolation tournament.

That rule was in place because if a team played in the NIT *and* hosted an NCAA regional game in its own building, it could detract from the "bigger" NCAA Tournament game and perhaps even hurt the local gate.

What did that mean to us?

Well, if we did not win the ACC Tournament to qualify for the NCAA Tournament, then we would all be going home for the second straight year with no postseason play. We would be a forgotten team that never reached its full potential. Our undefeated season of 1972-73 would mean nothing and would be regarded as a mere fluke.

Now *that's* pressure.

I'm not so sure that another team in basketball history ever faced a more do-or-die situation. The expectations our team faced—to win the ACC Tournament again in order to get to the big dance—were enormous. The incentive was great, but the potential reward was even greater.

Compounding the pressure to achieve was the fact that we had lost our two senior co-captains and emotional leaders, Rick Holdt and Joe Cafferky, to graduation. We felt confident, though, mainly because our core unit was still intact. Coach Sloan had prepared well by reloading the team with talent that would contribute and blend in very nicely.

Morris "Moe" Rivers was a prolific scorer from Gulf Coast Junior College. He was a little shorter than Joe Cafferky and didn't quite have Joe's outside shot. However, Moe was faster and a better overall defender.

Phil Spence was the perfect addition to our front line and became as valuable a sixth man as there ever was.

Coach Sloan told us during an October practice that we could be the greatest team in the history of college basketball. We believed him. There was one simple but monumental goal we shared: to win the national championship. We were convinced that this Wolfpack squad was superior in every way and that the championship was our very own prize to claim. Conversely, and more important, we felt that the title was ours to *lose*.

We envisioned ourselves holding up that trophy, having those basketball nets draped around our necks. We could taste and smell how it would feel to collectively experience the ultimate victory, and to then bask in the glory that would surely follow.

The first challenge Coach Sloan faced was to integrate our two new and very talented teammates into the Wolfpack style of play, an adjustment that took weeks to achieve.

Coach Sloan was up to his inspiring ways again as the season began. He always knew the right thing to do or say to get us focused, and he uttered a saying I remember to this day: "Constancy of purpose of individuals results in a team of champions." He made us understand our roles, and we performed accordingly. It was a profound philosophy that I bought into 100 percent and still do.

I sincerely believe that was the key to our success—a true team concept. Heck, Moe Rivers had averaged over 40 points per game in junior college, and Phil Spence was a junior college All-American, yet they sacrificed their individual game for the benefit of the team.

And our team was definitely unique. We were known in some media circles as "The Circus Team," because we featured a midget, a giant, and a high-wire act. The only thing missing was one of those little cars that holds a platoon of clowns.

The Wolfpack circus officially opened to rave reviews on December 5.

East Carolina came into our den, and we feasted like beggars in a buffet line. On the offensive side of the ball, it was apparent we were not firing on all cylinders as we scored just 79 points.

But on the flip side, we held the Pirates to a scant 47 points. Tommy Burleson controlled the boards, hauling down a game-high 13 rebounds. Big Tom also contributed 14 points, as did Moe Rivers.

I felt particularly good that game, hitting 13 of 20 shots for a total of 28 points. And the Raleigh faithful obviously felt fine, too, displaying their midseason form in December. They were well aware of the expectations that had been bestowed upon us by basketball scribes everywhere.

I will tell you this: It felt awesome to be back in the friendly confines of Reynolds Coliseum. If there was one place I felt comfortable, it was out on that floor.

The second sacrificial lamb to wander into the Wolfpack lair was the University of Vermont. On December 7, the Catamounts were literally ripped apart, 97-42, by a focused Wolfpack team on a mission.

The state of Vermont is primarily known for maple syrup, and we ran by them as if they were stuck in the stuff. I led the way with 19, while Monte Towe and Phil Spence had uncanny shooting nights, going a combined 13 for 16 from the floor and kicking in a total of 29 points. As usual, it was a superb team effort.

I will say this about the Catamounts, though: They had Burleson's number. In 24 minutes of action, our big guy only connected on one shot out of five for a game total of just two points. That was very un-Burleson-like, especially against a lesser team.

Rather than get discouraged, Tommy elevated the other aspects of his game. He had a game-high six assists and 11 rebounds. One thing about Burleson—he had the heart of a lion.

Tommy may have been looking past Vermont because our next game was against the top team in the country and the defending national champions, the John Wooden-coached UCLA Bruins.

The first UCLA game was not even on our original schedule. The television network had schemed right before the season started and figured out what a boon it would be for them if UCLA and North Carolina State played in an early-season dream matchup.

What most people don't remember about this famous game was that it was actually part of a doubleheader, with host St. Louis University—the Billikens—first taking on the Salukis from Southern Illinois. The day was billed as a "Basketball Spectacular."

I don't recall who won that first game, but you may find it interesting that St. Louis sported an assistant coach by the name of Dick Versace— the same Dick Versace who later coached the NBA's Indiana Pacers, was president of the Vancouver Grizzlies, and who is regarded as one of basketball's greatest ambassadors. Southern Illinois countered with a 6'11", 215-pound junior center named Joe C. Meriweather who went on to quite a productive NBA career.

But they're not who 18,000 screaming fans came to see.

UCLA had finished the 1972-73 season with an unblemished record of 30-0, duplicating their 30-0 season of the year before. With the great Bill Walton at center, the Bruins were an immaculate 60-0 with two national titles during Big Red's first couple years and were *78-0* (spanning three years) heading into that first game with us.

That was the longest winning streak in basketball history. Still is, in fact.

Of course, we weren't exactly chopped liver. We were on a 29-0 run ourselves and felt that if anyone could dethrone UCLA, it was us.

The game was played at the old St. Louis Arena, the site of the previous year's Final Four. Though certainly not home territory for UCLA, it was still more familiar to them than to us. They had won a championship in that same building only nine months before, and it's probably safe to say that they got a little sentimental when they stepped out on the floor.

It was a typical chilly, snowy, Midwestern day in December. As we came out of the hotel and headed toward the arena at 5700 Oakland Avenue, I remember thinking, "So this is what 'blustery' feels like." I was a Southern kid and didn't exactly take a shine to such extreme cold weather. Guys like Stoddard and Towe, who had seen their share of harsh winters growing up in Indiana, didn't even flinch. Must have been T-shirt weather to them.

Weather aside, my big concern was that we had not yet properly jelled into the precision unit I knew we could become. The bus ride to the game was tense as we contemplated our challenging mission. Nothing would have made us happier than to force an "L" into the loss column for UCLA after 78 successive wins.

UCLA was ranked No. 1 in the country, and we were No. 2. The network executives who put this game together sure knew what they were doing.

The players UCLA brought to the dance read like a Who's Who of College All-Americans: Keith Wilkes (who later became Jamaal Wilkes), David Meyers, Pete Trgovich, Tommy Curtis, Greg Lee, and two-time NCAA Player of the Year Bill Walton.

As confident as we were, we knew what we were up against: History, The Streak, Seven-Time Defending National Champions, The Wizard of Westwood—the list went on and on.

It would take our best individual and team efforts to defeat "The Walton Gang."

From the opening tip, it just didn't seem like it was going to be our kind of game. Actually, strange things happened even *before* the opening tip.

UCLA's dominating and slightly eccentric center, Bill Walton, strolled through our dressing room an hour or so before game time "to get taped." As he made his way through, he wished us all well. I'm sure it was meant to be some kind of psych-job, but it didn't work. We just thought it was kind of weird that the big redhead would appear in our locker room within an hour of game time on some kind of fool's errand.

I felt fine during warmups, but then the house came crashing down.

My game was off that day, and the refs called an excessive number of traveling violations on me early in the contest. The traveling calls robbed me of half my game, and Keith Wilkes took away the other half.

Wilkes played superbly, scoring a game-high 27 points on a dizzying array of jumpers from various sides of the court. He did an excellent job on me defensively, too, and that only added to my frustration. My shooting was abysmal, and I wasn't alone there. Tommy Burleson and I went a combined 12-36 from the field.

Amazingly enough, even with our errant shooting, we managed to lead at the half, 33-32.

A big contributing factor to that score was that Walton was on the bench the majority of the first half with four fouls. Unfortunately, that was no overriding problem for UCLA. They just replaced one near seven-footer with a real one. Ralph Drollinger, who was 7'2", filled in nicely for the foul-plagued Walton, scored eight points in 19 minutes, and grabbed five rebounds. Burleson did a good job on Drollinger just the same, as Ralph only went 3-10 from the field.

Since I wasn't playing well on the offensive side of the ball, I decided to crank up my defense. I hit the boards with reckless abandon and finished the game with 13 rebounds. Burleson took the same route and finished with 15 caroms.

With about 10 minutes left in the game, Wooden reinserted Walton into the Bruins lineup and thereby turned the tide in their favor. Walton hit a few key shots while Wilkes continued his torrid shooting. Suddenly, we were down by a few points.

Once we surrendered the lead, we flat-out panicked. Our desperation was palpable. We had been leading for most of the game, and we just did not want to lose. Not this game. Not against this team.

I missed several shots that I normally made, and I had company. Burleson had the same problem. It wasn't like UCLA was dominating us, or that we had difficulty containing Walton. In fact, it was close with three minutes remaining, but then a string of UCLA points down the home stretch padded their lead. The final score was 84-66 in favor of the Bruins.

My man, Monte Towe, had an excellent game despite the outcome. Our 5'7" point guard scored 14 points on 7-9 shooting against the two-time defending national champs. I always wondered what UCLA's taller and more highly recruited guards thought of that particular performance.

I know this much: Monte was definitely a gamer, and he was psyched up for this battle.

I was the leading scorer for us with 17 points, but it was still one of the worst shooting days of my career as I only connected on seven of 20 shots. I heard about it, too, in the form of some negative criticism from the fans and the press.

I received mail that said things like, "D. T., that was your first big game and you let the team down." That sort of thing stung and made me more determined than ever to always play up to my potential.

In the end, the Bruins had done their job. Their players were complimentary towards us, but you could just hear the arrogance in their voices. That just made us want to play them again. We knew we had not played our best and wanted another shot at redemption.

The one thing I always tell people about that game is that the final score was deceiving. We played UCLA tough throughout, and it wasn't until the end that they pulled away. The game was much closer than most people remember.

Coach Sloan said after the game, "We're more versatile than UCLA. We have something left to prove. And we still have Thompson. I like the odds." Good ol' Coach Sloan, playing mind games once again with the Bruins. He knew there was a good chance we'd meet again in the NCAA Tournament.

The loss really stung, but we weren't awed by them the least bit. It was a blow to our ego, but it didn't deter us from our overall goal of winning the championship. In fact, the loss actually brought us closer as a team.

A lesser team would have quit right there. Instead, we were insulted. We could have just sat there licking our wounds, but we decided to go out and whip every team we faced.

But first, we each had to deal with the loss in our own way. This was the only defeat we would suffer in two years, and it came in the biggest game any of us had ever participated in.

On the plane ride back to Raleigh from St. Louis, Monte lay down across a couple of seats with his face pressed into the cushions the whole way and wouldn't speak to anyone. Monte was so competitive that he took the loss personally. You know something is wrong when your very vocal leader shuts out the rest of the world.

The next day, Monte walked into Coach Sloan's office and announced firmly that the team needed some strict training rules. Sloan argued that strict rules were not necessary for this team because we were so skilled and focused.

Monte was resolute.

"Yep. Gotta have 'em," Monte said. Coach Sloan countered that we just had an off game against UCLA and that we would be all right.

Monte continued to argue for tighter team restrictions, and finally Sloan told him to gather all the players and come up with a set of rules they thought were necessary. Sloan warned everyone, though, that if anybody violated those rules, it would result in an automatic suspension of at least one game. Sloan was not going to have training rules without consequences.

The team readily agreed and all decided on an 11 p.m. curfew, which would cause problems later in the season.

Maybe we just felt like we had to punish ourselves for the UCLA loss. To add insult to injury, we dropped to fifth place in the polls, which did not sit well with us at all.

A little home cookin' was just what the doctor ordered. Georgia traveled to Raleigh three days after the UCLA loss, and we took out our frustrations on the Bulldogs, 94-60.

Feeling the need to reestablish my game, I tallied 28 points in 35 minutes and hauled down 11 boards.

Phil Spence played like a warrior as he snatched a game-high 15 rebounds in just 29 minutes, while adding 11 points. Burleson achieved another double-double with 15 points and 10 rebounds.

Christmas came and went, and before we knew it the time had arrived for the annual Sugar Bowl Tournament in New Orleans. The Sugar Bowl Classic began in 1948, so it was a tourney with a lot of history. And there were plenty of worse places to play than New Orleans.

On December 28, the Wildcats of Villanova became the fourth team to fall to the Wolfpack in the young season. In the opening game of the tournament, Burleson had his third double-double in a row with 20 points and 12 rebounds. I scored 26, but was most proud of my field goal percentage. I shot 12-19 from the floor.

Monte chipped in with 14, and Tim Stoddard added 11. No one will ever realize how important Stoddard was to this team. His role was unenviable, as he usually drew the toughest defensive assignments and was counted on to crash the boards every single game. But strongman Stoddard always did what was asked of him, and quite well.

And as if to prove he was still a bit ornery, Stormin' Norman picked up two technical fouls. Coach Sloan was fiery when he needed to be, that's for sure.

Memphis State was our worthy challenger in the championship game of the tournament. This was the same Tiger team that bowed to UCLA in the previous year's national title game, so we knew that this would be an effective litmus test. Even though Memphis State had lost their two star Larrys—Kenon and Finch—to the ABA, they were still good enough to enter this game ranked 16th in the nation.

Many experts believe this was the game where we finally put it all together. There was a noticeably improved cohesion, and the result was a thorough thrashing of the Tigers, 98-83.

Monte launched some alley-oops in this game that bordered on the ridiculous, yet somehow I managed to convert them all. Those lobs enabled me to reach 34 points to go with my 11 rebounds. I saw a lot of opportunities to get to the basket in this game, and I was fouled many times after I'd make my move. So off to the charity stripe I'd go and was fortunate enough to knock down 10 of 12.

Tommy was on a roll. The senior pivot man scored his fifth consecutive double-double, with 20 points and 15 boards.

The turning point had come for our maturing team, and we all sensed it. Rivers and Spence were now integral components, and we were performing like a finely tuned muscle car.

Witness our guards' play against Memphis State. Our very own "M&M" boys, Monte and Moe, combined for 28 points and nine assists. That kind of firepower from our backcourt, combined with our always-lethal frontcourt, began to strike fear into opponents before we even shook hands at tipoff.

With the advent of the new year came another annual rite of passage—the Big Four Tournament in Greensboro. And lo and behold, the Tar Heels of North Carolina were waiting for us with bated breath.

Dean Smith's bunch was a different unit from that of the previous season. They possessed a fleet-footed senior guard named Darrell Elston, who scored fewer than 10 points per game in 1972-73. One year later, he made the team a force in the ACC and would finish the year averaging better than 15 points per contest.

Add in fellow senior Bobby Jones and freshman sensation Walter Davis, who later acquired the nickname "Greyhound" for self-explanatory reasons, and you could see how much UNC had improved.

Ranked fourth nationally, they were right ahead of us in the polls. We were stuck at No. 5 thanks to the UCLA loss. The Tar Heels were more than ready to deal out some big-time payback for the three defeats they suffered at our hands during our undefeated streak of a year ago. So much so that this time they bolted to a 42-39 halftime lead. But this game would be one of the great thrill rides of our memorable season and a testament to our team's character.

With only minutes left and the Tar Heels up, 75-74, Burleson dropped one in and was fouled by Mitch Kupchak. Burleson missed the free throw, but State had grabbed the lead by one.

With 30 seconds left, Davis fired up a shot from the right side and missed, but the ball landed in the hands of Carolina center Ed Stahl, who also put the ball up and missed.

Moe Rivers captured the rebound and passed upcourt to a breaking Monte Towe. Monte turned, dribbled, and was fouled. As he would do time and again, Monte nailed the two foul shots under extreme pressure.

The score was now 78-75, our favor. With 20 seconds left, Carolina's Davis took the inbounds pass and raced upcourt at breakneck speed. Walter committed a huge freshman mistake at that point—he drove right at our 7'4" All-American center.

When the shot went up, Tommy's eyes got as big as saucers. Burleson not only blocked Davis's shot, but he also managed to hang onto the ball—only to have it stolen right out of his hands by Stahl. Stahl simply turned and made the easy layup.

Never-say-die North Carolina was now dangerously close, only down by one, 78-77.

There were only seven seconds left at this point. Unbelievably, North Carolina made another rookie mistake—they called for a timeout even though they didn't have possession of the ball. Coach Sloan dashed part of the way onto the court, facing the referees while waving his arms in the air in part protest, part disbelief. The referees paid him no notice. Those are the unfortunate breaks of the game, and you just try and make do.

Dean Smith, a master basketball tactician, now had time to set his defense. When the teams returned to the floor, it was Phil Spence who inbounded the ball for us. As Phil attempted to throw the ball in, it was knocked out of his hands by a Tar Heel. We should have been awarded a technical foul, or, at the very least, had another chance to throw it in since the rules state that a defensive player cannot interfere with the player inbounding the ball.

With no time taken off the clock, the ball was inexplicably awarded to North Carolina. My teammates and I were standing there thinking,

"This can't be happening! Are these the Russian officials from the 1972 Olympic Games?"

Inbounding for UNC, Davis spotted Stahl and got him the rock with a nice pass. Stahl faked once, but Burleson didn't bite. With only a couple of seconds left, Stahl launched an awkward shot and missed. Burleson got a hand on the ball, but a scramble ensued as he lost the handle. Rivers emerged from the melee with the ball and was tied up almost immediately.

A jump ball was called, but it was too late. Time had expired, and we escaped with a hard-fought 78-77 victory.

Burleson, the twin threat of points and rebounds, struck again with 14 of each. My line read like this: 20 points on 9-12 shooting, seven rebounds and seven assists.

Elston and Davis led the way for the Tar Heels with 18 and 12 points, respectively. Their team was a formidable foe, but we were better. That was our fifth straight victory over our in-state rivals over a two-year period. No easy feat by any stretch.

In the title match, we overpowered a solid 7-1 Wake Forest squad, which had beaten Duke 64-61 in the other semifinal. We topped Wake 91-73 to win the Big Four Tournament for the second consecutive year.

Tommy's double-double streak finally came to an end as he finished with 23 points and nine boards. Rivers had a nice game with 17 points, and I chipped in 20 myself.

We returned home from Greensboro with a definite spring in our step. Since our hiccup in St. Louis against UCLA, we had run off five straight victories and moved up one spot in the polls to No. 4. Only Clemson remained before we renewed our tense competition with the No. 3 team in the land—the mighty Terrapins of Maryland.

Monte must have had an axe to grind with the Clemson Tigers, because he took his game to another level that day. Leading all scorers with 19 points, Mighty Monte was 100 percent feelin' it. He went 9-11 from the field and was 1-1 from the foul line. To think Coach Sloan and I were once concerned about Monte playing in the oh-so-tough ACC.

Personally, it was a great relief to me to have been wrong about that. We were going to need Monte to play smart and effective as the Maryland game loomed ahead.

It wasn't just any game, mind you, but an epic battle of will and determination. It was a game I thought turned out to be "super," and so did about 25 million other people.

CHAPTER 7

SUPER SUNDAY

North Carolina State's basketball program got a huge public relations shot in the arm, thanks not to a bevy of well-paid flacks and sports writers, but, rather of all things, a pigskin.

That's because January 13, 1974, marked the second time ever that a college basketball game was televised on Super Bowl Sunday. For the second year in a row, we played Maryland on this sacred day usually reserved for football. Television folks have a habit of repeating things that work well, and the previous year's matchup had produced huge ratings, with more than 25 million people tuning in to our game.

Both the Miami Dolphins and the Wolfpack of NC State had won games on Super Bowl Sunday one year before, and here we both were again on the exact same stages with a chance to repeat history. The Dolphins were picked by oddsmakers to lose again, this time to the "Purple People Eaters"—the Minnesota Vikings—while Maryland came into our game ranked ahead of us.

Could NC State and the Miami Dolphins do it two years in a row? Were we somehow joined at the athletic hip? Were we each other's four-leaf clover?

For us, the answers would come at home in Reynolds Coliseum in one of the best games I would have all season. And we would need everyone's best, not just mine, because the third-ranked Terps were loaded once again. Maryland boasted three bona fide All-Americans on its roster.

Senior forward Tom McMillen, a Wolfpack nemesis if there ever was one, was undoubtedly one of the Terrapins' primary threats. Sophomore point guard John Lucas had lived up to his hype, providing a devastating combination of scoring, passing and court leadership. And senior center Len Elmore, a vacuum cleaner off the backboards, provided strength and scoring in the middle.

Lefty Driesell's juggernaut was 9-1 and out to prove that they were truly the "UCLA of the East." Unfortunately for them, the "UCLA of the West" had narrowly beaten them in the opening game of the season, 65-64.

Desperate to prove they could win the big games, Maryland came out swinging with everything they had.

As could have been expected, McMillen and Lucas were having big games as Burleson and Elmore practically neutralized each other. Though we took a four-point lead into the half, 45-41, the game was a seesaw battle all the way.

Great athletes talk about being in a zone, a place and time where everything seems to move in slow motion, making it easier to excel. That's exactly how I felt that day. In my mind, nobody could stop me. And nobody did.

While McMillen and Lucas would score 24 points each, it was overwhelmingly my time to shine. I had scored more than 41 points before, but *not* in a more important game. I was firing on all cylinders—jumpers, drives, alley-oops, you name it. I was also getting fouled a lot, meaning my game was purposely aggressive. It needed to be against a great team like Maryland.

I was successful on 13 of 17 free throws and shot 14-20 from the field, and we won the game 80-74.

It turned out that I had scored more than a point a minute, with 41 points in 39 minutes. Directly after the game, though, while the players were heading off the floor, something occurred that had even more impact than the big numbers I had just put up.

It had to do with Tommy Burleson.

Burleson had just completed a nightmarish game. After he had shot just 3-19 from the field, a horrific shooting game for Tommy, Terp center Elmore tried to rub his nose in it.

"You go tell that dude over there," Elmore said loudly, indicating Tommy, "that *I* am *the* center in the ACC."

Those words would burn in Tommy's head the rest of the season. Coach Sloan made sure of it by cutting out the newspaper article in which they appeared and taping it above Burleson's locker. It stayed there the rest of the year, a reminder of Tommy's mission the next time we faced Maryland.

Personally, I never understood where Elmore was coming from. Though Tommy missed 16 shots, his line easily stacked up to Elmore's. Elmore finished the game with 13 points on only 3-9 shooting and grabbed nine rebounds. Burleson scored 13 points and hauled in 10 rebounds. Tommy also dished out two assists to none for Elmore. And most important, he was on the winning team.

It wasn't like Wilt Chamberlain had just embarrassed Dale Schleuter! This was an evenly played matchup between two All-American centers. It's not like Elmore shot the lights out either, as his accuracy was only 33 percent from the field. But I guess he had to do something to boost his flagging ego.

Later that week we traveled north to Charlottesville, Virginia, to take on the Virginia Cavaliers. This game was more memorable for what happened off the court than on it.

Remember those team rules that we asked Coach Sloan to implement after the UCLA loss? They had resulted in a team curfew that suddenly came back to bite us in the behind. The day before we left for Virginia, Coach Sloan received a call at midnight from Moe Rivers advising him that he had missed curfew. But Moe wasn't chasing skirts or bending his elbow.

"Why?" Sloan asked.

"I got arrested," he told the coach. He was in jail.

Moe's story was that he had picked up a 39-cent box of aspirin in a convenience store, put it in his pocket, and forgot about it when he checked out. The storekeeper had him arrested for petty theft.

Sloan wasn't much interested in Rivers's protestations of innocence. That was for a judge to decide. But that he missed curfew was beyond argument, and Sloan decided to suspend Rivers for the next game.

When Monte found out, he told the coach that he was being unfair.

"Hold on! Wait a minute," Coach Sloan responded imperiously. Then he reminded Monte that the curfew was the players' own idea and now they had to live with it.

Monte negotiated like he was trying to save hostages, but Sloan was implacable.

The shoplifting charges were eventually dropped, but Rivers sat out the Virginia game. We won handily anyway, 90-70. Gus Gerard, a future teammate of mine on the Denver Nuggets and a 6'7" junior forward for the Cavs, had 20 points and 11 rebounds to lead Virginia.

The most notable thing about this game, other than Rivers's absence, was that we had three players with 20 or more points for the first time all season. I had 30, Big Tom had 22, and Monte tossed in 20. We basically put Virginia away in the first half, going into the locker room with a commanding 40-21 lead.

We then routed UNC-Charlotte, 104-72, and it was on to Chapel Hill for a January 22 rematch with the fourth-ranked Tar Heels. We had moved up to No. 3 in the polls and were cautiously optimistic. We never knew what would happen in Chapel Hill, and this game was no different.

But first, understand the significance of this contest. UCLA's incredible 88-game winning streak came to an end three days before at the hands of second-ranked Notre Dame, in South Bend, Indiana.

That put the Irish in the top slot, and we knew we had to keep pace. Though UCLA didn't slip far (they ended up at No. 2 after the Notre Dame loss), we knew an impressive performance against UNC would catch a lot of eyes.

We jumped out to a quick lead and held it as we hit the locker room at halftime, leading 42-36.

But North Carolina emerged from halftime with a vengeance.

Darrell Elston, their fine guard who had carried them all season, possessed the hot hand. He scored on a variety of shots and had 19 points as the game was coming to a close.

With 1:30 to play, and the Wolfpack ahead 82-76, Elston hit a shot from the far right side to bring them within four.

As Monte brought the ball up, the Tar Heels double-teamed him. The ball squirted loose. Elston grabbed it and drove the lane, but missed the layup. It was a frantic pace.

I rebounded Elston's miss and headed toward our end, facing Tar Heel pressure the entire way. There was only 1:05 left.

I passed to Monte, who slipped but maintained his dribble. He threw it back to me, and I let fly with a pretty jump shot that tickled the twine. But what should have been two points for NC State didn't count because Phil Spence had been fouled underneath before I took the shot.

I couldn't believe it. Was there anything else that could go wrong? Actually, there was.

Spence missed the front end of the one-and-one, and trotting up the court came Tar Heel freshman sensation Walter Davis. Davis probably remembered what happened the last time he wandered into the land of tall timber and wisely passed off to Elston, the player with the hot hand.

Elston connected from 10 feet out, and suddenly our lead was cut to a mere two points.

With 0:50 left, Spence had trouble getting the ball inbounds, but found me with only a second or two to spare. I passed immediately to Monte, who decided that he had seen enough.

It was time to break out the "Tease."

For the next 34 seconds, Monte and Mark Moeller played keep-away from the Tar Heels. The ball came to me with 11 ticks left on the clock, and I was promptly fouled.

I made the front end of the one-and-one, but missed the bonus shot. Carolina's Stahl gathered in the miss, and the Tar Heels instantly called time out with 10 seconds on the clock. The game was still up for grabs at 83-80.

Stahl inbounded the ball with a football pass that sailed the length of the court. Burleson intercepted and was fouled by Bobby Jones. Seven seconds remained.

Tommy went to the line and continued our poor free throw shooting, missing the first shot. Kupchak collected the rebound, just as I thought it would come to me. To make things worse, I was called for a foul with four seconds left in regulation.

Kupchak had a one-and-one opportunity. If he hit them both, it would be a one-point game. But he missed, and the partisan crowd gave such a loud, collective sigh, you would have thought everyone had just lost a loved one.

Mark Moeller hauled down the rebound and was immediately fouled by Elston, who had 23 points and seven assists that afternoon.

There were now four seconds left. Would the madness never end?

Moeller had not scored in this game, but could ice it with the free throws. Coach Sloan had us in a sort of "prevent defense." Moeller missed, but Burleson corralled the rebound and was fouled by Stahl with one second left on the clock. The refs then signaled that the game had actually ended, and we escaped Tar Heel land with an 83-80 triumph.

Monte scored 21 points, the high game of his career up to that point. I notched 26, which was about my scoring average, and we really controlled the boards as a team, winning the glass battle 41 to 32. Spence and myself garnered 10 each, and Burleson managed 11 to go with his 14 points.

So far, we had played the Nos. 1, 3, 5 and 16 teams in the land and beaten three out of the four. The next "easy" game on the schedule was against the Purdue Boilermakers. Purdue was a first-rate team that would finish the season ranked 11th in the polls.

So it was off to the hoops-crazy state of Indiana, home of the magnificent Rick Mount, Monte Towe, Norman Sloan and other basketball greats. Purdue's Mackey Arena was jammed that afternoon with 16,000 screaming crazies as the two teams took to the floor.

The Purdue game was the first big scare we experienced since squaring off against UCLA. We found ourselves down by 10 points at the half and were actually on our backs by 15 at one point, our largest deficit of the year.

But this time we didn't panic. We had learned our lesson in the UCLA game. We had more character and fought back like an angered junkyard dog.

But the Boilermakers still had a commanding lead at 81-74 with four and a half minutes remaining.

With 3:45 left, and the Wolfpack behind 81-76, I drove the ball to the left side of the court and launched a jump shot toward the rim. The ball found its mark, and now it was just a three-point ballgame.

Purdue had a wonderful freshman point guard named Bruce Parkinson. Parkinson, in fact, is still Purdue's all-time leader in assists. That tells you what kind of player he was, even though he was only in his first year when we faced him.

Moe Rivers had gone toe to toe with Parkinson all game, and with 3:23 left, stole the ball from the frosh point guard. As Rivers dashed the length of the floor and drove on Parkinson, he scored and was fouled from behind by Frank Kendrick.

After Moe nailed the free throw, it was all tied up at 81-81, with 3:19 remaining.

Now Coach Sloan ordered us to go into the Tease. Monte and Moe ran that thing to perfection, and Purdue didn't have an answer. It was a classic cat-and-mouse game, and we could really sense how well we were playing together at that point.

With 1:45 on the clock, I took the ball straight up the alley and scored. We had the lead at last, 83-81. Then, with about 12 seconds left, I was at the line and canned a foul shot, giving me 26 points for the night and putting us up by five, 86-81.

Purdue had not scored since the 4:31 mark. We had run off 12 consecutive points and won by a final score of 86-81.

Burleson amassed 17 rebounds and scored 13 points, while Rivers and Towe totaled 30 points between them. By late January, we stood at 13-1 and were ranked second in the polls. Notre Dame had stumbled to No. 3, and UCLA had regained the top spot. Naturally, we felt that that honor belonged to us.

We didn't have to look at the schedule to know who was up next. Burleson's behavior made it perfectly obvious. He had impatiently awaited the rematch with the Terps ever since Len Elmore made his arrogant remarks, and Coach Sloan would not let Tommy forget about it.

Big Tom exacted his revenge at Cole Field House that cold January day. It wasn't his best game, and he knew that, but all he had wanted was the win—and to outplay Elmore.

He accomplished both.

I didn't exactly duplicate my 41-point performance of Super Bowl Sunday, but I came close with 39. I started off very slowly, registering only eight in the first half. But shortly into the second stanza, with Maryland ahead 39-38, something incredible occurred.

Moe Rivers and I scored the next 30 points for the Wolfpack!

But it wasn't enough. With nine minutes left, Maryland had a 67-59 lead. As hard as we had battled back, we were still on the short end of the scoreboard.

We finally took the lead with six minutes to go, 70-69. With 51 seconds remaining, and the score 80-78 in our favor, I drove past a fallen Len Elmore and put the ball in the basket.

Tom McMillen was enjoying another monster game against us—he would finish with 28 points and 14 boards—and he drove the baseline with 38 seconds left. He pulled up for what looked like a sure-fire jumper. It caromed off the rim, right into Burleson's waiting mitts.

Tommy handed off to Moe Rivers, who was quickly fouled by star guard John Lucas with 16 seconds to go. Lucas fouled out, and Rivers went to the line for two.

Unbelievably, Moe missed them both. *Here we go again,* I thought.

Maryland moved swiftly upcourt, and Elmore took two shots in a row, missing both. Junior forward Tom Roy put the second missed shot by Elmore back up and in with just five seconds left.

The game was a two-point contest, 82-80. If Maryland could get the ball back and score, we'd have overtime.

As Monte received the inbounds pass, he passed to Tim Stoddard, but was fouled on the play by Terp guard Mo Howard. If there was one guy who could cure our free throw malaise, it was Monte. The smallest man on the floor coolly sank both shots, and we were ahead to stay, 84-80.

There were three seconds to go when Monte pulled off another miracle. Elmore tossed the ball in, but Monte stepped in front of the pass and stole it. With one tick left on the clock, Monte heaved up a long shot as the buzzer sounded.

Monte's moonshot found its mark and dropped straight through the cylinder. Had we been at home, they would have torn down the backboards.

The final score was 86-80, and I'm sure the good people of College Park were glad to see us go.

With the toughest part of our schedule behind us, we streaked into the month of February with an impressive 14-1 slate and a No. 3 national ranking. It turned into quite a month, both for us and that 800-pound gorilla on the West Coast.

UCLA would lose in February not once, not twice, but *three times.*

Meanwhile, the Wolfpack reeled off 10 straight victories in February, and when the polls came out February 19, we were finally the number one team in the land. UCLA had fallen to third, with Notre Dame occupying the second spot.

Our month started with Virginia and Duke falling in succession by scores of 105-93 and 92-78. The latter game was a headache for poor Moe Rivers, whose arrest for shoplifting the aspirin earlier in the season had not been forgotten by the fans in Durham, among the most ingenious in college basketball when it came to taking an issue and using it to taunt visiting players. When Rivers was introduced, you would have thought we were in a snowstorm. Aspirin tablets poured out of those stands like hailstones. It looked like it was an inch deep out on the floor. Workers needed about 15 minutes to sweep all the aspirin off the court. The Blue Devil fans should've held some of that back for themselves, because Rivers poured in 18 points to help us win, 92-78.

Next, we visited Charlotte for the North/South Tournament. We easily disposed of Georgia Tech in the first game, 98-54, and manhandled Furman for the championship, 111-91.

Davidson was no match as we crushed them, 105-78, on February 13. Then we rolled over Wake Forest (111-96), Duke (113-87), and Clemson (80-75), as I went on a scoring bender. I totaled 106 points in the three wins, with 31, 40, and 35, respectively.

The last two games before the ACC Tournament were against the fourth-ranked North Carolina Tar Heels, whom we beat at home after going on a huge second-half run, 83-72, and Wake Forest, who fell 72-63 in Winston-Salem.

Heading into our first game in the ACC Tournament on March 8 in Greensboro against Virginia, the pressure was mounting all over again.

If we didn't capture the conference title, we would all go home because we were locked out of the NIT.

We had a bye in the opening round by virtue of our first-place conference finish. Meanwhile, Maryland dumped Duke 85-66, North Carolina beat Wake Forest 76-62, and Clemson succumbed to Virginia 68-63.

The second round saw fourth-ranked Maryland soundly defeat a strong sixth-ranked North Carolina squad, 105-85. The Terrapins were firing a shot across our bow with the convincing 20-point victory against the Tar Heels. Maryland jumped out to a 16-point halftime lead and never looked back. It was one of the worst tournament losses ever suffered by a Dean Smith-coached team.

I knew I had to do everything in my power to ensure our entry into the NCAA Tournament, and so it began with Virginia. I scored 37 points against the Cavaliers and also pulled down seven rebounds. The first half was close, and at the break we clung to a two-point lead, 29-27.

But we pulled away in the end, and won convincingly, 87-66. Again, rebounding was our saving grace as the scales tipped in our favor, 47-33. Phil Spence had 13 boards and Big Tommy contributed 11.

Everyone got what they wanted—a Maryland/NC State conference final. This would be our sixth game versus the Terrapins in two years. We were 5-0 against them, but this game had more meaning than the 1973 final.

Maryland wanted to show not only that they could beat us, but that they could reach the NCAA tourney on their own merits. (They had advanced in 1973 only because we were on probation. Remember, we beat Maryland then to win the ACC title.)

Maryland had won 73 games in three seasons with two of the greatest players who would ever don a Terp uniform—Len Elmore and Tom McMillen. The Terrapins won the NIT in 1972 and made it to the NCAA East Regional Final in 1973.

Our sixth meeting took place the evening of March 9, 1974, and is called by many the greatest college basketball game ever played. I'm not about to argue with that.

It was the quality of play, more than anything else. As I mentioned before, Maryland loved to run with us. That made for a very up-tempo type of game, the kind where mistakes would be inherent.

But there wasn't one forced turnover in the first 40 minutes of regulation play. Not one. Not a three-second call, no traveling violations. Nothing.

You want offensive excellence? The *losing* team shot 61 percent and scored 100 points. When was the last time you saw statistics like that?

I still think about all those factors to this day, and it's so hard to believe. It was just a matter of two teams playing at their respective peak levels.

There was also the "Burleson Factor." Tommy felt he still had some payback to dish out to Elmore for his disparaging remarks the first time we played Maryland. He was almost foaming at the mouth in the locker room before we took the floor. I wouldn't have liked to be in Elmore's shoes that night.

Monte had been quoted in the press as saying that we were aware of how well Maryland was playing, especially after humiliating North Carolina the day before, and that we were going to have to raise our level of play higher than we had all year to beat them.

Ten minutes into the game, we knew that even that might not be enough.

The Terrapins broke out of the gate fast, and we were down by 12 before we even knew what hit us. Maryland looked so loose, and yet so focused. They were pushing the ball up the floor against us on virtually every possession, and their ball handling was flawless thanks to guards John Lucas and Mo Howard.

Coach Sloan said after the game that he thought we were in serious trouble.

Once again, Tom Burleson saved our hide.

Tommy was playing like a madman, swatting shots, scoring points, and taking away rebounds. He was out to prove to Elmore—and a national TV audience—that *he* was the best center, not only in the ACC, but in the entire country.

We cut the Maryland lead to five by halftime, and a big part of that was the guys who came off the bench and hit some big shots for us. Stoddard was one. Monte and I helped out, too. Despite a sluggish start, I scored 20 in the first half.

We knew that this was going to be a game for the ages. We were going to have to dig down deeper than ever before to come out on top.

Burleson came out of the locker room and began dropping hook shots—left-handed and right-handed—time and again on Elmore. Monte and I kept the defense honest by bombing from the outside so that the other interior Terp players could not help Elmore.

Tommy spun one way, then the other, hooking like Joe Frazier. He would finish with 38 points on 18-25 shooting, 13 rebounds, and his second consecutive ACC Tournament MVP award.

With five minutes left in the game, we finally pulled even. From then on it went back and forth. The Greensboro crowd was intense, cheering every basket that was made.

It came down to the final waning moments. With three seconds to play, Maryland swung the ball around to an open Howard on the baseline about 16 feet from the bucket. Not known for being shy with the ball, Howard opted not to shoot. It was a decision that still has people who saw the game puzzled. Instead, he passed out to Lucas, who fired up a frantic attempt that missed as the buzzer sounded.

Years later, Howard explained to reporter Bill Free, "I didn't take the shot at the end of regulation because I was afraid Burleson would block my shot."

It was only fitting that overtime would decide the ACC championship.

Both teams were on their last breath. Many of the Maryland starters had played almost the entire game and were worn out. Lucas had smacked his knee, and the swelling was noticeable. But like battle-bred warriors, they soldiered on.

Maryland jumped out to the lead again, 100-99 with 2:16 left. Then Lucas was at the foul line, trying to make the front end of a one-and-one. Fortunately for us, he missed. Suddenly, Monte had the ball and went dashing up the court. At our end, he dribbled patiently, searching for an open man with a good shot. Out popped Phil Spence from underneath, and Monte hit him perfectly for the easy layin—we led by one.

With just under two minutes left, Tommy made a beautiful block on Howard and got possession of the ball. At 1:30, Rivers was fouled by Howard. He missed the free throw. Lucas brought the ball up, closely guarded by Rivers. Moe, an excellent defensive player, forced a five-second call on Lucas. A jump ball was called. There may not have been any unforced turnovers during regulation, but the few that occurred in overtime were costly for Maryland.

The jump ball took place at the Maryland foul line with 33 seconds left. Lucas was taller than Moe, and he won the tip and walked the ball upcourt for Maryland.

They wanted the winning shot, and Lucas was looking for one of his talented big men, McMillen or Elmore. You could tell that the scrappy guard was dog-tired, and that undoubtedly was a factor in what happened next.

Lucas's pass, intended for Elmore in the middle with his eager hands out, went sailing past him with 23 seconds left. Our ball.

As Rivers prepared to throw the ball in, all 10 players were in the backcourt. It was a weird scene that showed what kind of pressure was on each of us with so much on the line, so late in this incredible game. Maryland was in a full-court press.

Rivers found Monte, and as he began to bring the ball back up he was fouled by Bill Hahn with six seconds to go. That was all Maryland could do to stop the clock.

Monte, who was 1-2 at the line up until then, hit two of the biggest free throws in college basketball history to make the score 103-100.

Maryland's Hahn took the inbounds pass and heaved a desperation shot at the buzzer, but to no avail.

The ACC championship was ours again, and, more importantly, we were headed for the NCAA Tournament. Burleson perhaps had the greatest game of his college career, scoring 38 points and hauling down 13 rebounds. Rightly so, he was given the Everett Case Award for the second straight year as the ACC Tournament's MVP.

While we cried tears of joy, the Maryland players' tears were sorrowful. They had wanted it so badly and had come so close. We honestly felt for them—and in the weeks ahead we were grateful to the Terps. Had they not pushed us so hard, forcing us to find the will to overcome their passion and skill, the rest of the season—and the rest of this story—could have turned out very differently.

After the game, Coach Sloan called it "as draining and exhilarating an experience as I've ever had. I still remember turning around on the bench at one point and just saying out loud, 'My goodness, this is a hell of a game!'"

I darn near collapsed walking off the court—I was that whipped. Playing basketball again in just five days seemed unthinkable. All we wanted to do was recuperate.

As we sat on the bus departing from the Greensboro Coliseum, Tommy spoke for everyone when he said he felt "felt like a dishrag that had been all wrung out. I had nothing left."

We were too spent to even talk to or congratulate each other. Coach Sloan cried on his wife Joan's shoulder. It was a scene I will never forget.

Suddenly the bus doors opened, and a man made his way up the steps slowly because he, like the rest of us, didn't have much energy left.

When he reached the top step, we all recognized him. It was Lefty Driesell, Maryland's fine coach.

Driesell first went over to shake Tommy Burleson's hand and have a word with him.

"That was the greatest game a center has ever played in the ACC. I've never seen a center dominate a game like that."

Then Lefty turned his attention toward the team.

"Men, I just wanted to tell you that I thought you played one of the greatest games I've ever seen," Driesell said. "I was proud of my team, and I am proud of you. You're a great team, and I hope you win the national championship. You deserve it."

We were stunned. It was one of the classiest acts I ever witnessed. For a coach to take time away from his own grieving players to congratulate and wish us well spoke volumes to me about the man.

Many years later, Driesell said that game cost him the national championship. He reflected on that historic night in 1974. "I don't usually go for that going into the other locker room stuff because I think it's phony," he said. "But that night, I did it because I really felt that way. I was disappointed we lost, but I wasn't upset. My team played its heart out."

They sure did, and I'm proud to have shared the floor with them. Maybe Maryland wasn't the "UCLA of the East," but thanks to the Terrapins, by the time the tournament was over UCLA would wish it was the "NC State of the West."

CHAPTER 8

PATH TO GLORY

hen I was playing high school basketball, my personal idol was Charlie
Scott. But the *team* I admired most was UCLA. My Crest High School
squad used to even pretend to be the Bruins. UCLA was one of the
great dynasties in sports back then, winning seven straight Final Fours
from 1967, when I was in the eighth grade, to 1973, when I was a sophomore at North Carolina State.

They steamrolled everybody, including some of my friends. They
beat Charlie Scott and North Carolina in 1968, the Purdue Boilermakers
in 1969, Artis Gilmore and Jacksonville in 1970, Villanova in 1971, Florida
State in 1972, and Memphis State in 1973.

The UCLA name was magical to a whole generation of basketball
fans. I'd see the Bruins on TV from time to time, always read about them
in the newspapers, and dream about being part of something as great and
grand and unstoppable as what Coach John Wooden had put together in
Los Angeles.

Coming out of high school, I knew that if I could just get with the
right coach and the right team, we could win the Final Four ourselves.
Most people in North Carolina hated UCLA because no matter how good
North Carolina or Duke or NC State or Wake Forest was—and those
teams were always good—as far as the experts and media were concerned,
UCLA was the nonpareil of college hoopsdom.

Of course, it wasn't exactly unwarranted.

Now, it was as if all my boyhood dreams were coming true.

As the NCAA Tournament began, we were fortunate enough to have earned a first-round bye by virtue of winning the ACC Tournament and also our No. 1 national ranking. We were fortunate in other ways, too.

The East Regional Finals were to be played on our very own home court, Reynolds Coliseum in Raleigh. Then, the Final Four would be played at the Greensboro Coliseum in Greensboro. Some experts still feel that playing so close to home factored into our winning the national championship that year. It was an advantage, I suppose, but hardly an unprecedented one. UCLA had played a few times in its own backyard during the Bruins' reign as college basketball's "Slaughterhouse Five." As recently as 1972, the Final Four had been held at the Los Angeles Sports Arena. I don't recall anybody complaining about an unfair advantage for the home team then.

First up for us in the regionals were the familiar faces of the Providence Friars. Though Ernie DiGregorio had graduated to the NBA, Providence was still formidable due to the presence of two of my teammates from the 1973 World University Games—power forward Marvin Barnes and all-everything guard Kevin Stacom.

Led by head coach Dave Gavitt, the Friars came into the tournament playing well. They had dominated the University of Pennsylvania, 84-69, in their opening game of the tournament. That and 18 rebounds by Barnes were enough for us not to take them lightly.

Stacom, a Holy Cross transfer, was a second team All-American, two-time Providence defensive player of the year, and a guy who took as much pride in his field goal percentage as I did. He is still No. 1 all-time in the school's history among guards, with 52.7 percent. We planned accordingly to not allow Kevin many uncontested shots.

Then there was Marvin "Bad News" Barnes. He led the nation in rebounding in 1973-74 (a goal he had set in the preseason), was a consensus first team All-American, and ended up as the leading rebounder in Providence history (his records still stand today). We knew we'd have our hands full with Marvin when it came to keeping him off the boards.

As if Barnes and Stacom weren't enough for us to worry about, there was also freshman forward Bob Cooper, who shot 57.2 percent from the field for the year with the Friars.

But on March 14, we were determined to show the world what it had missed the year before, and we accomplished that goal by handling the fifth-ranked Friars with relative ease.

Our crowd let us know that they were behind us, and that helped. Their vocal support also prompted some commentary from Providence coach Dave Gavitt. In an effort to stem any negative press for playing the regionals at home, Coach Sloan made a point of emphasizing that only 750 tickets had been allotted to NC State students for the Providence game.

Coach Gavitt wasn't buying it. "There's this biblical story about a fella who made a loaf of bread and a couple of fish go a long way," he said, "Man, State sure did a heck of a job with those 750 tickets."

Excited to finally be playing in the NCAA Tournament, I blasted off right from the opening tip. I had so much adrenaline coursing through my veins I ended up the only player on either team who never came off the floor the entire game.

Everything jelled for me, and I finished with 40 points (16 for 29 from the floor) and 10 rebounds in our 92-78 victory. It did get close at one point, but we just turned up the pressure.

Barnes (14 points and 13 rebounds) and Stacom (18 points) only shot a combined 13 for 31 from the field. Our defense caused them problems all game. Moe Rivers shadowed Stacom all night and came up with some important steals. When the Friars had the ball, Tim Stoddard guarded Barnes and accomplished his goal of making Marvin take the ball outside.

Barnes had to take Burleson on defense because of Tommy's height. The Friars had no one else of that size who could have handled him. Therefore, Barnes could not focus on me, which normally would have been the plan. That's how I was able to get open and create so many scoring opportunities.

Providence's 5'11" point guard, Gary Bello, guarded Monte Towe all game. Afterwards, Bello told a reporter, "Being short, I can relate to [Monte] well. And he really impressed me. He's a great ball handler and knows who to get the ball to—David Thompson. Thompson is the greatest I've seen in college. I've never seen anybody jump like him."

Burleson played like a 7'4" octopus in the middle. Marvin Barnes may have won the collegiate rebounding title, but Tommy was a monster on the boards that day. It's one thing to get 24 rebounds against insignificant competition—in fact, he had 11 in the first half alone—but to get that many against a fifth-ranked team with the top rebounder in the nation is the stuff of legend.

The only thing Coach Sloan was not happy about was our shooting. Providence wasn't the only team whose marksmanship was off. We connected on only 34 of 88 shots, or 39 percent from the field. Moe Rivers had an uncharacteristic day, going 3-16. Tim Stoddard followed suit with a 1-6 outing. Monte was off at 5-14. Even Big Tom had some trouble, going 7-19.

Chalk it up to opening-day jitters.

The very last play of the game is one I will never forget. Calling it "spectacular" doesn't do the play justice.

Providence took a shot and missed, and Tommy went high for the rebound. He caught Monte with a long outlet pass, and Monte saw me streaking to the basket out of the corner of his eye.

A Friar defender zeroed in on Monte as soon as he received Tommy's pass, so Monte flipped a perfect *behind-the-back* alley-oop pass to me just as I was going airborne toward the rim. When I caught the pass and made the shot, the place exploded into a chorus of Wolfpack cheers.

Marvin Barnes was awestruck by our performance and was quoted as saying, "You just try not to let David get 50. But how do you stop State? I mean, you can't leave Tim Stoddard, Tommy Burleson, Moe Rivers, or Monte Towe alone, either. I mean, there's Towe dribbling around two inches off the ground. And there's Thompson flying around—everywhere.

"There he was, flyin' around, all over the place like *Superman*. Now you all know why we call him Superman."

To get that first one out of the way was a huge relief to us all. We felt really loose heading into the Eastern Regional Championship game against the 13th-ranked Panthers from the University of Pittsburgh.

We were riding a 25-game winning streak and felt no team could stop us.

Something happened during the Eastern Regionals that we didn't know about at the time, but that had great significance in the history of college basketball.

It is well known that UCLA's head coach, the great John Wooden, did not scout other teams. UCLA would impose their game and their will upon all challengers—without fear of what the opponent might be planning for them. Only twice did Wooden request in advance information on a player his team would be facing.

One was Austin Carr from Notre Dame. The other was me.

Unbeknownst to us then, Wooden dispatched assistant Bruins coach Frank Arnold to Raleigh to check out this late-season version of the Wolfpack. Coach Wooden knew we were No. 1 and that we had not lost since we played his boys back in December, while his wonder boys had experienced as many losses this season (three) as they had the previous four years *combined*. Notre Dame, Oregon, and Oregon State had all cooled the Bruins' jets.

I've always considered that UCLA reconnaissance mission the ultimate show of respect to our team.

On March 16, two days after the Providence victory, we took the floor at home against Pitt. Pitt was strong, as evidenced by 22 straight wins at one point. But what started out as another routine NC State drubbing of another nationally ranked team ended up in near tragedy.

The Panthers had trouble breaking our press and found themselves down 14-5 almost instantly. I caught fire quickly again in this game and was three for four with eight points. But every time I took a shot, a Pitt player named Lou Hill would bump my elbow ever so slightly. I was getting really ticked off about it. The refs were right there and weren't calling anything. I became so uncharacteristically upset at one point that I almost drew a technical.

With about 10:30 left in the first half, Hill hit my arm again in midshot. The ball fell about two feet short of the basket, and I was embarrassed. Then I became angry and decided right then that something dazzling and dramatic was called for. As the Panthers pushed the ball up the court on the ensuing possession, Hill got the ball in the right corner and set for a shot.

Man, was I going to *show* him. I caught up with the play just in time and leaped as high as I could to block his shot. I began my lift-off from just inside the foul line and ended up around three or four feet in the air and I got a piece of the ball just as Hill released it. But right at the top of my jump I sensed my feet catch on something.

It was my teammate Phil Spence's shoulder. Phil had moved over to get in rebound position, and my foot caught his shoulder, knocking me out of orbit.

I cartwheeled wildly with my legs going every which way. It was the mother of all somersaults, ending when I crashed into the floor headfirst. Somebody later described the sound as that of a bowling ball dropped from the top of the backboard.

The 12,400 spectators who'd accompanied my ascent with a deafening roar were totally dumbstruck as I lay in a pool of blood on the court.

Chester Grant, our trainer, came running out immediately. Soon he was joined by two doctors and a nurse. My teammates feared I was dead. My eyes were rolled back in my head, and I was totally out. The sight sickened Coach Sloan, who later remembered, "I was numb. I wished I wasn't even associated with this team or this game."

Grant was scared because he initially thought that the blood was leaking from my ear, indicating possible brain damage. Upon closer examination, he identified a severe laceration on the back of my head. It was my scalp, actually. But there were other alarming signs. As I lay on the floor, my bladder released, usually a telltale sign of serious nervous system impairment.

Much later, assistant athletic director Frank Weedon said he, too, thought I was dead after that fall, mainly because of the blood. What struck him was the eerie, encompassing silence in the arena, like someone had suddenly turned off a blaring radio.

My teammates were totally distraught.

"It was unbelievably frightening to me," said Tommy Burleson, who was right next to me. "I was looking right at him when he fell. I've never seen a person take a fall like that. It was the worst accident I've ever seen."

"When I saw what happened, man, I was scared," said Phil Spence. "I panicked, I cried and I prayed."

After they wheeled out a stretcher, I apparently started to move a bit as I was wheeled out, but I have no recollection of that.

When I fully awoke I was in the back of an ambulance, with my mom sitting at my feet. It was so reassuring to see her loving eyes. I felt better almost instantly. It was like a strange prophecy had been fulfilled. I remember her always telling Coach Sloan, "That boy jumps so high that one of these days he's gonna fall and hurt himself."

I was taken to old Rex Hospital in Raleigh. Dr. Jim Manley, another of our team doctors, followed the ambulance there in a state trooper's car.

As Dr. Manley entered the emergency room in which I was being treated, he was handed a telephone. Calls were already flooding in from all over the country, and this one happened to be from legendary newsman Walter Cronkite, checking in on behalf of the *CBS Evening News*.

Dr. Manley explained to Cronkite that it was too soon to tell him anything, but the consummate journalist would have none of that. Fifty million viewers wanted to know my condition, Cronkite said, and he wasn't hanging up until he had something to tell them.

All that fuss over one college basketball player. Go figure.

After each phase of examination and treatment, Dr. Manley would relay the results to America's most trusted anchorman. Initial diagnosis, X-rays, the suturing of my scalp (15 stitches)—Walter Cronkite got a blow-by-blow account of it all.

The final word was that I had suffered a concussion, but would make a full recovery.

Unfortunately, the medical play-by-play was not available back at the Coliseum, and in the stunned silence that prevailed, ugly rumors began to fly faster than one of Monte's behind-the-back passes: I had died en route to the hospital; I was alive, but would never emerge from a vegetable state. Thankfully, neither was accurate.

There was 10:15 left on the first half clock, but my teammates did not want to continue the game. It took a lot of coaxing by Coach Sloan to convince them to retake the floor, because that's what I would want them to do. First, everyone huddled in prayer for my safe and speedy recovery.

It was Monte who was the most shook up. We were very close, and he literally played with tears in his eyes the whole time. He had to wipe them away as he dribbled upcourt.

Upon resumption of the game, Burleson led a spurt of 10 straight Wolfpack points. The score was 41-27 for us with 4:50 left. All of a sudden, the Wolfpack flatlined. Pitt put in eight straight points, and the lead dwindled to four, 45-41. Moments later, Steve Nuce broke the famine with a layup that made it 47-41 at the half.

Our locker room was as morose as a funeral parlor during the intermission. Nobody felt like playing absent any word about my condition. Coach Sloan himself was still so upset he didn't even know the score of the game. There was no review, no strategizing—just worry about me.

"I thought David had broken his neck," Monte Towe told a reporter in the locker room. "After he got hurt, I just went through the motions. Now I just hope he's going to be all right. I'm concerned about him as a person, not as a player."

That was nice, but in his hospital bed the patient himself was concerned about only one thing: victory. As the doctors sewed me up, I urged them to get my teammates the message that I wanted them to win.

My gallant teammates emerged from halftime still in a state of shock, but some of them, like Phil Spence, determinedly cranked it up a notch when the whistle blew, as if intuiting my message.

"Throughout the second half, I kept saying to myself, 'This is for you, David, this is for you!' I owed it to him. I had this guilty feeling about it," Spence recalled later.

The Wolfpack performed valiantly and played even better when, with the score 70-49 and with my friends firmly in control, an announcement was finally made over the loudspeakers that I was conscious and had suffered no serious injuries. When my plea for a Wolfpack victory was broadcast, the place erupted in prolonged cheers.

With 6:50 left in the game, Burleson was fouled and headed toward the free throw line. But all of a sudden he rushed off the floor, and Coach Sloan wondered for a moment if they had decided to quit after all.

Then there was a tremendous roar from the crowd as I re-entered the arena from a side door, just 48 minutes after I had left it on a stretcher more dead than alive. My teammates spotted me before anyone else, and I was mobbed by the most wonderful group of guys anybody could ever be associated with.

It was one of the most emotional scenes of my life. The crowd was on its feet giving me an ovation. The game was stopped for a minute or two, but we received no technical foul for delay of game, because I think even the refs were glad to see me back in one piece.

"The best thing about this whole ballgame is when [David] came back," Tim Stoddard told a reporter later.

With all the dire rumors about my condition flying around, we decided that I ought to return to the arena to put everyone's minds at ease. I was heavily sedated and looked like the fife player in that *Spirit of '76* picture, with a big white bandage wrapped around my head.

I was escorted to a seat on the bench next to Coach Sloan. Because of the medication given me, my speech was sort of halting. I asked Coach Sloan how the team was doing. "David, all they've cared about is you," he said. "They don't care about the game. But now they're doing fine."

To prove his point, there was Monte running around like the Energizer Bunny on speed, his face wreathed in a smile. "Way to go, Midget!" I yelled in slow motion-speak as he made a steal.

Everyone was so pumped that we thrashed the Panthers the rest of the way and won easily, 100-72. The hometown fans wanted that 100 points so bad. They screamed wildly when 6'11" freshman center Bill Lake was fouled with only seconds to go by a Pitt player named Disco, with the score 98-70. Lake made both shots, and bedlam ensued.

My teammates lifted me up to the basket rim to perform the net clipping ritual. I'm happy to report that they held on tight to keep me from falling on my noggin again.

Burleson (26 points and 12 rebounds), Stoddard (seven and six), Spence (10 and 14), Rivers (17 and eight) and Towe (19 points and six assists) all had fine games to secure the victory in my absence.

Billy Knight finished with 19 for the Panthers, and he made the East Region all-tournament team along with me, Burleson, Towe, and guard Bruce Grimm from Furman.

Not everyone was thrilled when I appeared back at the arena. Pitt coach Charles "Buzz" Ridl accused our school of bringing me back just to give our team a boost, as if there was something unethical about that. The fact is that Coach Sloan himself didn't even know I was returning. He was as surprised as anyone.

There was no postgame celebration for me. Dr. Manley took me right back to Rex Hospital for overnight observation. He thought it a very good sign when I announced that I was hungry. The hospital cafeteria was already closed, but Dr. Manley grabbed a phone and called his local golf club—Carolina Country Club. Before I knew it, a steak dinner was delivered right to my door.

Now *that's* what I call room service.

I was sprung from the hospital Sunday afternoon, just in time to have lunch with my teammates. They gave me grief about published reports that people from all over North Carolina had called and offered to pay my hospital bills. I laughed right along with them. There was no better medicine than their company.

I spent the rest of the day relaxing at Eddie Biedenbach's home, where I received two phone calls—one from the tenacious Walter Cronkite, the other from football star O. J. Simpson.

I returned to the dorm later that night, and my head bandages were removed the next day. It was a pretty miraculous recovery, and when I look back at it today I'm grateful to God for watching over me. And I'm glad that NC State didn't install the hard, unforgiving tartan floor surface in Reynolds Coliseum until my senior year, or they might still be sweeping up pieces of my skull.

And finally, I'm glad that big, Afro hairdos were the style back then, because I think mine may have cushioned the blow and saved my life. Now, I have no scientific basis for that claim, but going hairless sure didn't help Humpty-Dumpty.

Do you want to hear something really funny? Pitt Panther Lou Hill was actually awarded two points for that shot I blocked, because I was called for goaltending! Talk about adding insult to injury!

CHAPTER 9

GOLIATH, MEET DAVID

oach Sloan called off practice that Monday for two reasons. He had a standard policy of no heavy practices before big games anyway, and he wasn't sure of my status. I would rejoin the team on Tuesday as we began light drills in preparation for our first Final Four game.

The team was extremely uptight as we strode into practice on Tuesday. Everyone was looking at me like I might go into convulsions all of a sudden.

But other than a small headache, I was just fine. Nevertheless, doctors were present to monitor my every move, "just in case." During a team meeting in front of our locker room in Reynolds Coliseum, even Coach Sloan kept peeking at me just to make sure I wasn't slipping off into permanent slumber.

I decided to try to ease the tension by taking a page from a movie popular at that time. It was a huge blockbuster hit called *The Exorcist*. As Coach was going on about how easy we were going to take it that day, not doing anything strenuous. I suddenly dropped my head, then jerked it from side to side while rolling my eyes back and stiffening my body up. The only thing missing was the pea soup spewing from my mouth.

As the doctors bumped into each other to get to me—like a scene from *The Three Stooges*—Coach Sloan looked like he could use some medical attention himself, and I started to laugh.

Coach Sloan exclaimed, "David! You almost gave me a heart attack!" Well, it loosened everybody up and we went out and had a great practice. Approximately 8,000 fans had showed up, mainly to see how I was doing.

Coach Sloan usually held open practices, and our fans were always welcome. I hit a shot from halfcourt at one point that swished, and the throng of people in the stands went berserk.

When that shot went in, I knew something good was destined to happen. It was like a good omen of things to come. And the crowd? They didn't want to leave. Those people howled and shrieked and eventually had to be asked to leave the building. Security had to herd them off campus. They were ready to celebrate.

That was also the week that my friend and teammate Dwight Johnson gave me a nickname many people remember to this day: "TWA." When I had the laceration on my scalp, the doctor had to cut my Afro way down to sew in the stitches. So Dwight called my new 'do TWA, for "Teeny Weeny Afro." Man, did the media pick on that. I remember even seeing it in *Sports Illustrated*.

We drove the 70 miles to Greensboro that Friday, March 22. Some people who watched us head out said there was a halo following our bus, so I guess we were a true team of destiny after all.

NBC carried the Final Four with celebrated sportscaster Curt Gowdy and former Notre Dame and NBA star Tom Hawkins doing the announcing.

The fanfare and pageantry was something to behold. Signs of Wolfpack mania were everywhere. One poster proclaimed, "Even We Farmers Back the Pack." The whole state was behind us. Not a plow was turning in North Carolina on that March Saturday. Everybody wanted to see the Walton Gang thrown off the mountain.

The Bruins were a confident bunch, but they needed to realize that the NC State team they faced in December was not the same group now. That was before we had assimilated new talent and discovered just how marvelous a machine we could be.

This game was filled with historic overtones.

UCLA came in with 38 straight NCAA Tournament victories. They still had Bill Walton, Keith Wilkes and Greg Lee from their 1972 and '73 title teams that had gone 60-0. It was rumored that Bruins head coach John Wooden, "The Wizard of Westwood," might exit Pauley Pavilion along with the graduating Bill Walton. UCLA had all the motivation they needed.

Of course, there was also the "minor" fact of UCLA being the seven-time defending national champion.

We had some history on our side, too. We had just become the first team ever to go through the ACC undefeated two years in a row. That's no small feat in what was regarded as the toughest conference in the country at that time.

Coach Sloan was confident. He had even gone out and purchased a tie with little number ones on it after we were voted the top team in the country. He felt it, we had proved it, and now we hungered for redemption against the only team to beat us that year.

It was 3:10 p.m. EST and time to show our stuff in front of the 15,829 in the seats and the millions watching at home in front of their television sets.

Third-ranked Marquette University had held up their end of the bargain two hours earlier by easily disposing of a fine University of Kansas team, 64-51.

UCLA arrived in the Final Four by virtue of, first, outlasting a determined Dayton team in three overtimes, 111-100, in the West Regional semifinal. The Bruins scored 11 points in the third overtime to clinch the victory. Luck had definitely been on their side. Bill Walton had been up for six hours before the game studying for exams, and that might have had something to do with it, too. Bill was definitely a scholar, as were Keith Wilkes and Greg Lee.

Coach Wooden's defending champions then overwhelmed San Francisco, 83-60, in the West Regional Final to set up the much-anticipated showdown with us.

As game time approached, UCLA and Coach Wooden had something special planned for me. Using information gleaned during the East Region Final, they had spent extra time in practice the week before our game focusing on me and devising a gimmick defense the same way UCLA worked up a diamond-and-one to use against Elvin Hayes in the 1968 semifinal. Walton told me this himself about 20 years later.

When the players were announced one by one, the Bruins strolled out on the court in a very calm, cool and collected manner. Just another day at the beach...

Conversely, when Burleson's name was called, his arms were flying around and you could tell just how pumped up he was. He looked like he was going to hurt himself, a real sight to behold. All 7'4" of him was flailing and leaping. That got us even more fired up.

Just five seconds into the game, the crowd let the Westerners know this wasn't Disneyland. Walton controlled the tap, and junior forward Dave Meyers chased down the ball back in Bruins territory. But as he struggled to gain possession, it appeared that he double-dribbled by touching the ball twice. There was no call from the refs, but deafening boos rained down from the stands.

On that first UCLA possession, Burleson overplayed Walton just a bit too much. Meyers hit Walton with a perfect lob behind our defense and, just like that, the Bruins were up 2-0.

Burleson responded immediately with a right-handed hook directly in Walton's face. It was obvious that Tommy intended to fight the big redhead tooth and nail on every play, and that aggressive move proved it. It was Tommy's senior year, his last chance for that elusive championship, and he was going to leave it all out on the floor.

As UCLA brought the ball up past halfcourt, I stole a pass but stepped out of bounds. UCLA retained possession, and Walton scored again on a right-hand hook of his own. Walton wanted his third title desperately.

It was time for a little taste of our aerial assault. Stoddard and I would track very closely this entire game, and the first time it happened resulted in two points. Tim was 25 feet out when he tossed me a beautifully timed alley-oop pass. I had the easy part, and I converted for two.

When Meyers missed at the other end on the next play, I took Keith Wilkes right into the lane and was fouled. I needed to establish my own game this time and not let Wilkes get the best of me. I made one of the two foul shots.

My legs felt good, and I was determined to use them to the fullest. The next play was a good example. At the UCLA offensive end, Wilkes let fly with one of those soft 11-foot jumpers of his, but it missed off to the left. Walton rebounded and shot right back up toward the hoop from only three feet away. He pegged me out of the corner of his eye just as he released his shot and adjusted it to go a little higher than usual—but not high enough.

I timed my jump precisely and tipped the shot away. We gained possession, and my statement had been made. *Do not bring the ball inside if I am there. You will eat leather every time.*

UCLA had built a 10-9 lead when the first TV timeout was called. The pace was furious, and the fans were getting their money's worth.

When play resumed, UCLA had the ball. Greg Lee drove to the basket from the right side and dished off to Walton at the last second. As Walton soared above the pack on the way to the layin, he encountered a fast, black satellite—me. My block was executed with authority as I reinforced my message of intimidation to all Bruins who dared to enter my domain.

I was in total synch with the game. I saw that play coming, and I jumped when Walton jumped. I just happened to get up a little higher. The scene was one of mass, Wolfpack-red hysteria inside Greensboro Coliseum.

The game then became sloppy. Officials Rick Weiler and Paul Galvin were calling the game very closely. Burleson exited with about 11 minutes to go in the first half because of two fouls he picked up guarding the highly agile Walton.

On each of the next two UCLA possessions, the Bruins missed their shots. I didn't want to just grab those rebounds; I wanted to *terrorize their offense*. So I soared into the ozone each time to let them know what they were up against, even though I may not have needed to go that high to recover the missed shots.

Mistakes began to plague both teams. Wilkes and Walton were called for traveling on successive possessions, and even I threw the ball away twice within a minute—something that was definitely not typical of my game.

We implemented a mini-Tease with about 11:30 left for the sole purpose of looking for a good shot. We were patient, and with 10 minutes to go, we were ahead 15-14. A minute later, our margin was five.

UCLA fought back, like champions do, and with 6:35 remaining, our lead had been cut to 21-20. I knew I had to do more.

With about 5:30 left, and starting from the left side of the floor at the top of the key, I took Wilkes off the dribble. As I blazed toward the hoop I faked a little runner, and Walton bit. As he committed himself to me, it left Burleson wide open. I dropped the ball off to Tommy, and it was two more points for the Wolfpack.

With 5:12 to go, I attempted a shot from the deep right corner, and it found the bottom of the net. We took a three-point lead, 25-22. Walton countered by putting back a missed Bruin shot, and our lead was again down to one, 25-24.

Greg Lee's next shot missed the mark, and I went way up for one of my patented high-flyer rebounds. After I made the outlet pass, I raced down the court as fast as I could. Stoddard found me on the left side, and I took his lob going over more than half of the UCLA defense—Walton, Wilkes and Lee. They never knew what hit them as I scored my eleventh point, and our lead was 29-24.

As I said, the refs were calling this one close, and I became one of the casualties. I came out after picking up my third foul going up with Walton as he scored on a tap-in. Walton hit the charity shot for his eleventh point.

At the other end, Monte decided it was time to display his long-range marksmanship. From around 25 feet away, our leader launched a long jumper that went straight in. On our next trip down, Burleson—wanting to prove that he was every bit the center Walton was—backed big Bill down in the blocks and scored. That made it 33-29 in our favor.

After a UCLA score, Moe Rivers tossed in a jumper from the right side that gave us a four-point lead. Wilkes came right back and hit a shot of his own to make it 35-33.

Coach Sloan called for the Tease again with 0:55 seconds left. For 50 of those seconds, we waited and hunted for a good shot. Rivers drove for the hoop with five seconds left, but was called for traveling.

Then Dave Meyers re-entered the game for UCLA.

It was a good thing for them that he did. Tommy Curtis inbounded the ball to Greg Lee, who quickly passed to Meyers 30 feet away from the basket with two seconds left. Right before the horn sounded, Meyers chucked an ugly shot toward the rim with Phil Spence in his face. Somehow the shot went in, and the score was knotted 35-35 as both teams went to their locker rooms. It really was an amazing shot.

I don't remember much of what was said in our locker room, but I'm sure Coach Sloan re-emphasized that if UCLA had an Achilles heel that year, it was that they were not particularly good at a slowed-down game and that they did not play well with the lead. The fun just wasn't there for them when we deliberately forced a sluggish pace. It was a cat-and-mouse game we played, speeding up the tempo when behind, and slowing it down when ahead.

UCLA drew first blood as the second half opened. Walton was the Bruins' ace all year, and he lived up to that billing by nailing a turnaround jumper in the lane that gave UCLA the lead, 37-35.

Stoddard and I tried to regain our alley-oop magic from the first half, but failed on our first attempt. When Walton tried the same shot he used to open the half, he missed and Burleson snared the rebound. He threw a hard bounce pass over to Monte, and it went right past him out of bounds.

A Dave Meyers short jumper from the left side gave UCLA a four-point lead, 39-35. We had not yet scored in the second half, and the next time down court, I was called for traveling. Coach Sloan had seen enough and called time out to settle us down.

The respite didn't help. At time-in, Walton shot and missed, but grabbed his own rebound and scored. It was now 41-35, and UCLA had outscored us 6-0 since the beginning of the second half. It wasn't until Stoddard was fouled and connected on one of two free throws that our drought ended.

As UCLA came back our way, I anticipated a Greg Lee pass and picked it off. I went the distance for a nice layup to put us within three, 41-38. UCLA then stole the ball from Burleson, and Meyers completed the play by scoring and restoring the Bruins' five-point lead. Soon thereafter, Burleson picked up his third foul and headed to the bench.

We were performing like an average team, and UCLA capitalized on it. Tommy Curtis fired a line-drive jump shot from the free throw line that went in like a laser. UCLA now had their biggest lead at 45-38, and it would only get worse for us.

After Monte launched a stray missile, Curtis made his second shot in a row—a jumper off the glass from the left side. Now it was 47-38, and we were letting the game get away from us.

When Stoddard and I tried the alley-oop again, Wilkes fouled me as I went up. Tossing the ball in after the Wilkes foul, Spence passed inside to Burleson, only to have the ball sail directly through Tommy's outstretched hands. We might as well have been playing blindfolded.

On the next UCLA possession, Wilkes drove hard from the right but missed the layup. Walton was "Mr. Offensive Rebound" again and made the put-back to give him 19 points and his team an 11-point lead, 49-38.

Moe Rivers ended up with the ball on our next possession and was tripped as he entered the middle section of the lane. The Bruins tied him up, and a jump ball was called. It just seemed like we couldn't get anything positive going. We had already committed five turnovers in the second half.

Maybe we weren't playing with sufficient aggression. Possibly we had taken UCLA too lightly, if that was possible. Whatever the cause of our poor play, it was time to remedy the situation right then and there, or just pack it in. Enter the next phase of this famous game, one I will call "The Wolfpack Comeback—Part I."

I fired up a long, errant jump shot that Walton reeled in directly underneath the basket. But just as Bill got his hands on the ball, Burleson knocked it right out and then laid the ball in for two. That basket broke an 8-0 UCLA run and resulted in a 49-40 score. Our 7'4" center began to assert himself once again.

Burleson continued to have his way with Walton. A right-hand hook over the top of the UCLA All-American made it 49-42. Then Curtis took a back-door pass from Meyers and went straight at the Newland native. Bad idea. When Curtis shot, Burleson almost swatted the ball down his throat as the crowd roared.

At the other end, Big Tom scored his sixth straight point as he put back a missed 24-footer by Stoddard. The Bruin lead was now down to five. Curtis came right back for UCLA with a 20-foot shot from the right side of the floor, but Monte answered with a long 25-footer of his own. It was one beautiful shot, hitting nothing but net.

After two Wilkes free throws and back-to-back baskets by Walton and Meyers, the UCLA lead was back up to 11, 57-46.

Stoddard got us back on track as he drained a long jumper from the right corner. That was the beginning of "The Wolfpack Comeback—Part II," where we scored 10 unanswered points. It was 57-48, and time was becoming a big factor.

A few plays later, I found the range from almost the exact same spot where Stoddard had launched his lengthy jumper. It was my fifteenth point, and now we were only down by seven, 57-50.

The next time we had the ball, Monte drove the length of the floor and put up as pretty a one-handed floater, in the lane, as you'll ever see. The ball never touched the rim—it just sailed right through.

UCLA's Curtis attempted a long bomb, and when he missed, the rebound sent the ball all the way out to Monte. He spotted a streaking Moe Rivers, who had started his break when he saw that Curtis's shot was off. Towe's pass to Rivers was on the mark, and Moe hit the layup to get us within three, 57-54.

After another UCLA miss, Tim Stoddard drew a charging foul on Wilkes, and UCLA began to make some uncharacteristic mistakes. It was the fourth foul on Wilkes, and the crowd was going crazy with 8:31 to play. Then Walton scored underneath but was called for traveling—no basket.

After a myriad of turnovers by both teams, Stoddard ended up with the rock and tossed in a long six-foot layup over a flat-footed Walton. We had clawed back to within one, 57-56.

UCLA finally broke their scoring drought on a Meyers jumper and increased their margin to 59-56. But I came down the other way and tossed in a shot of my own from the left corner to keep us within one, 59-58. Keith Wilkes banked in a shot from 15 feet out and the Bruins went back up by three. With only 5:43 left in regulation, Monte then drove in from the left side of the court, circled into the lane, and flipped in another of those sweet one-handed floaters from eight feet out.

Stoddard spotted me cutting to the hole again and sent in a beautiful lob. I caught the ball and laid it into the basket all in one motion, and was simultaneously fouled by Meyers. For the first time in the second half, we had the lead, 62-61.

I stepped to the line for my bonus attempt, and put the ball up. No good—but UCLA was called for a lane violation, another crucial Bruin mistake late in the game. I sank the re-do, and we were up by a deuce.

That lasted until Walton fed Meyers for a layup and the junior forward converted. With 4:36 to go, we were all tied up at 63-63.

We decided to frustrate the UCLA defense by bringing out the Tease once again. With Monte, Moe Rivers and myself up top, Burleson in the middle and Stoddard off to the right, we ate up almost two full minutes of precious time.

I had the ball with 2:39 left when I was fouled by Lee as I went by him. I missed the front end of a one-and-one, and the rebound sailed far right. Stoddard picked up a foul as the ball flew out of bounds, and Coach Sloan called a timeout with 2:36 remaining.

On the very next play, UCLA's Big Red took a pass from Lee and sent up a high-arching, 13-foot jumper from the left side that kissed off the glass and went cleanly in. Walton was definitely a master of the bank shot, even when a lunging Tom Burleson—with albatross-like arms outstretched—came directly at him. UCLA had regained the lead, 65-63.

It was time for an encore of the Stoddard/Thompson circus act. This time I elevated well above both Meyers and Walton to receive Tim's pass from 18 feet out. The announcers said that my elbows were actually above the rim when I caught the ball and scored the bucket. It was my 21st point; once again we were at a stalemate, 65-all.

What many felt was the true national championship game was living up to the hype.

It was UCLA's turn to be patient in looking for their best opportunity. There was too much at stake to force a shot. With 51 seconds on the clock, Walton decided it was up to him to be the hero. He lofted a baby hook with the right hand from 10 feet away, but the ball bounded off the front of the rim, and Burleson swept away the rebound.

We would play for the last shot, the win, all the marbles, and the glory.

With 23 seconds left, Coach Sloan called our last timeout. When play resumed, Monte dished the ball to Stoddard, positioned 23 feet from the basket on the right side of the floor. In retrospect, that may have been just what UCLA wanted because of what happened next.

The man guarding Stoddard, Dave Meyers, fell off him and collapsed into the middle with Walton—accomplishing two things at once. First, he was daring Tim to take the last shot. UCLA must have determined those were good odds. Second, clogging the middle made it impossible for Burleson or me to create something inside. That was a smart play. You don't win seven titles in a row by playing dumb.

Tim stood with the ball searching for an open teammate for at least six or seven seconds and then realized time was running out. He decided to let 'er rip with five seconds left. It was actually a nice-looking shot, but it caromed off the back of the rim.

Though Wilkes was guarding me closely, I maneuvered myself enough away from him to jump up and try to make a tip in if the ball were to come my way—no such luck.

Instead, the basketball shot all the way out to Greg Lee, and UCLA used their last timeout with two ticks left on the scoreboard clock. When play resumed, Meyers passed the ball in to Lee, who attempted a last-ditch shot that wasn't close, and that was the end of regulation play.

After an intense, fiercely contested 40-minute war, nothing had been decided. Regulation ended in a 65-65 tie. Overtime was needed to unmask the real number-one team in the nation.

The referee tossed the ball up into the air, and overtime began with Burleson winning the tip. My teammates worked the ball over to me, and I fired a 12-foot jumper over Wilkes that missed. UCLA came down the other way and Meyers found Walton underneath, but threw it away. The Bruins were still making careless mistakes.

Burleson drew first blood with a stunning spin move to his right that left Walton befuddled. But Greg Lee tied it right back up from the left side with a 22-foot swish. Rivers had played off him a little because up to then Lee had not shown himself to be a potent scoring threat.

Amazingly, we were only 1:12 into the extra stanza, and that's all the scoring that would be done in that period. Not that there weren't ample chances, mind you.

On a failed alley-oop to me, Burleson was fouled by Meyers. Tom missed the front end of the one-and-one just off the front of the rim. Then Stoddard stole a Lee pass intended for Wilkes, and we regained possession with 3:18 left.

Once again, just like at the end of regulation, we held the ball for what seemed an eternity. UCLA didn't know what to do. With 15 seconds left, Coach Sloan called a timeout.

After the break, Moe Rivers threw the ball in to Monte, who caught it just behind the halfcourt line. He tossed it back to Moe, and then it came to me. With time winding down, I lobbed a pass into Burleson, who decided he was going to end this marathon slugfest. Closely guarded by Walton, Tommy faked left, went right and put up a five-footer with Walton right in his mug.

No good.

The ball popped out to Lee again and he hurled another desperation shot down the floor, but it hit the Coliseum scoreboard because of how high he had thrown it.

We couldn't believe it. Two chances to win it at the end, and both missed. Nothing against Tom, but I don't think he had ever taken a potential game-winning shot with so much pressure attached. After Burleson missed at the end of the first overtime, Monte came over to me and said, "David, if it comes down to that situation again, either you or I are going to take that shot."

I heard you, my man; I really heard you.

Round Two began at 67-all, and we won the tip. I decided I was really going to assert myself more in the next five minutes and began with a long jump shot that missed. Burleson fouled Walton trying to get the rebound. Not a good start.

Walton drained the two foul shots. It was as if he was telling his teammates, "Follow me. I know the way." UCLA was back on top 69-67.

On our second trip into UCLA terrain, Burleson twirled for a sweet reverse layup attempt around Walton. As the ball tap-danced up on the rim ever so softly, Stoddard tipped it in and the basket was disallowed. You can't touch the ball while it's in the cylinder. We were now 0-2 from the field in the second overtime, and UCLA was gaining confidence.

When UCLA brought the ball up, Lee passed inside to Walton. Bill faked once on Burleson, dribbled once to his left, and launched a perfect jump shot over Tommy that swished in for Walton's 27th point. The Bruins had bolted out in front, 71-67, and only 1:50 had passed.

Rivers's shot missed at our end, and Tommy Curtis pushed the ball up hard for UCLA. When he reached the foul line, he sent a bounce pass to Wilkes, who subsequently scored and was fouled by Stoddard. The Bruins had not missed a free throw all day, performing at a perfect 9-9 clip.

Wilkes continued the string by making the shot, and UCLA was up 74-67 with 3:27 remaining. We were in trouble, but our luck was about to change.

As Monte charged upcourt with the ball, Curtis committed a silly foul. Monte went to the line as confident as ever and sank the first of two shots. When he made the second one, we all breathed a collective sigh of relief as we were now only down by five, 74-69.

As if to return the favor, Monte fouled Curtis in almost the same situation. Curtis continued the Bruins' flawless free throw shooting by hitting the first shot. But he muffed number two—still, UCLA by six, 75-69.

I knew it was now or never. I had dreamed of this as a young boy, and the hour of reckoning was here. The next time I touched the ball, I powered down the lane, took a shot and missed, but went skyward to tip in my own shot off the backboard.

Monte and I had talked about taking over at the end, and now it was his turn to make something happen. As Curtis brought the ball up the floor, he made a quick move on Monte to the left to get by him. But Monte's quick feet kept him squarely in front of Curtis, and the UCLA guard was called for charging.

With the ball back in our hands, I let fly with a 24-foot jumper, but missed. Meyers corralled the rebound, and Wooden called for a timeout. As soon as play resumed, UCLA turned the ball over.

Monte tried a shot from around the foul line, but didn't make it. Burleson was Tommy-on-the-spot, however, and tipped that baby back in even as Walton actually had a hand on the ball.

The score was 75-73 UCLA, but the Wolfpack rally was on.

Walton tried to catch Wilkes back-door, but Stoddard slapped it away with 1:50 left. As we set up our offense at the other end, Burleson was posting up Walton big time. When Tommy got the ball, he gave a little fake and Walton took the bait. As Walton's feet left the ground, Tommy went up and was fouled. Burleson hit the first one to bring us within one, 75-74, but he missed the second shot.

Incredibly, the ball bounded out to Stoddard. He tossed to Burleson, who missed a 15-foot jumper. Walton tried to tap the rebound out to Curtis, but Moe Rivers intercepted it. The ball went over to Monte, who missed on a shot deep from the left corner.

I was starting to wonder if we would ever get the job done.

Stoddard fouled out trying to get a rebound away from Dave Meyers. Coach Sloan consoled him with a pat on the back and told him what a great game he had played. Meyers missed his free throw, and up, up, and away I went for the rebound. That one wasn't going to get away.

There was 1:10 remaining. It was my time. Pressure time. Glory time.

I drove firmly to the right, just outside the lane, with Wilkes matching me step for step. I pulled up as quickly as I could and banked home a nine-footer for a 76-75 NC State lead with 50 seconds left.

We had overcome a seven-point deficit in less than two and a half minutes against the mighty Bruins. We were not about to let this one slip away.

UCLA passed the ball around to Greg Lee for a 25-foot jump shot. He missed, and as I went for the rebound, I was pushed from behind by Keith Wilkes and the foul was whistled on him. With 34 seconds left I strode to the line.

I notched my 27th and 28th points as I converted both tries, and we were on our way. The Wolfpack lead was up to 78-75, with 30 seconds left.

As Lee brought the ball up for UCLA, Rivers almost picked his pocket but lost the ball out of bounds. For some reason Lee then tried to inbound the ball all the way down to Walton, who was only about eight feet from the basket. Burleson knocked it away over to Rivers. Tommy, sensing the sweet scent of victory, raised his arms high above his head as he trotted down court. The crowd howled along with each step he took.

The fans were in a frenzy now. Raw emotion was spilling out from the stands, but we still had work to do.

Monte was running around, killing the clock, when he was fouled by Curtis with 12 seconds left. If he made both free throws, we could introduce ourselves to Marquette. They say that cucumbers are cool, and if that's the case, then Monte is the coolest of them all. Our pint-sized guard with the heart of a lion crushed UCLA single-handedly with two gorgeous foul shots.

The score was 80-75, and there wasn't much else UCLA could do.

The Bruins got the ball down court quickly and fed Walton, and he took a shot that rolled all over the rim before falling through with six seconds left.

I grabbed the ball so we could put it right back into play and finally get the heck out of there. I spotted Burleson to my right about five feet away, tossed it in high, and up the ladder Tommy went.

UCLA jumped all over him in the left corner and a foul was called with one second left. Security guards were trying to keep anxious fans off the court as Tommy missed the front end of the one-and-one. Meyers grabbed the rebound and tried to whip it down toward his basket, but the ball fell just beyond midcourt and into the waiting hands of Monte Towe, who tucked it under his arm and made for the locker room. On his way there, Bill Walton intercepted him for a congratulatory hug.

College basketball would finally have a new de facto champion after seven years of domination by UCLA, and glory now had a permanent home in Raleigh, North Carolina.

"We knew it couldn't go on forever," said a gracious John Wooden after the game. "We were very close to keeping it going. I thought we had the game in hand on two different occasions."

State's locker room was a Times-Square-at-midnight-on-New-Year's-Eve mob scene. I remember telling a reporter it was the happiest moment and biggest thrill of my career.

"I had nothing personally to prove, really," I said. "But as far as the team was concerned, we did. We knew we could play a lot better than we did in St. Louis. I don't feel this was an upset. I have felt all along we were the number-one team."

Beating UCLA felt like we had climbed Mount Everest, but the reality of the situation was that we still had one more step to take before the Wolfpack would occupy the most exalted peak in college basketball.

CHAPTER 10

THE WINNER TAKES IT ALL

Noah's Ark finally hit Mount Ararat, the sun did eventually set on the British Empire, the Titanic sank, Rome declined and fell, the glaciers went back, and the dinosaur vanished. Even Methuselah died.

Hey, nobody's perfect. Not even UCLA.

Jim Murray, the great writer from Los Angeles, also wrote, "Great kings are felled by great adversaries. Caesar had Brutus; Napoleon, Wellington. Lee had Grant. But this was more like the dinosaur succumbing to the tsetse fly." I know what he meant. That Bruins team had won 88 straight games, and many believed it was Coach Wooden's finest. I knew just one thing, though.

UCLA was *dead*.

We honorably drew the sheet over the monarchs of basketball and then basked in the glory of what we had accomplished—for about three hours.

Coach Sloan was very fearful of a letdown after the emotional victory over UCLA. How could he not be? There would've been nothing more embarrassing than for us to beat UCLA and then lose the national championship game to Marquette.

So he worked to keep us focused on the task at hand as we headed back to the motel in Greensboro.

The Albert Pick Motel was always our home away from home when we played in Greensboro—which was more than you might think when you consider that the annual Big Four and ACC Tournaments were held there. Those four to five games made up approximately one-fifth of our schedule each year.

The manager at the Albert Pick was Art Flynn, and his place became known as "Flynn's Inn" to Wolfpack fans everywhere. We enjoyed a hearty celebration that Saturday night.

My parents were celebrities that night. People came up to them the entire evening asking questions about me. "What did you feed that boy?" was a favorite. I think that was one of the happiest times of their lives. They loved coming to the games and getting wrapped up in our whole atmosphere and feeling the electricity in the air. Someone gave my dad a Superman shirt to wear with my name on the back. My brother was there, as were many other members of my extended family.

But as I said, Coach Sloan was one Nervous Nelly as the national championship game approached.

Al McGuire, Marquette's fiery coach, was quoted after the Warriors' win against Kansas as saying, "On paper, we're not as good as UCLA or North Carolina State, but we'll make sure that whoever we play hears some footsteps."

When Sunday arrived, there was a big press conference at the Coliseum, and all four teams worked out. (At that time, there was a consolation game for the two teams that didn't make the final.) The big question that was on everyone's mind had nothing to do with the Marquette/NC State national championship game.

Inquiring minds wanted to know if Bill Walton was going to play against Kansas in the consolation game.

The 6'11" redhead had already let it be known that he felt like sitting out the consolation round. "I'm due for a rest," he said. Likewise, Greg Lee said he would just as soon pass on the game against Kansas.

Coach Wooden had no problem with that. He was on record as saying that he always detested the game that determined third place. "I think consolation games are for the birds," said the sage of Westwood. "Several of my players probably won't play, and it will be all right with me."

As it turned out, Walton and the other Bruins ended up playing, and they beat Kansas handily, 78-61. But I always found that situation interesting. Since when did the vanquished get to call the shots?

When we arrived at the Coliseum for our scheduled practice, Marquette was just finishing up. We had the final time slot. While we were standing there watching the end of the Warriors' workout, no fewer than three scuffles broke out—and Coach McGuire was involved in two of them. Guys were shouting at each other and playing very aggressively, until finally an NCAA official came in and forced them off the floor.

As he came off the floor, Coach McGuire stopped and waved his finger in Coach Sloan's face.

"You know, you only get an hour!" McGuire yelled. "Just because you're the last one here doesn't mean you can stretch it out!"

Coach Sloan just chuckled and said, "Hey Al, you can have 15 minutes of my time. I'm enjoying this."

We took an entirely different attitude onto the court. We were fooling around, trying to drop-kick field goals football-style, posing for pictures, being silly and totally having a good time. After only about 15 minutes, we chased each other into the locker room.

Yeah, you could say we were pretty loose.

Before the season had even started, Coach McGuire remarked that his Warriors probably had an outside shot at an NIT berth. But as the season progressed, his gutsy team gained confidence and built up some serious momentum that eventually landed them squarely in front of us for the national championship.

Marquette had a catchy slogan that captured the essence of their tournament run and unlikely appearance in the title match: "Everything is falling into place." We wanted to make sure they fell on their face.

McGuire's team was loaded, but young. The lone senior was team captain Marcus Washington, a sometimes dazzling, sometimes exasperating 6'1" guard. He was joined in the backcourt by sophomore Lloyd Walton, a 6'0" jet of a playmaker.

It was up front, though, where the Warriors were most talented. Earl Tatum, a 6'4" sophomore, whom McGuire had christened "the black Jerry West," was an excellent defensive player who occupied one forward spot.

The center was another of my former World University Games teammates—the Enforcer himself, 6'9", 215-pound junior Maurice Lucas. Maurice was Marquette's true leader, and he provided the emotional spark that made the Warriors go. Coach McGuire referred to Lucas as his "Secretariat," referring to the 1973 Triple Crown horse race winner.

But it was a freshman to whom McGuire always pointed to explain why Marquette was such a surprise that year. Maurice "Bo" Ellis, a 6'9",

200-pound, lanky forward, was the key factor in carrying the Warriors beyond McGuire's preseason NIT level forecast.

"I'd never seen him play, so I had no idea how good he was," McGuire said at the Final Four. "If I'd known," he added with that streets-of-New-York wit, "I would have paid him more." Actually, Ellis was paid handsomely his senior season when Marquette won the national championship in McGuire's last year on the bench.

All five Marquette starters would be drafted by NBA teams, and two, Lucas and Ellis, would go in the first round of their respective drafts. The only player not to make an NBA roster was Washington. Needless to say, we took Marquette very seriously.

Exactly 15,742 fans heralded our entrance in to the Greensboro Coliseum on March 25, 1974. Millions tuned in that Monday night to watch the game on NBC-TV. I'm not sure how many Marquette fans were in the house, but it didn't sound like many. Or maybe it was just the Wolfpack faithful drowning them out as they prepared for the inevitable.

Actually, this game could have ended up closer than a lot of people think.

Even though we felt a bit sluggish after the hard-fought win over UCLA, we jumped right out to a 10-2 lead. But in the snap of a finger, Marquette had us all tied up at 12.

The Warriors played a very physical brand of ball against us, but we just gave it right back to them. It was exactly this bruising style of play that cost them late in the first half.

With 2:48 left before intermission, Marcus Washington, the quick Warrior guard, was whistled for charging into me after he completed a driving layup that put Marquette ahead, 28-27. The contact was slight, but our bodies did meet under the basket and we both slowly fell to the floor.

The call was a little delayed by referee Jim Howell of the Southern Conference, and Coach McGuire rose off the bench and screeched at him for it. Then McGuire stomped his foot and clasped his right hand around his clenched left fist to make the "choke" sign. Howell immediately zapped him with a "T."

I went to the line and dropped the foul shot on McGuire's technical. Then I buried the next two free throws for Washington's charging foul. We then got the ball out of bounds. Burleson made a beautiful turning jump shot, and we led by four, 32-28.

With 1:55 to play in the half and State now ahead 34-28, Phil Spence drove in for a layup that seemed to be blocked cleanly, on its upward arc, by Bo Ellis. Official Irv Brown of the Western Athletic Conference didn't see it that way, however, and called Ellis for goaltending.

McGuire exploded for the second time, storming out onto the court, stomping his feet and screaming. Brown promptly called another technical foul on him.

I scored another free throw on the technical, and, with Spence's basket on the goaltending call, we were ahead 37-28. We had scored 10 unanswered points in just 55 seconds.

McGuire would later admit, "I cost us the game. I lost the game for us because of those technicals. In effect, it was two five-point plays, and the game was over."

Those technicals definitely gave us a lift. So did something else that happened right before the first half ended, although Coach Sloan would dispute that.

For all of his four years at State, Tom Burleson's dream was to, just once, take the ball coast to coast—on the dribble—baseline to baseline and make a layup. Trouble was, 7'4" centers aren't exactly the most adept ball-handling wizards, and Tommy was no exception.

With the seconds winding down, Big Tommy grabbed a rebound and decided now was the time. Coach Sloan saw what was coming.

"He's not going to pass the ball," he screamed in disbelief. "He's going to try and take it all the way!"

Tommy the giant guard made it as far as the Marquette free throw line before the Warriors stole the ball from him. Fortunately, there wasn't enough time left on the clock for Marquette to attempt a shot, but that didn't get Tommy off the hook where Coach Sloan was concerned. Had Burleson passed the ball instead of running his furlong, we might have headed into the locker room with a psychologically imposing double-digit lead instead of just nine points, 39-30.

Coach was so upset at Burleson that he got right in Tommy's face and was letting him have it good. I felt so bad for my friend.

Finally I tugged at Coach Sloan's sleeve ever so gently and said, in a pleading way, "Coach, we're up by *nine*." Coach Sloan stepped back, went out into the hall, composed himself, and came back inside to calmly discuss our strategy for the second stanza.

The second half was vintage Wolfpack. We built a 19-point lead five minutes into play, and the outcome was never in doubt from that point forward.

Monte bombed in a couple from 20 and 25 feet, and our defense harassed the Warriors into 18 turnovers for the game. Tommy and I had some nice blocks, and I'm sure the Marquette players had the yips every time they got near the rim.

Then there was Moe Rivers, who finished the game with 14 points and dished out five assists. "Tonight was Moe's best basketball game of the season," said Coach Sloan afterwards. "He came up with key steals. He was quick as lightning. He has been a super guard all season."

We went into the Tease delay after securing the big lead, and Marquette only came close once—to within nine—before we put the lid on the national championship game, 76-64.

I sent our fans home with an extra memory with 18 seconds left to play in the game. Lloyd Walton drove the lane and put up a high-arcing layin attempt. I saw it coming and blocked that baby right into the stands.

I don't even know to this day if they realized or even cared that I had been called for goaltending. That's how crazy the place was.

With 14 seconds left, Moe Rivers was fouled, and something unbelievable happened. Marquette's volatile head coach, Al McGuire, walked onto the court and congratulated several of us players. He was really impressed by Monte and made sure to shake his hand and tell him how much he enjoyed watching him play. It was Monte, not me or Tommy, whom Coach McGuire felt was the one who made us great. That's one heck of a nice compliment from one of the greatest coaches who ever lived.

Moe knocked down his two free throws for his 13th and 14th points, and the title was finally ours!

Monte, who finished with 16 points, was later quoted as saying, "We played eight great minutes of basketball. We had three good minutes at the end of the first half, and five at the start of the second half.

"The other 32 weren't too good, but you have to attribute that to Marquette. They played strong defense and a very physical game."

To be fair, we committed 23 turnovers to Marquette's 18. This was not exactly our best game, but it was good enough.

Our guards, though, did play great defense. They held Marquette star guard Marcus Washington to a 4-13 shooting night, and fellow guard Lloyd Walton went only 4-10.

Tim Stoddard had an excellent game with eight points and seven rebounds.

I suppose the Marquette game was kind of anticlimactic after our Ali-Frazier duel with UCLA, but Monte spoke prophetically when he told a reporter, "Tomorrow I will probably go crazy."

Once again, our team was not dominated by one player. We all knew our roles, accepted them, and executed as well as any group ever has. For example, Phil Spence and Mark Moeller saw playing time and contributed much to the win.

Burleson closed out his college career with 14 points and 11 rebounds. During Tommy's three-year varsity run, the team went 73-11. I believe he lived up to his press clippings. "It's been a lovely four years at NC State," he said. "It's hard to believe it's over."

I tied Maurice Lucas for game-high honors with 21 points on seven-for-12 shooting. I also contributed seven rebounds and two assists and was named MVP of the Final Four. I made the All-Tournament team along with Monte and Tommy, Lucas from Marquette, and Walton from UCLA.

I became the only non-center, undergraduate player to average more than 23 points per game during an NCAA Tournament.

Additionally, I was named the ACC Player of the Year for the second straight season and National Player of the Year for the first time. Monte joined me on the All-ACC team, becoming the smallest player at that time ever to win All-Conference honors. Maryland's Len Elmore and John Lucas and North Carolina's Bobby Jones completed the first team.

Surprisingly, Burleson and Tom McMillen from Maryland—two seniors who had made first team All-ACC as sophomores and juniors, failed to make the first team this time. They both landed on the second team. How Tommy ended up an All-American, but not first team All-ACC still has me scratching my head.

The best news, of course, was that we had fulfilled Coach Sloan's prophecy at the beginning of the season, when he said that we could become one of the greatest teams ever.

Our 57-1 record over two seasons solidified our place among the greatest college basketball teams of all time, and the 1974 national championship became our ticket to immortality.

If you want to truly understand what we accomplished in 1973-74, and the toll it took on us, consider the following: In the history of the NCAA Tournament, no other team has ever had to face as many highly ranked teams as we did in 1974. In the final three weeks of the season, we had to beat No. 6 North Carolina near the end of the regular ACC season, No. 4 Maryland in the greatest ACC championship game of all time, No. 5 Providence and No. 13 Pittsburgh in the Eastern Regionals, No. 2 UCLA (winner of seven consecutive championships and 38 straight NCAA Tournament games) and No. 3 Marquette to win the title.

No team before or since has ever had to defeat six teams ranked in the top thirteen in the final three weeks of a season, on the way to winning a national championship.

Never.

The mood on our bus ride from the Coliseum to the motel was surprisingly calm and silent. It was almost like we couldn't believe what we had accomplished. Sometimes when you aspire to achieve something so strongly, it's almost surreal. Like it didn't even happen.

The scene at Flynn's Inn was also subdued. Unbelievably, people wanted to know about next year already. Who would replace Burleson? What were our chances? We just wanted to relax and smell the roses.

That night, Monte, Moe Rivers and I rode around Greensboro talking about the game. Monte and Moe had dates, but I didn't. That was OK, though. I had the best win of my life to keep me warm.

Back in Raleigh, our fans tore through Hillsborough Street, the road that runs alongside the campus. Their celebration was a precursor of a much bigger one the next day, Tuesday, March 26, 1974, when we took the bus back to Raleigh. More than 10,000 fans were there to greet us and lay eyes on the national championship trophy. Coach Sloan stood at the podium and told the crowd: "It was a tough road; they wouldn't be defeated. They're an unbelievably beautiful bunch of young men on the court and off the court. I just wanna tell ya that to have the honor and the privilege and the genuine sheer ecstasy and pleasure of standing here to represent this group of champions is the highlight of my life."

Every one of us knew those words came directly from Coach Sloan's heart. We couldn't have asked for a better coach and mentor than Norman Sloan.

Coach then introduced every one of the players, starting with the underclassmen. We each made a short speech.

After the freshmen and sophomores finished, it was Monte's show. He was jumping up and down like a jack-in-the-box. That Indiana charm bubbled right to the top. "Ya'll are very beautiful people. I've been up all night partying, and I just want to continue doing it the rest of the day. I'll let Thompson do the talking...he hasn't stopped all night!"

I didn't do much of it when it was my turn. After a 45-second standing ovation, I said, "I would just like to say that I love you people and thanks a lot for helping to make us number one. All right! Let's go!"

Not exactly the Gettysburg Address, but nobody complained.

Then came one of those moments I will never forget. Senior forward Greg Hawkins, a native West Virginian, was invited by Coach Sloan to come up next, which Greg did—*walking on his hands*. The howling echoed through Reynolds Coliseum. This perfectly set the stage for the last player to speak—our towering senior center and the man who was the primary reason I chose NC State—Tom Burleson. Tommy brought the house down when he referred to Hawkins's previous hand-walking act.

"When I was a freshman here, I couldn't even walk on my feet, let alone on my hands," Tommy said.

His voice choked with emotion, Tommy told the crowd, "This has been the most wonderful four years of my life. You don't know how much I love this damn team." With that, Burleson retreated from the podium to a second standing ovation and sank slowly down into his chair as the tears streaked down his cheeks.

Also speaking were Raleigh mayor Clarence E. Lightner (who proclaimed Raleigh as the "City of Champions"), lieutenant governor Jim Hunt ("This is Wolfpack Year in North Carolina!") and NC State athletic director Willis Casey.

The final word went to Coach Sloan: "UCLA didn't get beat by Dayton; we beat 'em. And we had to go through the toughest conference in the country before getting there. When people talk about us for at least another year, they'll be talking about the defending national champs."

We were even lauded in the nation's capitol. Representative Walter B. Jones, D-NC, a proud NC State graduate, was warmly applauded on the House floor when he spoke of the Pack's achievements. His remarks were even inserted into the Congressional Record for posterity.

And with that, our enchanted season came to a close.

All that joy and happiness, and what an achievement to celebrate. I never even realized that something else was happening to me that was putting everything I had accomplished at tremendous risk—jeopardizing my name, my reputation, my very life.

I went to a lot of beer parties as a freshman in 1971. I was only 17 and not yet of legal drinking age, but frat bashes were around every corner. I succumbed to peer group pressure and became a social drinker.

But as I got older, my drinking progressed.

At the end of my tenure at NC State, I graduated from a social drinker to an everyday drinker.

I recall one night during college when I was driving pretty fast from a party headed toward my dorm room. I was feeling quite relaxed from after an evening of convivial drinking and was barreling down a back road with my tape deck blaring the sounds of the Isley Brothers and Stevie Wonder.

Suddenly, an oncoming car crossed the center line and was headed right toward me. I swerved to avoid a collision, my wheels hit some loose gravel on the side of the road, and my Pontiac Grand Prix slammed head on into a tree.

I could have been hurt, paralyzed, or even killed, but the good Lord was definitely looking out for me that night. After I collected myself and assessed the situation, I ran back to the dorm and called the police. Like a typically immature kid—and a besotted one at that—I lied and reported the car stolen. It's something I deeply regret today, but I knew that if I told the truth I'd be charged with driving under the influence and sent to jail.

Who knows what that devastating news would have done to the school and me? It would have cast a definite pall on team morale and adversely affected our season. No way was I going to be responsible for that, even if it meant difficulty looking at myself in the mirror for a while.

That was the first time I was aware that I might have a serious drinking problem, and I stopped.

For two whole days.

I didn't realize it then, but it was hard to stop drinking when you're constantly the toast of the town.

CHAPTER 11

THE SPOILS OF SUCCESS

T he summer of 1974 brought more basketball and fanfare, even beyond the city limits of Raleigh.

The people of Converse, Indiana, decided to honor their favorite native son, Monte Towe, with a special homecoming celebration for his role in our championship. Converse was a typical Midwestern, one-stop-light town. It was typical in another way, too. It was all white.

Doc Towe (he was actually an electrician, not a doctor), Monte's father, had called Coach Sloan to see what he thought about the homecoming, and of course Coach Sloan gave his blessing. Northwestern Bank in Wilkesboro had an old DC-3 they used as a company plane, and they lent it to us for the occasion. Wilbert and Dwight Johnson, Monte, myself, and a few other players made the trip.

We flew into Marion, which was only a few miles from Converse. Marion was also where Coach Sloan's parents were living at the time.

There must have been 500 people waiting for us at the hog barn inside the fairgrounds in Converse. The barn was decorated in red and white in honor of the Wolfpack, and the Converse High School band provided the music; they were in full pep rally mode.

The master of ceremonies was George Smith, a diminutive local athletic booster who juggled his notes nervously as the band played an off-key version of the National Anthem.

"We are all here today to honor the greatest college basketball player in America," proclaimed Smith to open the program. I wonder if anybody would've laughed if I had stood up right then—probably nobody harder than ol' Monte himself. But it was his day, and I was proud to just be there among his legion of fans.

Besides, to be perfectly honest, I was already skittish about the kind of reception I would receive. Even though the landmark Civil Rights Act had been in effect for just over a decade, there were still plenty of places where black people were about as welcome as mosquitoes at a nudist colony.

Leave it to Mighty Monte. When the man of the hour was called to say a few words, Monte made them about me. He spoke about our friendship and our shared experiences. Then he called me up to the podium, and, as we embraced, the specialness of the moment and of our friendship spread warmth throughout the place that overrode all pre- and misconceived judgments.

When it was my turn to speak, I took the microphone and spoke directly from my heart. "Monte talks about Converse and you people all the time, and what wonderful people you are," I said. "I've been looking forward to this chance to come here and meet you. You're better than he said you were. I can now see why Monte has so much affection for you."

Maybe they all weren't ready to go out and join the NAACP, but clearly there was some big-time bonding going on.

In fact, the whole experience was wrought with high emotion. It was a landmark event in rural Converse, Indiana, and one I will never forget because I managed, if only for the moment, to effect change through something other than a basketball.

The rest of the summer was fun, if nothing else. We were feted all over town and invited to homes for dinner, shopping malls for autograph sessions and appearances, and parties. That national championship was better than a credit card, because we rarely picked up a check. We were celebrities, and we were even invited up to the Governor's mansion for a visit.

Everybody knew who we were, and the attention was unbelievable.

The honors kept pouring in. An "All-Time ACC Team" was named, and after only two varsity seasons I was named on every first-team ballot. Joining me was my boyhood idol, Charlie Scott of North Carolina. Also included were Art Heyman of Duke and Scott's fellow Tar Heels Billy Cunningham and Lenny Rosenbluth. It was quite an honor considering I still had one year of eligibility left.

Next, it was off to the Far East for the Wolfpack of NC State. Everybody went, including incoming freshman sensation Kenny Carr. We spent almost three weeks playing against competition from the Philippines, Japan and China. We went 8-0, and Coach Sloan experimented with a two-guard, three-forward formation that seemed to click.

Without Burleson, we were smaller but quicker. As September rolled around, we played against the Russian national team in a six-game tournament that took us all over the country, including Spokane and Seattle, Washington, Los Angeles, and two games in North Carolina.

Our team was composed of one-half NC State players, and the other half college All-Stars, including Junior Bridgeman from Louisville and Ron Lee from Oregon.

We sent the Russians home with five losses and only one win against us. The Cold War was in full frigid flower then, so it felt good to dominate them so thoroughly. Our confidence was soaring as we finished 13-1 against the international competition.

Then there was the riveting saga of a talented recruit by the name of Moses Malone. Moses may well have been the most highly sought-after high school player in history, including Lew Alcindor.

Hailing from St. Petersburg, Virginia, Moses was courted hard by Lefty Driesell at Maryland. Moses also made a visit to NC State, and Jerry Hunt and I escorted him around the school. Moses ended up choosing Maryland, but then broke Coach Driesell's heart when he joined the Utah Stars of the ABA without ever playing a game for the Terrapins.

How Malone ended up in the professional ranks by way of Maryland, instead of NC State, is a story unto itself. It begins with the strange odyssey of Tom Barker.

Barker, a native Texan, was a 6'11", 225-pound junior college All-Star who committed to the Wolfpack for the 1974-75 season. He tore up the junior college ranks playing one year for Southern Idaho Junior College in Twin Falls, Idaho. Assistant Wolfpack coach Eddie Biedenbach scouted Barker at a basketball camp in New York during the early summer and had made a strong pitch for him to join the No. 1 team in the land. Barker was amenable to NC State, but made it clear to Biedenbach that he was interested only if State gave up its pursuit of Moses Malone.

That wasn't a big deal, because Biedenbach had a strong inkling that Malone would choose Maryland anyway. When Barker committed to NC State by signing his letter of intent, all of us felt that Tom Burleson's re-

Current photo of my boyhood home—35 years later.
Photo courtesy of David Thompson.

The Thompson family at the World's Fair. Front row, from left: Bernard Smith, Brian Smith, Tarngy Lattimore, Charlotte Smith, Chad Smith. Middle row, from left: Trini Lattimore, Pecora Malachi, Etta Smith, Chris Brown. Top row, from left: Vellie Thompson Jr., Me, Todd Brown.
Photo courtesy of David Thompson.

KYWALKER

My senior picture at Crest High School in 1970.
Photo courtesy of David Thompson.

NC State freshman track, 1972, on my way to a school record in the triple jump.
Photo courtesy of David Thompson.

Me with my mom and dad, Ida and Vellie Sr., at Carolina's Athlete of the Year banquet in 1974. Check out my '70s gear.
Photo courtesy of David Thompson.

On the floor with full body cramps in the ACC Tournament semifinals against Maryland in 1975.
Photo courtesy of Rick Clemons.

Tommy Burleson and me holding Monte Towe—a photo Monte hated.
Photo courtesy of Rick Clemons.

Blocking a shot against UCLA great Bill Walton.
Photo courtesy of Rick Clemons.

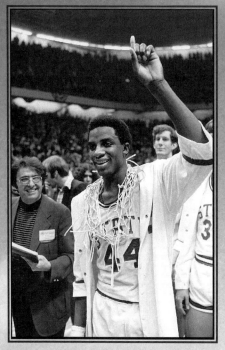

Wearing the net around my neck after winning the NCAA tournament. Photo courtesy of Rick Clemons.

Rookie preseason game against the ABA New York Nets in 1975. Photo courtesy of David Thompson.

One of my most memorable moments—cutting down the net after the NCAA finals. Photo courtesy of Rick Clemons.

…e, Monte Towe, and coach Sloan as members of the South team at the Aloha
…lassic All–Star Game in 1975. Photo courtesy of David Thompson.

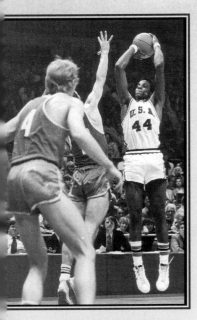

…laying with Team USA against
…e Russian National Team.
…hoto courtesy of Rick Clemons.

David, Tim Stoddard, Moe Rivers, and I
sign autographs after a barnstorming
game in 1975. Photo courtesy of David Thompson.

Me soaring as a Nugget.
Photo by Larry Berman.

Driving to the basket against the Nicks.
Photo by Larry Berman.

I pass to a Seattle teammate during a game against the Atlanta Hawks.
Photo by Scott Cunningham/ NBAE/Getty Images

Me, Cathy, and our good friend Jim Gray at the NBA All-Star Game.
Photo courtesy of David Thompson.

One of my favorite pictures—me with Julius "Dr. J" Irving and George Gervin– two of the greatest players of all time. "ABA royalty."
Photo courtesy of David Thompson.

Me and Michael Jordan at the NBA All-Star Game in Washington, D.C., where they honored 50 years of All-Star Game MVPs.
Photo courtesy of David Thompson.

SKYWALKER

Hickory Sports Club Event with Tommy Burleson (far right), Bill Walton (second from left), and Chris Edwards (far left). Photo courtesy of David Thompson.

Me being honored at NC State University. Photo courtesy of Rick Clemons.

From left, my wife, Cathy Thompson, Masako Oishi, Amy Zwieback, and my daughters, Erika and Brooke Thompson by the Statue of Liberty—our first family trip to New York. Photo courtesy of David Thompson.

placement had been found and that we had a great shot at repeating our title run.

Not so fast.

While Barker went so far as to have a trunk of his clothes sent to Raleigh, that was as much of him as we would ever see. All of a sudden, the guy became scarcer than Howard Hughes. Biedenbach couldn't track him down at all, and our missing-in-action star recruit seemed to have totally dropped off the face of the earth.

When Barker finally turned up again, he was in Hawaii. He had a girlfriend who had just enrolled at the University of Hawaii and apparently wasn't into long-distance relationships. Aloha, Wolfpack.

It also turned out that our love-struck recruit had signed two letters of intent, one with NC State, the other with Hawaii. Biedenbach called UH Rainbows coach Bruce O'Neal for confirmation that Barker had enrolled there, but O'Neal never got back to him. Apparently, O'Neal was having his own problems with the peripatetic Barker, because the latter eventually ended up playing college ball at the University of Minnesota. After that, he had two subpar seasons in the NBA before permanently sinking into oblivion.

Barker or not, we were not all that worried heading into the 1974-75 season. We had played well during the summer tours with our two-guard, three-forward offense, and we returned four of five starters, including our sixth man, Phil Spence.

As I previously mentioned, we also had one of the top freshman players in the country in Kenny Carr, who went to DeMatha High School in Hyattsville, Maryland, one of the most storied high school programs in the country. Carr, a 6'7", 220-pound forward, would garner a gold medal in the 1976 Olympic games.

Two other notable freshmen were guards Craig Davis and Robert "Bobo" Jackson.

We prepared for the upcoming season with Phil Spence at center, Tim Stoddard and myself at the forward positions, and Moe Rivers and Monte at the guard slots.

Rounding out the team were Mark Moeller, Craig Kuszmaul, Bill Lake, Jerry Hunt (my Crest High School teammate), Bruce Dayhuff and Dwight Johnson. Mike Buurma had to sit out the year due to injury.

When Coach Sloan was asked about the loss of Burleson, he replied, "We will not even try to replace him. He cannot be replaced." That was not a slap at Phil Spence. It merely spoke to Tommy's dominant role on our team the year before.

It meant we would be rolling out a new three-forward offense and a stingy man-to-man defense, as opposed to the zone we played a lot the year before. You really need some size to execute an effective zone defense, and we didn't have it. And with the man-to-man, we would apply pressure and try to cause turnovers.

We opened the season ranked No. 1 by the Associated Press. *Sports Illustrated* had us at No. 2 behind Junior Bridgeman and the Louisville Cardinals. Denny Crum's Louisville team was ranked No. 8 by the AP, so I don't know what the good folks at *SI* were thinking.

We knew the road would be tougher in my senior year for many reasons. Tommy was gone, everyone would be gunning for us, and it seemed that every team in our conference was stronger, if only because they were all a year older. Multiple ACC teams were loaded with returnees, all looking to knock off the defending national champs.

No fewer than five ACC teams cropped up in the AP Top 20 throughout that season. That made for a bumpy Tobacco Road.

Everywhere we looked there was newness, down to the floor of the Reynolds Coliseum. Installed was something they called "Astroturf," although it wasn't turf at all.

It was a hard, tartan surface. Tartan was an extremely stiff, solid rubber that could tear a player's knees up over time. If I had come down on my head on that surface during the Pitt game the season before, I don't think I would be here today.

We handled all the changes just fine as we opened the schedule on November 30, 1974, against East Carolina before a packed house at home. Approximately 12,400 fans saw Phil Spence put any doubts about being able to play center to rest. Phil torched the Pirates for 22 points, 17 boards, and eight blocked shots en route to a 98-81 victory. It was our 29th consecutive win.

I felt good for our first game, too, and amassed 33 points, mostly from inside baskets. I also added five steals. Our pressure defense wore them down and created turnovers just like we had practiced, with most of the havoc created by Moe and Monte, our all-everything guards. East Carolina committed 36 turnovers.

But it was Phil who was the man of the moment. Monte said after the game, "This is gonna be his year. People expect a lot from him and he can do it. He'll do the job."

It was obvious Phil raised the level of his game once he became a starter. "Last year I would play a little, and if I made a mistake, Coach Sloan would take me out, sit me down, and talk to me," Phil said in comparing the two seasons.

The only time Coach Sloan took Phil out now was for a much-needed rest.

Kenny Carr also did well in his first game, contributing seven points and nine rebounds.

We christened UNC-Asheville's new civic auditorium on December 3 with a 111-68 rout of the Bulldogs. And though I achieved my varsity career high of 42 points, besting by one the total I scored against Maryland the year before, my new record would stand for only one game.

We welcomed the Buffalo State Bengals into Reynolds Coliseum on December 5, and I decided to let it all hang out that night.

I set an ACC single-game scoring record of 57 points as we defeated the Bengals with no problem, 144-88. I also set an ACC field goal mark with 27, and Monte broke a school record with 14 assists. During a 1:20 span, I reeled off 15 quick points. I had 30 by the half, and Monte and I worked the Alley-oop no fewer than eight times throughout the game. I also plucked down 17 rebounds.

Said Buffalo State head coach Tom Borschel afterwards: "There's no way you can stop David. If somebody can stop him, I would like to see who it is."

I continued my torrid shooting in our next five victories over Virginia (101-72), undefeated and 16th-ranked Oregon State (86-73), Davidson (95-79), Kent State (99-61), and Pitt (86-70). My scoring for those respective games: 24, 28, 43, 39, and 20. Pittsburgh was our 36th victim in a row, and we headed confidently into the Big Four Tournament in Greensboro, seeking our fourth championship in five years.

But it was not to be, as 1975 was ushered in with a resounding thud. The first game of the new year, and of the Big Four Tournament, was played on Friday night, January 3, against an upstart Wake Forest team.

The Demon Deacons came out on fire and shot 58 percent in the first half. They perfectly executed coach Carl Tacy's 1-2-2 zone defense, which effectively held me to only 15 points on 5-20 shooting. I did pull down 13 boards, but it was not nearly enough.

Our 36-game winning streak, our 33 straight ACC wins, and our No. 1 national ranking all were taken from us when Wake Forest won, 83-78.

It was our first taste of losing since that fateful game in St. Louis against UCLA in December of 1973.

"We knew defeat was possible," I told reporters in the locker room, "but we didn't think it would come. And certainly not here. Not this soon."

Ever the optimist, I closed by saying, "We sure wanted to keep the streak going. We'll just have to start over."

Optimism was a good thing as we took on the eighth-ranked Tar Heels of North Carolina the very next night. We beat them, 82-67, and showed that we could bounce right back after a tough loss against even tougher competition. I attribute that to Coach Sloan, who knew just the right buttons to push to get us ready for what lay ahead. Dwelling on defeat wasn't in his playbook.

Backed by my 26-point performance, we dropped North Carolina in front of 15,381 fans anxious to see if our stumble the night before would turn into an outright pratfall. Our pride may have been wounded, but our bite was still lethal.

After laying waste to Western Carolina on January 9, 119-61, one week later we traveled to Cole Field House for our first game of the ACC season against the fifth-ranked Terrapins of Maryland. The result was even worse than the Wake game.

Maryland, which had graduated Len Elmore and Tom McMillen, sported new starters to go with now-junior All-America guard John Lucas. The new-look Terps burned us on 65.1 percent shooting and prevailed 103-85.

Their place was teeming with 14,500 fans, who had keen and acidic memories of some great games and close losses against us the past few years. The fine trio of Terrapin guards combined for 63 points. Durham native Lucas torched us for 30, fellow junior Mo Howard found his way for 18, and star freshman Brad Davis followed with 15.

When I heard the raucous "Amen! Amen!" chant with about 10 minutes left and Maryland up by 20, I thought I was going to be sick to my stomach. Losing was not something I particularly enjoyed, especially against

Maryland. We had beaten them six times in a row, and we were getting our comeuppance.

Our offense totally stalled, with only two of our players reaching double figures—me with 33 and Rivers with 16. Also, we weren't getting the job done defensively as Maryland riddled us with every shot in their arsenal.

With two losses in our last four games, something was clearly wrong. Coach Sloan had been concerned during our preseason workouts that we were not as committed as the year before, and he was right. He felt he wasn't getting the same effort when it came to weightlifting and general conditioning. He was also getting reports that his players were partying to the point of excess.

Monte was our leader, and he told Coach that the expectations were too great and that if we sacrificed as much as we had the previous year—and didn't win it all—then we'd have nothing.

When Monte suggested to Coach Sloan that we were good enough to win it all without killing ourselves in practice, Coach Sloan put his foot down. He told Monte that poor conditioning would catch up with us at some point, and that while we might still win it all while not being 100 percent focused, it was highly unlikely.

Monte was also reminded that it was just a year ago when he'd come to the coach after the loss to UCLA and, on behalf of the team, demanded stricter rules for the players. Why, wondered Coach Sloan, should those rules be relaxed after just two setbacks?

It was a team decision, Monte told him. The consensus, after vigorous in-house debate on the issue, was that the players could now get the job done on their own terms and in their own way without all the sacrifice.

Coach Sloan realized that Monte and the rest of the team were well aware of the expectations placed on us and decided to let us do it our way the rest of the season.

I don't know if it was just a matter of the other ACC teams being better that year, or if Coach Sloan was right, but we ended up dropping six games that season, compared to just one in the previous two campaigns.

We were tested at every turn. The next game, on January 18, was at home against our rival, North Carolina. It was without a doubt one of the classic duels in State's long history with the Tar Heels.

We won it in overtime, 88-85, overcoming a six-point deficit in the last 1:27 before a howling, disbelieving Saturday afternoon crowd at Reynolds Coliseum.

I led the team in scoring with 20, though I played most of the second half with four fouls. In the second half the lead changed 16 times, and after I was called for charging early, Stormin' Norman lived up to his nickname by picking up two technical fouls.

Next, we got our revenge against Wake Forest on January 25, 106-80, in front of our home folks. It was our 36th straight win at Reynolds.

A blistering pace was set right from the opening bell, a run-and-gun type of game that saw us make 48 of 85 shots for a sizzling 56.5 percent field goal percentage. Spence came up big with 18 points and 15 rebounds, while I broke free for 29 points and 11 boards of my own.

Kenny Carr was highly productive, contributing 17 points in only 18 minutes of action, and Moe Rivers showed his worth with 14 points.

We throttled Duke next, 95-71, as Kenny and I led the way with 22 and 21 points, respectively. The Blue Devil defense kept dropping off Kenny onto me, and he made them pay with short jumpers from all over the court. Moe Rivers had a great game, too, with 20 points.

That brings us to the February 1 rematch against Maryland on our home floor. Unbelievably, they dropped us again, 98-97, as Lucas, Howard and Davis shot superbly, combining for 59 of the Terps' 98 points. Howard had a career-high 29, shooting a spectacular 12-14 from the floor.

The Maryland win broke our three-year, 36-game unbeaten streak in Reynolds, and they did it with a national TV audience watching.

There were only two seconds left when freshman Brad Davis looped a 12-footer over Carr, bringing the Terrapins perhaps their biggest win in three years. The winning goal was a driving shot that capped a day filled with such plays.

With 38 points I broke the school scoring record, passing Sammy Ranzino's 1,967 points, but it didn't ease the anguish I felt. I was crushed, and it showed in the locker room. I faced a wall as I dressed when reporters asked me about the game.

"I always thought we'd win," I struggled to say. "Even with one second left, I thought we'd win.

"Losing is painful no matter where you are. We did want to win all of our home games, especially the seniors. But that's gone now."

It would be a different story against Maryland if we met again, I vowed with as much defiance as I could muster.

We found our rhythm again as we thumped Clemson, 92-89, and Georgia Tech, 101-66. I scorched the nets for 39 and 31 points in the two wins. The Georgia Tech game was the opening match of the annual North/South Classic, and we met Furman in the second game the following day, February 9. I had the hot hand again, scoring 35 as we demolished the Paladins 102-87.

I was leading the nation in scoring with a 31.9 points-per-game average and had moved into third place on the all-time ACC scoring list with 2,077 points. Buzzy Wilkinson from Virginia set the mark with 2,233 points from 1953-55. But scoring points and setting individual records came a distant second to the winning I desired so badly.

We beat Virginia on February 12 in a low-scoring affair, 59-46, and I scored 19 points—with nine of them coming from the foul line.

On February 15, we took our No. 4 ranking into Winston-Salem to play our rubber match against Wake Forest. The 89-87 victory wasn't sealed until I sank a pair of free throws with four seconds left.

I would be remiss if I didn't mention the play of our fearless freshman guard, Craig Davis, in the waning moments of that close contest. Davis helped engineer our spread attack in the final four minutes, dished off for a key basket, sank a pressure free throw and drew a charging foul against the Deacons' leading scorer, Skip Brown, that blunted Wake's last hope for victory.

Duke was an easy mark on February 19, falling to us 92-78. We thought that the young Clemson Tigers would succumb just as easily three days later. We thought wrong.

Clemson handed us our fourth loss of the season, 92-70, on their home court. A 22-point defeat to such a young team was a hard thing for us to accept. Clemson's 6'4" freshman guard Skip Wise had actually been brash enough to predict a win in Littlejohn Coliseum after we beat them at our place, and then walked the walk by scoring 30 points.

Again I picked up four first-half fouls. I'd never been one to complain about the officiating, but it was apparent that something was going on. I fouled out of the game with 16 minutes remaining. I don't think that ever happened to me before. My absence was widely cited as the key to the Tigers' win.

I was so disgusted with the bad calls that when I collected my fourth foul I flipped a towel high into the air at midcourt. It was my own personal protest and was very uncharacteristic of me.

We now stood at 19-4 and 8-3 in the conference. We had won the much-cherished bye for the ACC tournament the past two years, but it didn't look good this time around.

Our last game of regular conference play was on February 25 against the Tar Heels in Chapel Hill. We desperately needed a win, but for the only time in my career at NC State, we lost back-to-back games.

It had been three long years and nine games since Carolina had tasted success against us. And if Tim Stoddard's 20-footer had found the range instead of rimming out with two seconds left, UNC's diet of failure would have continued.

Tar Heel guard Phil Ford was spectacular in the first half, gunning in 19 points and dishing off four assists. As the half ended, Ford fired in a 30-footer at the buzzer and left the court in a mad dash the length of the floor. North Carolina was sky high.

Coach Dean Smith had Ford and the rest of the Tar Heels run their Four Corners slowdown offense for 18 minutes in the second half, hoping to keep this one close and play for the win at the end.

With the score 75-70 for UNC, they missed the front end of a one-and-one opportunity with 47 seconds left. Phil Spence then notched his tenth point from underneath, and Coach Sloan called time out with 38 seconds showing on the clock.

Next, Stoddard intercepted a Tar Heel pass and dished it to me. I swished home a 20-footer for my 32nd point. It was 75-74 as we called for another timeout. Carolina then had trouble getting the ball across midcourt, and when they finally did, Tar Heel Mickey Bell was fouled immediately.

Bell hit the first foul shot and missed the second, and Spence gathered in the rebound. We spent our last timeout with nine seconds left mapping a play for the last shot. We didn't get the shot we wanted, and when Moe Rivers was pinned in the corner, he flipped the ball over to Stoddard, who let fly.

There was still one second left when the ball flew out of bounds off the miss, but the Carolina crowd didn't wait to start its celebration. The Tar Heel players were engulfed by cheering fans whose celebration of their team's first win over us since 1972 went on for some time.

The last home game of my college career came against the 49ers of UNC-Charlotte, on March 1, 1975. A Reynolds Coliseum crowd of 12,400 saw my jersey retired in a pregame ceremony, and school chancellor John Caldwell paid tribute to seniors Monte Towe, Moe Rivers, Tim Stoddard, Mark Moeller, Craig Kuszmaul, and myself.

It was Coach Sloan who announced to the fans that my jersey was being retired. I was genuinely humble as I addressed the hushed crowd. I was the first Wolfpack player ever to have his jersey retired while still in uniform.

"I have mixed emotions," I said. "I'm happy for the honor of having my jersey retired, but it's sad to be playing my last game here.

"These have been four great years for me. I wouldn't trade the memory of them for anything in the world."

UNC-Charlotte featured future NBA star Cedric "Cornbread" Maxwell and came into the game 22-2, riding high on a 16-game winning streak. We knew it wouldn't be easy, but we also knew that we would die before we lost three games in a row and certainly not our final home game as seniors. It was one of the most focused, intense efforts of the season as we pulled away for a 103-80 victory.

The 36 points I scored moved me to within eight of the all-time ACC scoring record. I was 14-22 from the field and a perfect 8-8 from the line. Not included in that is the bucket that almost blew the roof off ol' Reynolds Coliseum, a basket that is remembered by many even today.

With 3:39 left in the game, I received a long pass from Tim Stoddard that resulted in a wide-open breakaway. As I galloped down the court, it occurred to me that the stage was perfectly set for a Kodak moment that would define the last four years for me and the NC State faithful and leave them with a memory even more shining than my jersey hanging from the rafters.

Instead of laying the ball into the basket, I threw down a sweeping, thunderous, backboard-rattling dunk that sent the crowd into a frenzy and left everyone in the building with an indelible imprint of my passion for the game. People were jumping up and down in the aisles and hugging each other.

Even Coach Sloan gave me a standing ovation. He said the dunk was "the Thompson touch—a touch of class."

For four years I hadn't been able to dunk in a game, and I thought that was wrong. That was my statement on the subject for all to see in plain view. Sure, they disallowed the basket and called a technical foul on me. The score was insignificant in my mind anyway because we had such a large lead.

It was the *dunk*, and what it meant metaphorically, that was principal to me.

Our overall record entering the ACC tournament was 20-5, and we were ranked eighth nationally.

We opened against the Virginia Cavaliers on March 6. Maryland earned the first-round bye by virtue of their first-place, 10-2 record. We knew we would have to have three great games to advance to the NCAA Tournament and defend our national title.

We had finished the regular season in a three-way tie for second place with an 8-4 record—the same as North Carolina and Clemson. We lost a coin flip, and instead of being the second-rated seed, we ended up being the fourth-rated seed. That meant if we beat a tough Virginia team, we would have to play top-seeded Maryland in the semifinals.

We advanced with a 91-85 win, and the ACC had a new all-time leading scorer. I tossed in 38 points against Virginia, added 10 rebounds, and was glad the season wasn't over. It could easily have turned out that way as we frittered away a 22-point first-half lead before finally subduing the tenacious Cavaliers.

Hello again, Terrapins. Heading into our third matchup against Maryland that season, I was determined to honor my vow after our last meeting that the Terps would not defeat us again.

The Friday night game was described by some as frantic and furious. It was also downright unbelievable.

With 3:54 left in the game, we had an 84-69 lead, and easy victory seemed a lock. I had 32 points and checked out with 9:56 remaining with the most severe leg cramps I had ever experienced. The muscles completely locked up on me, leaving me temporarily handicapped. The trainer and doctors said they had never seen cramps like that in their lives. They had to carry me off the court and into the dressing room. No biggie, though—not with us up by 15, right?

You can probably guess what happened next. The Terps went on a 16-0 burst. Maryland senior forward Owen Brown sank two foul shots to bring them to within one, 84-83, with only 26 seconds to go. Monte missed a one-and-one and three seconds later was charged with a controversial blocking foul on Terp guard Mo Howard.

Howard hit both shots, and Maryland had the lead for the first time since late in the first half, 85-84. Then freshman guard Craig Davis brought the ball down the right side and cut toward the key, but lost control of the ball off his knee.

Moe Rivers alertly picked it up, drove two steps toward the basket and dished off to Kenny Carr on the right side of the lane. He drove straight for the basket, made a layup off the glass, and was fouled by Maryland forward Tom Roy. Carr made the foul shot, and we were up 87-85. Maryland's John Lucas attempted a 30-foot shot at the buzzer, but it clanged off the front of the rim. We'd proven that we could beat Maryland when it counted most.

Next was North Carolina for the fourth time in one season. This time it was for the golden ticket to the big dance—the ACC tournament championship, which would be our third straight. My legs still ached from the leg cramps in the Maryland game, but if necessary I would will myself to play.

It was March 8, and this would be my last college basketball game. The Tar Heels, led by gifted playmaker Phil Ford, dethroned us and took the final, 70-66.

Ford received the tournament MVP trophy, tallying 24 points in the title game and dishing out five assists.

My legs never really felt good in that game, and I managed only 16 points on 7-21 shooting. Freshman Carr served notice of things to come as he scored 16 points and pulled down 14 rebounds.

North Carolina earned the automatic bid to the NCAAs, and the second automatic ACC berth went to Maryland because of their better overall record (22-4) compared to ours (22-6).

In our somber locker room, Coach Sloan said a few comforting words about what a great run we had and how we would be remembered as one of the great teams in college basketball history. Then he produced a telegram that had just come, inviting us to the NIT.

"That's a great tournament and used to be *the* tournament," Coach said. Therein lay the problem. The NIT was for schools that weren't good enough for the Big Show. It was the losers' bracket, and no matter what the final score of the North Carolina game was, we weren't losers. We still had pride, and so we decided right on the spot that the NIT was no place for us.

Later, Coach Sloan said it was the last time he would ever give a team a choice in such an important matter. It was clear, he said, that we were not in a proper emotional state of mind to handle such a decision, and he was right.

Two days later, on Monday, March 10, Monte and a couple of other players went to Coach Sloan and told him we had changed our minds. We would play in the NIT after all. But it was too late, as the tournament roster had already been filled. My college career was suddenly over.

We finished as the seventh-ranked team in the nation, while UCLA surprised many and handed Coach John Wooden his 10th national championship in 12 years.

I averaged 29.9 points per game that season to finish as the country's third leading scorer (a school and conference record). I had become the ACC's leading scorer in history with 2,309 points, was named the ACC Player of the Year for the third straight time, was National Player of the Year, and made first team All-America again.

However, that all paled next to the one list I didn't make—the graduation list.

While I did stay in school all four years when many top players were leaving early for the pros, I did not graduate with my class at NC State. I was three classes short of qualifying for my bachelor's degree. With the previous summer's games in the Far East, the tour here in the States against the Russians, and various other types of All-Star games, I fell behind in my academics.

That was a constant source of disappointment and guilt, too, because I promised my mother when I enrolled at NC State that I would leave with a degree. However, I am proud to say that as of this writing, I have earned my sociology degree at NC State.

I did it for myself, of course, but just as importantly to honor that promise I made to my mother three decades ago.

CHAPTER 12

THE HOT TICKET

My four years at North Carolina State were coming to a close. I finally understood how a teary-eyed Tom Burleson had felt the year before up on that stage after our championship run, telling a packed house at Reynolds just how much he'd miss them.

Time had traveled too quickly, and now I was stepping into a whole new world going through its own changes. The country was going through an identity crisis, and people were trying desperately to figure out exactly who we were as a nation and what values were worth holding on to as society coped with a myriad of problems and strife.

Though our troops had been fully pulled out of Vietnam, Americans were still divided by that prolonged and costly war. Inflation and high unemployment had brought the swift and envied U.S. economy to a grinding halt. Approximately 7.8 million Americans were out of work.

The president was asking companies to trim their employees' hours, the general population to turn down their thermostats, and for the speed limit to be reduced to 55 miles per hour to conserve gas. The energy crisis was real, and the 1973 oil shortage and embargo were stunning developments to a generation that never had to contend with such restrictions before.

Watergate and its aftermath taught youth of the day not to trust its leadership, and they didn't.

It was definitely a time of social and political uncertainty.

Culturally, people were literally moving their feet in brand new directions. There was the advent of disco music and the mirror-balled discotheques where people could dance to the beat-laden music. The exercise boom was in its infancy. Enthusiasts discovered that jogging freed them of their daily troubles and allowed them to think more clearly. The connection of mind, body and soul was coming together.

The public also turned its eyes and ears toward the entertainment world for relief, soaking up TV comedies like *M*A*S*H*, *The Mary Tyler Moore Show*, *All in the Family*, *Happy Days* and *Sanford & Son*. Movies such as *The Godfather Part II*, *The Sting*, and *Blazing Saddles* allowed folks to escape their personal demons for a few hours. Of course, almost as if to mark the mindset of the times, there were disaster pictures like *The Towering Inferno*, *Earthquake*, and *Airport 1975*.

Then there was the music, my personal escape. Two albums I remember fondly were Stevie Wonder's *Innervisions* and *Fulfillingness' First Finale*. Also, The Stylistics ("You Make Me Feel Brand New"), Al Wilson ("Show and Tell"), and Earth, Wind, and Fire ("September," "Shining Star," "That's The Way of the World") were all on my personal playlist.

With the Vietnam War ending, people were trying to come together again. But it was not an easy thing to do. No one was sure where they wanted to go with their lives, so they started experimenting. By the end of my rookie year, I would do some experimenting of my own.

I was just a 20-year-old kid from Boiling Springs, North Carolina, who wanted to play hoops. Surfing through the waves of social chaos was a bit frightening, and I was just trying to find out where I fit in. Basketball was the one place where I found solace and confidence, and thankfully my talent allowed me to fulfill my childhood dreams and live in that world.

With great social change comes idealism, and the sports world was not immune. In the early to mid-1970s, The World Hockey Association took on the National Hockey League, and the World Football League challenged the highly popular National Football League. The upstarts created competition for the best players, and they had taken their cue from a renegade league that bounced along to the colors of red, white, and blue.

The American Basketball Association was spawned from these same idealistic roots. This was Charlie Scott's league, the place where Connie Hawkins finally was unleashed, and where Rick Barry, Joe Caldwell and Billy Cunningham found refuge from their financial dissatisfaction in the NBA. This was the oasis where the great "Dr. J" strutted his stuff night in and night out in virtual anonymity.

But I knew all about the ABA. These were the guys who played for the Carolina Cougars in Raleigh, Greensboro, and Charlotte. The Virginia Squires, who had Charlie Scott, George Gervin and Julius Erving at one time or another, were the team I admired and had had a lot of exposure to while at NC State.

To me, the ABA had the best young and exciting players in professional basketball. Therefore, when it came time for me to choose the team that would pay me to do what I loved most, the NBA did not have the upper hand. It was a 50-50 proposition as far as I was concerned.

I had a few things to take care of before I entered the professional ranks. I played in the Aloha Classic college All-Star game in April and then participated in a barnstorming tour with a group of guys I wanted to help out. One of the players was my college teammate, Dwight Johnson.

Dwight gave up his athletic eligibility to join the barnstorming team, but retained his scholarship, completed school and earned his degree. And since each of the players received a percentage of the gate—$15,000, to be exact—Dwight promptly went out and bought himself a Porsche. I believe he thought things worked out just fine for him.

Then came the Pizza Hut All-Star Classic in Las Vegas. Our East team was coached by Norm Sloan, and Monte was a member of the squad, too. In fact, when Coach Sloan inserted Monte into the lineup, he and I hooked up on at least three alley-oops. The West team was tough, though, sporting UCLA All-America forward David Meyers and UNLV grad Rickey Sobers, a super-quick guard.

Our team emerged victorious, and 6'7" Bill Robinzine of DePaul (a first-round pick of the Kansas City-Omaha Kings) was named MVP. I think of Bill occasionally because he committed suicide in September of 1982, just five short months after he left the NBA. He was a good guy, and it was sad to see him succumb to personal problems.

On a much happier note, I met a young lady that summer who really turned my head.

There was a basketball camp held on our campus that I was involved in. One night I took a group of the camp counselors to Fass Brothers Fish House located near Avent Ferry Road. I really liked Fass Brothers and was disappointed to find it was already closing for the evening.

The night manager of the restaurant was a beautiful young lady, and when I poured on the charm—or so it seemed to me—she was kind enough to let us in to eat.

The very next day, I was washing my car when I happened to notice the same attractive girl waiting in line directly behind me. I walked up to her and asked, "Are you following me?" She assured me she wasn't, and we had a good laugh.

The following night I was at a popular dance club called Hillsboro Square located directly across the street from the main campus. I couldn't have been there 10 minutes when, to my amazement, I noticed this same gorgeous creature standing not too far from me. I figured if destiny was tapping me on the shoulder that hard, I had better make a move or risk bad luck for the next 20 years.

Cathy Barrow was the daughter of Bradley and Helen Barrow, and we liked each other instantly. I asked her out for a date that night, and she accepted. We began dating, but were not an exclusive item immediately. That took some time.

I will tell you this, though. Five years later I would ask her another important question, and the answer she gave me provided me with a vast amount of long-lasting joy.

Cathy was very friendly, outgoing—and did I mention attractive? We liked a lot of the same things, including dancing and music. She was a California girl who had lived in New Jersey, and ended up in North Carolina. Cathy lived with her parents at the time. She worked for the North Carolina State Revenue Department during the day and was managing the fish house at night.

Our relationship raised a few eyebrows in Raleigh because Cathy was white. Interracial dating was still unacceptable to a lot of people. I could not have cared less what anybody else thought. The fact was that there were very few blacks attending NC State at the time, so you dated whomever you could. I'm sure I was cut some slack because of who I was, but out in the cold, cruel world there would be more problems.

Basketball was still at the forefront of my mind as the NBA and ABA college drafts approached. In late April, about a month and a half after the season had ended, Coach Sloan huddled up with me in his office to go over a list of prospective agents to represent me. There were about five people we talked to, but Larry Fleisher ended up being our guy.

Fleisher, who passed away in 1989, was the executive director of the NBA Players Association. A Harvard-educated lawyer residing in New York City, Fleisher was the man who put the teeth into the NBA Players Association that Celtics great Bob Cousy helped create in the 1950s. In

Cousy's heyday, the players did not have things like salary minimums, life or accident insurance, pensions, or even a collective bargaining agreement.

Larry Fleisher came along in 1961 and changed all that.

By 1976, the players didn't even have to carry their own bags on the road. The league salary minimum had jumped to $109,000, and this was when the major-league baseball minimum pay was $17,000! The players now had trainers, pensions, and many other things that Fleisher negotiated on their behalf. But Larry never strong-armed the NBA into agreeing to unreasonable demands and never struck a militant posture.

He always sought the intelligent win-win outcome, and I knew he was the kind of man I wanted on my side. Because Larry represented the NBA players, he knew every one of their contracts inside and out. His reputation was flawless, and he was such an articulate, direct and honest man that picking him as my agent was a no-brainer.

With his thick glasses and slicked-back hair, Larry seemed the epitome of what a sharp New York lawyer should look like. He always laid everything right on the line, a very direct and to-the-point kind of guy. I thought he was a great businessman, and no one could argue with his credentials.

When Coach Sloan and I asked Larry what we could expect in terms of a contract, Larry replied, "I figure I can get you the highest contract ever for a rookie." Larry figured that since I was a two-time Player of the Year, possessed a wholesome and clean image and was bringing an exciting style of play to the pros, such a deal would be no problem. I think he was excited to represent a player of my stature because I was a real hot ticket.

Fleisher wanted his company to handle all my financial business in addition to my contract negotiations, but Coach Sloan thought I could save a lot of money by keeping my business affairs separate. I went with Coach Sloan on that one, and it turned out to be one of the worst decisions of my life.

Coach Sloan had an acquaintance from Greensboro named Ted Shay who was a financial advisor. Ted worked for Northwestern Bank and had handled some of Tom Burleson's business interests. That was good enough for me.

In hindsight, I should have listened to Larry Fleisher. Larry represented the game's top players, like John Havlicek and Oscar Robertson, and helped players like Marvin Webster make a lot of money from investments like Gulf & Western.

What I would give to have had the wisdom then that I have now. I literally paid for my ignorance.

We still had to figure out which league I would go with. The NBA was experiencing a lot of change. Kareem Abdul-Jabbar, one year removed from an NBA finals loss to the Boston Celtics, took his skyhook from Milwaukee to Los Angeles. The Lakers sent 7'1" center Elmore Smith, second-year guard Brian Winters and top draft picks Dave Meyers and Junior Bridgeman to the Bucks.

Ironically, the next year Milwaukee would finish in first place in their division and make the playoffs, while L.A. would finish in next to last place in the Pacific and not make it into the postseason.

The Knicks—getting long in the tooth and desperate to inject some talented youth into their lineup to keep their ultra-demanding fans happy—unsuccessfully tried to hook either me, Indiana Pacers strongman forward George McGinnis (who signed with Philadelphia), or Jabbar. They resorted to buying Spencer Haywood from the Seattle Supersonics for $1 million.

Charlie Scott went to Boston for Paul Westphal, adding to the Celtics' already potent offense. Dave Bing wanted to go home to Washington, so Kevin Porter was sent to Detroit in return.

There was also change at the top in the NBA front office. Walter Kennedy retired as commissioner, and Lawrence O'Brien took over. O'Brien was a prominent political figure who had been associated with President Kennedy and whose office as chairman of the Democratic National Committee had been the target of the bungled Watergate burglary.

O'Brien was a basketball fan and native of the sport's birthplace, Springfield, Massachusetts. He possessed exceptional administrative and mediating credentials, as well as valuable connections in Washington, all of which were expected to help with the anticipated NBA-ABA merger.

The ABA also had a new man at the top as it began its ninth season of operation—former NY Knick great Dave DeBusschere. DeBusschere was taking over for Tedd Munchak. Also, four of the league's 10 franchises were under new ownership.

Just as the season was about to start, the two strongest teams in the ABA—Denver and New York—applied for entry into the NBA. This couldn't be acted upon immediately because the players' antitrust suit (named the "Oscar Robertson Suit," because the Cincinnati star was head of the players' union) had not been settled. More on that important lawsuit later. But the move by the Nuggets and the Nets made inevitable the eventual demise of the ABA.

When the NBA draft dust settled, the Atlanta Hawks had chosen me as their first pick, the Lakers went with Dave Meyers at number two, and Atlanta chose again at number three, taking Morgan State's Marvin "The Human Eraser" Webster. The Hawks had secured the number-one pick by virtue of the previous year's deal that sent "Pistol" Pete Maravich to the New Orleans Jazz.

We figured that Atlanta was serious, even though they were said to be financially struggling and experiencing a change of ownership.

We'd gotten a strong foreshadowing of Atlanta's interest in me when head coach Cotton Fitzsimmons said, after watching me perform in Hawaii at the Aloha Classic, "Probably at this stage of his career, Thompson can do more things than anybody who ever played the game. And I saw Oscar Robertson, Jerry West, and the big guys—Bill Russell, Wilt Chamberlain, Kareem Abdul-Jabbar and Bill Walton—when they were collegians.

"I believe he's the best ever."

When asked after the draft if he was concerned about Denver signing me or Marvin Webster, Hawks President John Wilcox replied, "Where's Denver? I never saw them on TV." That was the kind of arrogance the Hawks and the NBA wore on their sleeves. A number-one pick had never gone to the ABA, so why would one now? That was the prevailing attitude.

For all their attitude, the Hawks were pretty stingy. On my visit to Atlanta, a trip that allowed me to see a quiet throng of 3,000 people at their new arena, The Omni, Cotton took me to McDonald's for a Big Mac.

By contrast, the Nuggets—who felt they would somehow figure out a way to secure my rights—flew Monte and me to Denver in early April to witness a Western Division semifinals playoff game against the Utah Stars (Denver won the series, 4-2, but was upset in the Western Division Finals 4-3 by the Indiana Pacers). There were banners that read, "Welcome, David Thompson!" and more than 7,000 screaming fans packed into a building whose legal capacity was 6,900. As an added bonus, I got to see Dancing Harry, the 1970s flamboyant boogying fool. The Nuggets capped off the evening by introducing me during the game. It was a nice touch. There was a steady stream of fans coming up to me for my autograph.

The Nuggets pulled out all the stops. We were chauffeured all around Denver—and not to McDonald's—in a limousine. We were often accompanied by head coach Larry Brown, complete with designer jeans, sweater, and clog shoes—his trademark garb. We stayed at the same hotel the Pacers were staying in, and one night big George McGinnis and some of his teammates stepped into the elevator with me. I had never seen anybody that big in college before, and I said to myself, "I have to go up against guys like *him*?"

All of George's teammates said hello and congratulated me, and McGinnis himself was very cordial. But man, did that guy have huge mitts when we shook goodbye!

Coach Brown even took us over to what would be my new basketball home, McNichols Arena. It was basically finished, except for the landscaping. I could see myself doing great things there in front of 17,500 fans. It was a fantastic feeling.

The Nuggets had just gone 65-19 to achieve one of the best records in ABA history. They had my old friend from North Carolina, Bobby Jones, and coach Larry Brown was a man I knew well and respected greatly. I had even met general manager Carl Scheer while he was with Coach Brown as part of the old Carolina Cougars franchise.

Coach Brown was the *man*. I appreciated him because he had excellent basketball credentials: 1964 Olympic Gold Medal, ACC player and All-American at North Carolina, All-Star ABA player. Larry turned pro at 27 when the ABA was formed and spent five years in the league. He led the league in assists three times, played in 376 games, 47 playoff games, three All-Star games, and dished out over 2,500 assists and scored more than 4,200 points. All this, and he was just 5'9" and 160 pounds.

Maybe subconsciously he reminded me of my good friend Monte.

As a coach, his complex defenses, picked up when he was Dean Smith's assistant at North Carolina, revolutionized ABA play.

The colorful league also appealed to me for other reasons. In October of 1972, I had seen Julius Erving and Pete Maravich play against the Carolina Cougars in Raleigh, in one of the few games they played together for the Hawks while the Doctor was trying to jump leagues. Man, that was some show.

It seemed to me that many of the game's most exciting players were in the ABA. Dr. J, George McGinnis, Moses Malone, Marvin Barnes and George Gervin all shot the red, white and blue ball.

In the end, Denver and the ABA looked pretty big-league to me. Where was the downside? You tell me. There seemed to be plenty of that to the Atlanta Hawks' proposition.

The Hawks were rebuilding, and I didn't want the pressure that was put on Maravich while he was with the Hawks or what he was experiencing in New Orleans as the so-called savior of that franchise.

The press in Atlanta was also notoriously negative. Atlanta Braves baseball players Ralph Garr and Dusty Baker said that fellow star Dick Allen refused to report to Atlanta when traded there because of the volatile treatment the players received from the press. Garr and Baker were convinced that was one of the main reasons I shied away from Atlanta. To a certain degree, it was true.

I had seen how they skewered Pete Maravich there, and I wanted no part of that. In fact, there was a series of articles that ran around that time in the *Atlanta Constitution* entitled "Loserville, U.S.A." detailing the woes of their professional sports franchises.

The Hawks were in a classic economic Catch-22. They needed me and Webster to generate high ticket sales to help the franchise out of its dire financial straits, but because they were low on cash, they could not afford us.

Not only were the Hawks suffering at the gate, but they also had to contend with a $400,000 fine levied by the NBA Board of Governors for tampering with Julius Erving in 1972 while he was still property of the Milwaukee Bucks even though he was playing in the ABA for the Virginia Squires.

The Milwaukee Bucks owned the draft rights to Dr. J, so when Julius tried to jump leagues and go to Atlanta, the Bucks screamed bloody murder. When the dust cleared that September, Julius was back in Virginia, the Bucks were $400,000 richer, and the Hawks had lost a superstar and a lot of greenbacks.

In a last-ditch effort to woo me, Atlanta picked Monte in the fourth round and said he'd have a crack at making the team.

Over in the ABA, the Monday draft was a mess. The Kentucky Colonels argued that they owned my rights because they had chosen me in my freshman year at NC State. The Memphis Sounds (then the Tams) also chose me as the second overall pick (Bill Walton went No. 1 to San Diego—his hometown team) in the 1973 "undergraduate" draft. But those teams forgot that if the drafted player did not sign at that time, they went back into the pool and were fair game for all teams the next year.

The Virginia Squires had the actual territorial rights to me only because Tedd Munchak had shut down the Carolina operation and the franchise relocated to St. Louis and became the Spirits. The Squires' owners—Van Cunningham and Ted Broecker—knew they could never pay me, but they also knew what I was worth in trade value to Denver. It was for the latter reason they made me the initial pick of the 1975 ABA draft.

The Memphis Sounds, which would become the Baltimore Claws before the season started, took Lonnie Shelton from Oregon State at No. 2, and the San Diego Sails grabbed Kevin Grevey from Kentucky at No. 3.

The Nuggets plucked Marvin Webster with a special "bonus choice" awarded by the league. They chose high school phenom Bill Willoughby with their second-round pick (just in case they couldn't sign Webster) and took my good friend Monte Towe in the third round. In June, Monte accepted a one-year, $50,000, no-cut contract to play with the Nuggets.

Regarding Webster, the Nuggets reportedly offered him $1.5 million. In Baltimore, Marvin told the press, "I have mixed emotions about Atlanta. But I am certainly favoring Denver strongly right now."

There were last-minute pleas to Webster from Hawks head coach Cotton Fitzsimmons, but when the *Atlanta Constitution* asked the coach for a progress report, Fitzsimmons flatly replied, "He turned us down."

Now it was time for me to decide. The offers from the two leagues were identical—$2.5 million over six years—although a physical contract never materialized from Atlanta. My mind wandered back to the days when I was shooting balls into a homemade basket with my brother Vellie, Jr., and to see everything happening was literally a dream come true.

The Hawks had wised up to my wanting to play in Denver, and, fearing that they would become the first NBA team to lose a No. 1 pick to the ABA, they panicked.

The New York Knicks coveted my services immensely, and they let their feelings be known to both Larry Fleisher and the Hawks. Had the NBA had a rule in place like that of the ABA, whereby any team that could afford to sign a player the drafting team could take its best shot—just to make sure the player stayed in their league—there was a chance I might have suited up in a Knicks uniform. It was only a slight chance because I had my heart set on Denver; but there was that one percent.

Knicks general manager Eddie Donovan was quoted as saying, "We made every effort that if Atlanta was not successful in their negotiations with Thompson, we would have liked to negotiate with him and his attorney. We were ready to compensate them well."

The Denver Post quoted Cotton Fitzsimmons on July 16, 1975, as saying that the Hawks had offered me in a trade to the Knicks. In the article, Cotton said, "We indicated that if [Thompson] wanted to play someplace else, it could have been worked out."

Even Larry Fleisher wanted me to go to New York because of the media exposure I would receive and the related income-earning potential that would go with just being in the Big Apple.

But the Knicks' offer could not overcome the strong sense of belonging and comfort I got from the ownership, the players and the fans in Denver. It was the last day of June, and I took 10 days to consider the matter before I made any decisions.

Many experts believed that landing the choicest picks of 1974's draft was the greatest coup for the ABA, with Bobby Jones (Denver), Len Elmore and Billy Knight (Indiana), Marvin Barnes, Maurice Lucas (who had declared hardship) and Gus Gerard (all three with St. Louis), and Moses Malone (Utah) all going to the newer league.

Jones, Elmore, Barnes, and Lucas were all first-round NBA selections. The NBA had never seen so many blue-chippers vanish into thin air. Granted, Malone (just out of high school) and Gerard (an undergraduate from Virginia) had been ineligible for the NBA draft, but that was just another guerilla tactic that the ABA used to snare top talent right from under NBA noses.

For all that, the upstart ABA, it was said, had never landed the top-of-the-pile, grade-A, number-one, college glamour players. Jimmy Walker (1967), Elvin Hayes (1968), Lew Alcindor (1969), Pete Maravich (1970), Sidney Wicks (1971), Bob McAdoo (1972), Doug Collins (1973), and Bill Walton (1974) had all gone into NBA-land. If I didn't follow them, it was suggested, my whole career would be diminished.

You know what? I really didn't care. I did what I felt in my heart. There were so many things to consider, but I chose the Nuggets because they were a young and winning team. I knew Monte and Bobby Jones and was very impressed with Coach Brown, and the city of Denver was perfect for me because of its small-town feel.

All the Nuggets had to do was provide ample compensation to the Virginia Squires to acquire my draft rights. Denver ponied up first team All-Star guard Mack Calvin, starting center Mike Green, reserve forward Jan van Breda Kolff, plus $250,000 in cash. Bingo! The Squires turned over my rights to the Nuggets and threw in forward George Irvine as a bonus.

I informed Coach Brown on July 9, 1975 that I was going to sign with the Nuggets. On July 14, a very hot Monday as I recall, I became the first No. 1 pick of the NBA to sign with the ABA when I inked the largest rookie contract ever—just like Larry Fleischer had predicted.

Monte Towe and soon-to-be University of Indiana senior Quinn Buckner, another of my close friends, accompanied me to the press conference at Denver's Stapleton Plaza to announce my signing. It was quite the festive deal, with a large audience that included Denver Broncos owner Gerald Phipps and head coach John Ralston, among other civic notables.

First, at the press conference, the Denver Nuggets' owners were introduced by Nugget GM Carl Scheer. They were a corporation—Nugget Management, Inc.—with 29 members in the group, including Scheer. Then, after a highlight film of mine was shown in the theater room, Scheer told the assembly, "It is an exciting time for all of us. It is an awesome thought, [signing Marvin Webster and David Thompson]. We had planned on it, and Larry [Brown] asked me, 'Why not?' But it didn't seem possible. Yet here we are today, and it is a reality."

When I was introduced, I told them what they wanted to hear, and meant every word: "Denver is the type of city where I feel comfortable. It's got a lot to offer young people—the mountains and entertainment. Denver is a relatively big city that retains a small-town atmosphere as compared to other cities such as Chicago and New York. I'm very satisfied with how this has turned out and I can't wait to get started.

"People are probably gonna expect too much of me, but I'm gonna work hard to help bring the city a championship."

I was becoming quite the speechmaker. That same week I was in New York City at the Americana Hotel for another speech, and I remember New York Nets owner Roy Boe beaming from ear to ear because of what my signing represented to his and *all* the teams in the league.

The signing of Marvin Webster and myself showed the ABA's new muscle, greatly improved its stature in professional basketball, and hurt the NBA right where it lived—in the prestige department.

The American Basketball Association was now an official member of the country club.

It was as if my signing gave the league some pedigree. Columnist Leigh Montville wrote that my signing was akin to the ABA marrying the top debutante in town. Montville also compared the signing to that by the football N.Y. Jets of a quarterback from Beaver Falls, Pennsylvania, by way of the University of Alabama, who chose the much-maligned AFL over the established NFL. His name was Joe Willie Namath, of course.

My commitment to the ABA was said to be the final piece of the puzzle that brought a national TV deal for the league, something that the cash-starved teams needed badly to compete with the NBA.

Commissioner Dave DeBusschere was negotiating that very TV contract when the Nets and Nuggets applied for NBA inclusion before the start of the season. The secret maneuverings of the ABA's two marquee teams with the NBA brought Big Dave's TV discussions to a screeching halt. He was not exactly thrilled with Carl Scheer at the time.

My signing with Denver was so significant that it gave the Nuggets immediate and solid footing in any merger talks. Not only was my signing good PR and image enhancement for the ABA, but it also helped strengthen two franchises in one fell swoop.

Virginia now had ABA All-Stars Mike Green, Mack Calvin (first team in 1974-75), Willie Wise and Dave Twardzik.

There were other excellent teams in the ABA, like the Julius Erving-led N.Y. Nets, but they did not draw well at home primarily because Nets fans could not identify with the opposing team's players. The visitors to Nassau Coliseum were largely unknowns.

That all changed on July 14, 1975.

More evidence of the impact of the dual signings was that Nugget season ticket sales immediately jumped to 6,000, versus only 2,200 the year before.

The Atlanta Hawks now had the dubious distinction they had so dreaded—being the first NBA team to lose its top pick to the ABA. The poor Hawks had only 1,100 season ticket holders at that time, and it shrunk from there. When they traded Pete Maravich to the Jazz, they were in essence banking their future on me and Marvin. When we didn't sign with them and their biggest star, "Sweet" Lou Hudson, only played in 11 games due to an elbow injury, the Hawks were grounded.

Atlanta's only move was to sign their second-round pick, 6'8" high schooler Bill Willoughby. Which ABA team had drafted Willoughby? The

Nuggets, naturally. But Scheer and assistant GM Bob King said that Willoughby was only an insurance pick in case they couldn't sign me or Marvin, so they let the Hawks have him.

As confident as I was about playing in the ABA, Larry Fleisher was doing everything he could to protect me. Afraid that the ABA might not make it past the 1975-76 season, Larry put a clause in my contract that released me from Denver if the league folded. I signed a five-year contract with an opt-out clause after three years.

It's now time to put to rest a rumor that has been around for years. Contrary to popular belief, the Nuggets did not sign Monte Towe as a condition of signing me.

In fact, the Nuggets passed over me and chose Marvin Webster with their bonus choice pick because Coach Brown felt they had a better chance of signing Marvin than me. Denver didn't want to waste the pick in case I went with the Hawks of the NBA. Therefore, there was no "package deal" for Monte and me.

Monte was an excellent player in his own right and earned his spot with the Nuggets by virtue of his basketball talent. "We feel he can stand on his own and play for us," said Nuggets spokesman Ted Malick when questioned as to whether Monte's signing was a condition of my playing in Denver.

I did say during my April visit to Denver that I hoped to play on the same team as Monte in the pros, but I never held a gun to anyone's head to make that happen. I definitely had a strong desire to remain with my point guard friend, and if it could be worked out…then great. But I never insisted that Monte and I were joined at the hip.

Now that I had come into big money, I decided to give back to the two people who meant the most to me and were responsible for the person I had become.

I was quoted as saying that I would provide my parents "with any extravagances that they might want." I subsequently put a large down payment on a home they picked out in Shelby, a two-story, corner-lot house with a front and back porch. They moved in immediately, and I paid that house off for them three years later.

The last thing I remember about the fervor over my signing with Denver was that it was the final nail in the NBA's coffin that would force them into a merger with the ABA.

By the end of the season, that prophecy would be fulfilled.

CHAPTER 13

A SEASON OF FIRSTS AND LASTS

t's been said that any successful business or organization is a reflection of its leadership. The Nuggets were one of the ABA's most successful franchises after Carl Scheer and Larry Brown arrived in the summer of 1974.

Scheer, a native of Springfield, Massachusetts, spent his first two years in pro sports as the NBA's assistant commissioner. From there he went to Buffalo and spent one summer as president of the Buffalo Braves before leaving for the Carolina Cougars of the ABA. He served as the Cougars' president and general manager for four years before leaving for Denver.

Once the Carolina franchise moved, everybody knew that Carl Scheer and Larry Brown would end up in the same place because they were a package deal. Incumbent Denver head coach Alex Hannum was glad to go, because his highly disciplined style was no longer in vogue and he thought the drug element in pro basketball was getting out of hand.

Scheer and Brown turned the Nuggets into an amazing 65-19, first-place club in 1974-75 after a next-to-last Western Division finish the year before. In the dynamic duo's first season, Denver lost its first game, but won the next nine in a row and became the hottest ticket in town. The team scorched opponents at home with an amazing 40-2 record.

Scheer was a marketing madman. He ran all sorts of promotions—gimmicks for cars, fur coats, basketballs and T-shirts. Upon his arrival in 1974, Carl started a contest to choose a new name for the Denver team. Continuing as the Rockets didn't make sense any more, since former owner

Bill Ringsby—who named the team after his trucking company—was no longer there. Thus, the team became the Nuggets.

Obviously an ambitious individual, Carl was named the ABA's Executive of the Year for the 1974-75 season and had assembled the ownership group that purchased the Nuggets when outgoing owner Frank Goldberg decided to head off to San Diego to improve the Sails' situation.

My arrival changed the whole face of the Denver team. To secure my rights, the Nuggets had to give up their second and third leading scorers, guard Mack Calvin (19.5) and center Mike Green (17.4), to the Virginia Squires. Calvin had also topped the ABA with 7.7 assists per game. Guard Ralph Simpson remained, along with his team-leading 20.6 points per game.

Bobby Jones remained at the forward position opposite me, and Marvin Webster was to be the opening-night center. Scheer and Brown considered the following guards to replace Calvin as the fifth starter: Memphis's Chuck Williams, Utah's Al Smith, San Antonio's Bobby Warren and George Karl (current Milwaukee Bucks head coach), and San Diego's Jim O'Brien (current head coach at Ohio State University).

Fatty Taylor was the starting choice if we didn't get any of the aforementioned players.

Jones, a 1972 Olympian, was making a name for himself in the ABA. He had finished only one vote behind the St. Louis Spirits' Marvin Barnes in the previous year's Rookie of the Year balloting. He also led the ABA in field goal percentage at .605.

Byron Beck, one of the most popular Nuggets ever, was a 6'9", 240-pound forward. A Denver player since the franchise's inception in 1967, he had attended Denver University. Byron was an outstanding shooter with a deadly hook across the lane and a soft outside jumper.

The 1974-75 Nuggets set an ABA record for field goal accuracy, making 50.9 percent of their combined two- and three-point shots, matching the 1970-71 Milwaukee Bucks' mark. Of course, the Bucks didn't have the constant temptation to make long-range, three-point buckets.

The Nuggets had also averaged a league-leading 118.7 points per game in 1974-75, thanks to a high-octane offense that was always on the move. The fans bought it, and the Nuggets sold out their downtown digs—antiquated Auditorium Arena—more often than not.

I was psyched heading into my first pro training camp and didn't waste any time getting into the spirit of things.

"David seems to really like to practice," commented Coach Brown to the press after our first team workout. "He really competed in all the drills. For a guy to come in with his kind of reputation and still work extra hard proves to me that we've got a winner in him."

What I recall most about the first scrimmage we ran that day was that I had four dunks—something I was unable to do in college. It felt really, really good to finally slam 'em home.

Two watershed events occurred before the start of the season—one just as the team reported to training camp at the Air Force Academy in Colorado Springs, and one just before the regular season started.

Our other prize rookie, center Marvin Webster, showed up at training camp with a broken foot—cause unknown. On top of that, Marvin had ballooned to a totally unacceptable weight, and he informed management that he also had contracted a liver ailment, which may or may not have had something to do with the hepatitis he had been battling since his junior year in college.

His afflictions would keep Marvin on the sidelines until very late into the season. We were all so high on "The Human Eraser" because he had averaged 17.5 points per game in 114 varsity college contests, averaged six blocked shots, and was a rebounding machine as his 19.9 per game attested.

Now what were we supposed to do for a true center? The uncertainty threw Scheer and Brown into panic mode.

The Nuggets had willingly given up Mike Green, last year's pivot man, in the deal to get me. Other than Byron Beck, there really wasn't anyone else who could fill the middle. All of a sudden a finger-lickin' deal fell right into our laps.

John Y. Brown, owner of the defending ABA champion Kentucky Colonels, Kentucky Fried Chicken magnate, and eventual governor of Kentucky from 1979-1983, was having a fire sale in Lexington. Citing extreme financial losses, Brown offered All-Stars Artis Gilmore and Dan Issel to the highest bidder.

Dan Issel was both the victim and ultimate beneficiary of Brown's machinations. When the Baltimore Claws, a team that had just moved from Memphis, claimed him, Issel called the Brown residence to remind the future governor that he had a no-trade clause. He ended up talking with Mrs. Phyllis Brown, former Miss America and TV personality, who proceeded to go point-counterpoint with Dan about the deal. When Issel wouldn't be charmed or bullied from his position, Mrs. Brown finally turned him over to John Y.

Dan could legally have fought the trade, but in the end he realized that Brown's losses in Kentucky meant that the franchise might not even survive the current season anyway—even though the Colonels had just won the ABA championship. Dan agreed to go to Baltimore, and his contract was said to have brought the Colonels a much-needed infusion of up to half a million dollars.

The Claws needed an identity, a player who would bring strong basketball recognition. The team also needed positive PR that would create strong, loyal fan support. Issel gave them all of that and a truckload of credibility, too. The Claws had shot themselves in the foot in the credibility department right off the bat when the new owners anointed their franchise the "Hustlers." Needless to say, that that name didn't fly with the ABA brass.

Some hustling was what Dan Issel ended up doing when it became apparent that the Baltimore poobahs couldn't come up with the money promised to Brown for him. Issel made some calls to other ABA teams and found out about Marvin Webster being sick and that Carl Scheer was frantically looking for a new center.

Stiffed by the Claws, John Y. Brown cut a new deal with Issel. Brown was skewered by the Lexington press for letting their favorite Kentucky son go. Brown told Issel that he would broker a Denver deal in return for some favorable public remarks to help calm the roiled waters.

Issel agreed and told the press that as far as he was concerned Brown had only made the Baltimore deal because it was good business, that nothing personal was involved, and he wished John Y. nothing but happy trails. That's how Dan ended up in Denver, giving us all the ingredients for one of the most dominant offensive front lines in all of basketball.

Fate was really smiling on Dan. The Claws played only three exhibition games before the team folded on October 20, 1975, only five days before the regular season started. The Baltimore franchise was only in business for 40 days, and not one of their players was ever officially under contract. It was so bad that players were getting thrown out of their hotel rooms because the team wasn't making payment, and they weren't even receiving their meal money. Dan said the only paycheck he ever received from the Claws bounced just like a basketball.

We headed to North Carolina in early October for a series of exhibition games, including several against NBA teams. We proved that we more than belonged on the same court with them by running up a 4-2 record against the supposedly superior NBAers.

I took advantage of the opportunity to see Cathy again when we played the New Orleans Jazz in Raleigh in early October.

We rekindled our relationship, and Cathy moved out to Denver with a friend later in the year. She had been looking to make a move from the South because she wasn't all that fond of the region anyway. That's when we became an exclusive item. It was so nice to be in love and be able to have someone like her to lean on during such a transitional phase of my life.

Of the 10 preseason games we played that year, one contest really stood out and taught me a valuable lesson about pro ball.

We were playing against the New York Nets and the fabulous Julius Erving one night. At one point in the game I had a breakaway and was going in all alone. Being a young, cocky, naïve rookie, I thought I could outrun anybody and lay down a pyrotechnic slam that would get the word out once and for all that there was a new sheriff in the league.

I went up kind of leisurely, slowly floating toward the basket, when the Doctor materialized out of nowhere and smacked my attempted dunk right up against the backboard. I just couldn't believe it. From that point forward, whenever I had a breakaway I threw that baby down *hard.*

I have so many fond memories of that first year in pro ball. I shared a condominium with Monte Towe on the southeast side of Denver, and it was just like college again except that we were getting paid very well.

My jersey number was 33. Ralph Simpson already had my college number, 44, so I opted for the other and kept 33. I kept that number my entire career until I was traded to the Seattle Supersonics in 1982. Then I went back to 44.

That red, white and blue ball in the ABA was an adventure unto itself. Whenever I was chosen as a game captain, I would always look for one that was a little roughed up, because the fresh paint on the newer balls made them almost impossible to handle. Slick was all right when I was the one being that way. I didn't need a ball stealing my thunder.

For the first eight years of the ABA, the league used the 30-second clock. In preparation for a possible merger, the league went to the 24-second clock in 1975-76, which is what the NBA used.

Our club was built on speed and quickness, not physical strength. Webster was supposed to have provided our bulk, but now it was the nimble Issel in the middle instead. Everything considered, our prospects were as high as the nearby Rockies.

My first regular-season game as a professional came on October 24, 1975, when we opened against the San Diego Sails in San Diego.

I learned an important difference between the ABA and the NBA on that Friday night in late October. The ABA was the equal of the NBA on the court and by any index you can name—except one. The ABA sure wasn't the NBA when it came to putting people in the seats. Actually, the ABA wasn't even *NC State* when it came to that. There were always 10,000-12,000 fans in Reynolds Coliseum to watch our Wolfpack play. In San Diego, where the Sports Arena held 14,600, there were a whopping 3,060 people to watch the professional debut of David Thompson.

I should say that the *announced* attendance was 3,060. As I found out later, in the ABA they had a habit of "stretching" the truth when it came to official attendance figures. Either way, the place was practically vacant.

I was thinking there was, at least, going to be some television coverage and press hoopla concerning my first pro game, but none of that happened. It was then that I realized that I was no longer at NC State. I was in the ABA.

Though not many people saw it, I tallied 28 points in a convincing 120-108 Denver victory. Ralph Simpson led the scoring parade with 30, and Dan Issel—also making his Nuggets debut—scored 21, making 11 of 12 from the foul line.

On November 11, 11 games into the season, the 3-8 San Diego Sails sank beneath the waves, never to be seen again.

A few days later, we beat the Utah Stars in Denver, and by early December the Stars joined the Sails in the graveyard of defunct ABA franchises.

The season had started with nine teams, and now we were down to just seven. The Virginia Squires would teeter on the verge of bankruptcy for the whole season, and nobody knew what was coming next. The ABA leadership scrapped the two-division lineup, and all the teams just became one undivided league.

But all was well in the Mile High City. We went 16-3 in our next 19 games and even had a nine-game winning streak in there, including two wins against the New York Nets and Julius Erving—one at home and one on Long Island.

As the midpoint of the season approached, attention was centered on the All-Star game. The ABA owners and league honchos realized that the eyes of the basketball world would be upon them thanks to several factors, including the tenuousness of the league itself, the increasing prospect of a merger with the NBA, and the fact that the game was being nationally televised on Home Box Office.

The ABA didn't just need to put its best foot forward; it needed to provide a compelling spectacle that would showcase the league and prove it worthy of a national television audience and a possible merger with the NBA. The brain trust took a great risk by unveiling two concepts that had never been tried before.

Since there were no longer two divisions, a creative format had to be developed that would allow for two "All-Star" teams to play each other in Denver, chosen the previous year to host the 1976 game because of the opening of McNichols and the state's centennial-bicentennial celebration.

It was Denver's Carl Scheer, the ABA's Jim Bukata, and league financial director Jim Keeler who decided that the team in first place at the All-Star break—which would be the Nuggets, with a 32-11 record—would play a squad made up of the best players from the remaining six teams.

But Scheer, Bukata and Keeler still needed a hook to draw public attention and make the game a memorable and resounding success.

When it came right down to it, the ABA was really known for two things: the athleticism of its players and dunking. The dunk was a masculine badge of honor that many of us ABA players wore proudly. Apologies to Bob Cousy, but is there anything more exciting and awesome in the great game of basketball than a monster dunk? That idea captivated their imaginations and spawned an innovation that lives on to this day—the Slam Dunk Contest.

Bukata claims credit for it, but it was *Sports Illustrated* who called it "the best halftime invention since the restroom."

To save money, the league only asked players to participate who would already be at the game. They figured that wouldn't be a problem since the league's best players would all be in attendance. That short list of invitees included the most creative high flyers the ABA possessed: Artis Gilmore, Larry Kenon, George "The Iceman" Gervin, Julius Erving and me. The winner would get $1,000 and a stereo system.

Even before the game format and Slam Dunk Contest were conceived, Scheer and Bukata worried that they might not have a sellout based only on the merits of the game. They decided something else was needed to get people into the arena long before the game even began. And the best way to do that, they concluded, was to provide some musical entertainment by two of the biggest names of the day.

Charlie Rich, the "Silver Fox," and "Rhinestone Cowboy" Glen Campbell performed a two-hour pregame concert. Campbell, sporting a beard and longish hair representative of the times, was dressed in black pants and a black shirt trimmed in rainbow colors. His large belt was adorned with ornate silver medallions.

Scheer, the marketing wizard, had done it again. The game had sold out within 24 hours of tickets going on sale.

Let me tell you—1635 Clay Street in Denver, the address of McNichols Sports Arena, was the place to be that incredible January evening in 1975. Even the NBA Phoenix Suns' general manager Jerry Colangelo was there on the grounds that this was a major basketball event not to be missed.

By the time the game began, 17,798 basketball crazies were packed into McNichols. It was a red, white, and blue bonanza.

The ABA All-Stars started Billy Knight from Indiana and New York's Julius Erving at forward, Artis Gilmore from Kentucky in the middle, and San Antonio's James Silas and New York's Brian Taylor at guard. The All-Stars' coach was Kevin Loughery of the Nets.

We responded with Bobby Jones and myself in the corners, Issel at center, and Chuckie Williams and Ralph Simpson at guard. The referees were Norm Drucker and Ed Middleton.

The game was close right from the opening tap. Every player on the floor knew that this might be the last ABA All-Star Game ever, and with a national TV audience watching along with an arena full of people, each of us was performing at peak level.

The first period ended with the Nuggets in the lead, 32-31. But the All-Stars outscored us in the second period, 25-23, and took a one-point lead into the half, 56-55. The game was living up to its billing.

There are few truly "classic" moments in sports—events that are so indelibly imprinted on the public's mind that, over time, they not only become legendary, but actually provide a sense of *identification* with a sport or league that is both highly personal and emotional.

The Slam Dunk Contest was all of that, wrapped tightly in a 20-minute rift in time on a cold January night in Denver. I venture to state that there is not one true basketball fan who can't recall at least some of the details of that historic night. Simply put, heroes were created.

The non-participating players were told that they could go into the locker room at the half, but they didn't. They formed a semicircle around the basket, giving them the best seats in the house for the sport's version of the shootout at the O.K. Corral.

Two extra backboards and rims were at the ready in case somebody brought one down. Doug Moe, our assistant coach, and Julius Erving reportedly had a $1,500 side bet on whether the Doc could actually dunk from the foul line—something Erving said he had successfully done in practice before. While Doug appreciated the Doctor's abilities, he doubted that even Dr. J could perform such a feat.

The judges for the contest were Larry Faye from Fayline Productions, a local promoter; some high school player whose name I don't recall; a lady I didn't know; and some dignitary who may have been a local politician. Not exactly a panel of experts, but the thought was that their layman's perspective might dispose them to greater appreciation of our virtuosity.

They were supposed to judge us on innovativeness, artistry, body flow, and crowd reaction.

The rules required five dunks: two compulsory moves—one from underneath the basket, the other from the bottom of the foul circle; and three freestyle dunks—one from the left, one from the right, and one from the baseline.

The predetermined order was Gilmore, Gervin, Kenon, me, and Doc.

In the week leading up to the event, I had a good case of butterflies. I knew what I could do and wanted to put on the performance of my career. Monte and my other teammates helped me decide which dunks to showcase.

As we warmed up before the contest, I performed my "Rock the Cradle" dunk. That was where I got way up above the rim while cradling the ball in my left arm, and then punched it through the hoop with my right fist. Jim Bukata said it was "probably the most spectacular dunk of the night, and it didn't even count." It was also a very *dangerous* dunk for me because I had to get up really high so my arm could be above the rim when I punched it through.

Not using the "Rock the Cradle" in the actual competition may have cost me the dunk crown.

The first dunks were not that special because of the mandatory slams that had to be performed. Gilmore was all about power. He wanted the ball to actually go through the floor when he was finished with a dunk. Artis's most impressive dunk was when he picked up two balls, jumped up, and dunked them both.

Gervin had two balls when he lined up for his dunk from underneath the basket, but then dropped one. "I know I can throw one through, but I ain't gonna try something I know I can't do," he said. "I might get hurt." He then proceeded with a one-handed windmill dunk. The Iceman had some pretty dunks, but he did miss one.

Kenon was what we called a *long* player—body, arms, everything. He had some nice dunks, too, but missed one just like Ice did. That pretty much sealed both their fates.

Then it was my turn.

Facing the basket, I started off with a two-handed stuff where I had brought the ball all the way from behind my head and jammed it with severe authority. I actually ended up on the right side of the rim when the ball went though.

Dunk number two was a running, one-handed, windmill, tomahawk sledgehammer. I started from the left side of the floor out by the halfcourt line, took off running and jumped right at the bottom of the foul line circle—about 12 feet away from the basket. I brought the ball back and threw it down very hard with my right hand. I had so much momentum that I ran into the basket support past the out-of-bounds line.

On my third attempt I tried for something even more flashy. Beginning on the right side of the court this time, at approximately the three-point line, I swooped in and completed a perfect double-clutch backwards slam.

The players were rolling around on the ground, high-fiving each other and pointing. I knew I was doing something right and the crowd joined in.

It was on my fourth try that I made a fatal mistake. I started again from the left side, out by the three-point line. Moving toward the basket, I jumped up and tried to kiss the ball off the glass with two hands while twisting my body to finish with a backward, two-handed dunk. It was a jam I'd done more than once before.

But this time, after I touched the ball to the backboard, I was slightly out of alignment as I turned, and the ball bounded off the back of the rim, to the crowd's disappointment. Now I had to finish with something that would not only redeem me, but also bring everyone out of their seats.

I took the ball over to the far left baseline, sized up my target, and began my assault on the basket. When I reached my liftoff point only a few feet from the rim, I performed a complete 360-degree, two-handed stuff that some said was the best dunk of the day. As I lightly completed a two-point landing, McNichols Arena exploded with deafening applause for the hometown hero.

Dr. J said later that it was his absolute favorite dunk of the competition, and that meant a lot to me. As I walked over to the sideline where Julius was sitting, he put out his hand so I could slap it. We were competitors, yet members of a mutual admiration society.

Because the replay has been seen so many times, many people think that Erving's famous dunk from the foul line was his last one of the contest and the one that won it for him. In fact, it was only his second dunk.

Here are the Doctor's five dunks, in order. First, for his standstill dunk, he took two balls, jumped up, and slammed them both through—one after the other—with almost no effort at all. That was the same dunk Gervin did not want to attempt, and the Doc made it look like child's play.

When Julius started pacing off his 10 steps for his second dunk—the historic one where he would take off from the foul line—Doug Moe and my teammate George Irvine moved to the side of the court to verify where Julius was taking off from. With big money reportedly on the line this time, Doug wasn't taking any chances.

As Erving walked off his steps cradling the basketball in his huge hands, people were going berserk in anticipation of what was to come. Then, when Julius reached the top of the opposite foul circle and turned to face Everest, the place suddenly went eerily silent. The fans knew they were going to see something special—something they would one day tell their grandchildren about.

When Julius took off down the court, he looked as graceful as any human could. As he achieved liftoff from a few inches inside the foul line, I don't think there was a person in the whole place who wasn't holding his breath—including me. It wasn't until the ball hit the ground after Julius rammed it through the hoop with one sweeping motion that the place went absolutely ear-splitting crazy. I'm surprised the noise didn't trigger avalanches at ski resorts all over the state.

No surprise, then, that the top prize went to the Doctor. The whole thing was subjective, of course, but it was all great fun and I could not have lost to a better man.

The game resumed, and the All-Stars took it to us in the third quarter. As the final period began, the Nuggets were behind 97-92.

I didn't win the slam-dunk competition, but I did win the last ABA All-Star game MVP award with my performance in the fourth quarter. I scored 15 points in the final stanza, helping Denver to a 144-138 win.

The game had been played at breakneck speed, and there was one spectacular play after another. It was a fitting showcase. Because of the pregame concert and the Slam Dunk Contest, play ended well after midnight, and by then, many fans had left and missed a record 52 Denver points in the fourth quarter.

It was the highest-scoring ABA All-Star game in the nine-year history of the event. I scored a game-high 29 points and was the third Denver player to win an MVP award.

Bobby Jones contributed 24 points and 10 rebounds, and Dan Issel and Ralph Simpson each tossed in 19. Byron Beck and Claude Terry both played pivotal roles off the bench as each man scored 14 points.

Erving led the All-Stars with 23 points, while Billy Knight and James Silas each scored 20.

When league play got back under way, there was some good news on the Marvin Webster front. His condition had initially been considered so dire that it was feared he might never play basketball again. But thanks to an excellent dietician, Marvin lost 30 pounds and was pronounced fit to play by the All-Star break.

In his first three minutes of play against Virginia at home on January 30, 1976, the Human Eraser slapped away three Squires shots. But his offensive play needed more work. We didn't care, though; we were just glad to finally have him in the lineup.

The grind of the long season was wearing on me a little, but I managed to hide it well. On February 27, in a game at home against the Spurs, I scored my season high of 50 points (17 of 20 shots from the field and 16 for 19 from the foul line). We easily won the game 140-116.

Finishing first in the league after taking 10 of our last 15 games, we secured home court advantage throughout the playoffs. Our final record was a stunning 60-24—five games ahead of Erving's New York Nets—and included a 26-game win streak at home.

It was the first time in ABA history that a team had achieved back-to-back 60-win seasons.

We drew the defending champion Kentucky Colonels in our first round after they got by Indiana 2-1, and knew that series would be no cakewalk.

Though we won seven out of 12 regular season games against the Colonels, they were all back-and-forth affairs. Not many people were surprised when the series came down to a deciding seventh game, played on April 28 at the McNichols Sports Arena.

There weren't many times in my career when I wasn't able to boost my level of play in a big game, and I didn't disappoint this time, either. It was one of the few times I really remember having an exceptional game against Kentucky forward Wil Jones, but I did everything I wanted to do that night. I came out very aggressive, and we ran away with a convincing 23-point victory, 133-110.

It was on to the ABA finals to face the New York Nets.

The fans got what they wanted in the championship series—a show-down between the league's two premier teams, and between the league's All-Everything, All-World player and the new young gun from the Rockies. A Broadway playwright couldn't have come up with more drama.

On paper, we looked to be the favorites. The Nets had not beaten us at home all year long, losing seven consecutive games at McNichols. In fact, they had lost 11 straight to us there if you included the end of the previous season. The Nets were only 15-7 overall against us the past two years.

And even though we managed to win only two of seven games at Nassau Coliseum in 1975-76, we should have been all right since we owned the home court advantage.

But it didn't turn out that way, thanks to Mr. Julius Erving. If ever there was a case where one player won a title for his team, this was it. In my opinion, in the entire history of Dr. Naismith's game, no one ever went out and single-handedly won a championship the way Julius Erving did in early May of 1976.

The Nets had reached the finals by disposing of the San Antonio Spurs four games to three. The Spurs held a 2-1 lead after three games, but the Nets took the last three out of four to win the series.

Julius had a gut feeling that this would be the ABA's last hurrah, and he badly wanted to go out a champion. It would only be a fitting farewell since the young doctor had grown up on Long Island, a stone's throw from Nassau Coliseum.

The Nets did have some challenges. They were thin at forward because Larry Kenon had been traded to San Antonio earlier in the season for center Swen Nater (who was dealt to Virginia later), and chief enforcer Wendell Ladner had been killed in the worst single-plane disaster in U.S. history up to that time at New York's Kennedy airport in June of 1975, just a few months before the season started.

The Nets were still a solid team, though. Brian Taylor was the ABA's version of Walt "Clyde" Frazier—quick hands, always sniffing a steal, who could back guys down and shoot over them. "Super" John Williamson was 6'4" of muscle, loved physical play, and was a clutch performer. Rich Jones was an excellent forward opposite Julius.

The chronological format for the finals called for two games in Denver, two in New York, one in Denver, one in New York and one in Denver. We simply could not afford to lose either of those first two games at home. The trouble was that Dr. J was at home wherever he played.

Game 1: May 1, 1976 in Denver. New York 120, Denver 118

An all-time league record 19,034 people jammed McNichols Arena. Five hundred extra seats were added, and even then it was standing room only.

The first quarter was relatively even, with the Nets a single point up at the buzzer. Erving really got going in the second period, though, scoring 13 points on an array of creative shots. He'd noticed in the past and filed away for future reference that defensive ace Bobby Jones had always played him closely, denying him the ball and the lanes to the basket. So this time Erving moved out farther so that he could receive the ball in better position and have more area in which to operate.

The strategy definitely worked against us. The score was 90-84 in favor of the Nets at the end of the third quarter.

Entering the final period, the game was shaping up as one of greatest professional contests ever played. Too bad it was only shown on television in Denver and New York.

With four seconds left, we were tied at 118 apiece. The Nets had possession, and anybody who had to guess who would get the ball for the last New York shot should not have been allowed to leave his house alone, drive a car or operate heavy machinery.

When the Doctor got the ball, Bobby Jones was draped all over him. Julius wanted to take it inside and at least get fouled if he couldn't get open, but Bobby played him to perfection. With nothing left for him to do, Julius floated up an 18-footer from the far right side with his legs spread-eagle. Try it sometime.

To get the shot off was, in itself, stunning. To hit nothing but net with it was impossible—but that's what happened. We lost by two, and maybe a blister.

After chasing Erving around all night, Bobby had developed a nasty blister on his right heel. On that last play, Jones's blister burst just as Erving took his shot, and Bobby has always maintained that the pain broke his concentration just long enough for Julius to get off the toss.

I scored 30 points on 13-19 shooting from the floor, but the stat that mattered was 1-0, in New York's favor.

Game 2: May 4, 1976 in Denver. Denver 127, New York 121

In front of a second straight record-setting crowd of 19,107 I scored 24 points to help even up the series, but Erving's performance this time was even better than his first. He scored 11 of New York's last 13 points, eight of them on dunks, and the other on a three-pointer. He finished with 48 points, 14 rebounds, and eight assists.

Game 3: May 6, 1976 in New York. New York 117, Denver 111

It was odd that Nassau Coliseum did not sell out. Only 12,243 fans showed up, leaving 3,700 seats empty. The Nets' performance in Denver apparently did not make the New York news.

Julius got into bad foul trouble early and sat on the bench a good while. When he reentered the game with only 1:50 left to play, New York was leading 109-108. The Nets had proven they could stay with us even when their superstar was out. John Williamson and Rich Jones had picked up the slack with excellent performances.

Only seconds after coming back in, Erving hit a spectacular jumper to give the Nets a three-point lead. But I answered right back with a three-point play, and we were all tied up at 111.

The Doctor blocked a couple of shots down the stretch, but it was a controversial charging foul called against me with 23 seconds left that put the game away for New York. When the call was made, we had a chance to tie it up again. But the Nets ran away with it. Erving scored four more points on a dunk and two free throws, and New York won 117-111 and took a 2-1 series lead.

Julius finished with 31 points, 10 rebounds, four assists, four blocked shots and two steals. After the game he told a reporter, "I feel like I can do just about anything that I want to." Who could argue with him?

Game 4: May 8, 1976 in New York. New York 121, Denver 112

More of the same—the Nets took a 3-1 series lead as Erving totaled 34 points, 15 rebounds, six assists, two steals, and a blocked shot. Dr. J had several stuffs and threw it down every which way you could imagine.

Through the first four games of the series, Dr. J had amassed 158 points, 51 rebounds, 22 assists, seven blocks, and eight steals. And that was against a great defensive player like Bobby Jones. It was such an awesome performance that *Sports Illustrated* plastered him on its May 17 cover with a headline proclaiming, "Dr. J Slices 'Em Up."

Thankfully we were headed back to Denver.

Game 5: May 11, 1976 in Denver. Denver 118, New York 110

Given the way things were going, it's not surprising that ABA public relations maven Jim Bukata brought the championship trophy from New York to present to the Nets after the game.

His plans were upset in more ways than one. In the first place, we won. In the second place, Bukata left the trophy in a rental car overnight and someone stole it. Had New York won, there would have been no trophy to present to them. As it was, when the Nets won the championship in New York in Game 6, they had to accept the same trophy that they won in 1974. Only months later did the stolen trophy materialize, showing up in the league office in a package mailed from Denver—without a return address.

Even though we took Game 5, Erving was still the man. In this one he scored 37 points, had 15 rebounds, nine assists, five steals, and two blocks. God in Heaven!

Game 6: May 13, 1976 in New York. New York 112, Denver 106

Nassau Coliseum was rocking with a sellout crowd this time, and the game was televised live by HBO.

The fans' screaming was so loud from beginning to finish—even when we were once up by 22—it was almost scary. Guess they were making up for their earlier apathy.

I really thought we'd win, considering Dan Issel was on his way to 30 points and 20 rebounds, and I achieved my series high of 42 points—27 of them in the first half alone. We took a 13-point lead into the intermission, 58-45.

By the end of the third quarter, though, Erving already had 29 points, even though his team was down by 14. He would finish with 31 points, 19 rebounds, four blocked shots, five assists and five steals.

But it was John Williamson who really came alive in Game 6 for New York. The Nets' muscular streak shooter scored 13 points in the final 8:35 as New York played determined catch-up ball. Super John scored 16 of his 28 points in the fourth quarter when the Nets claimed the lead for good and the championship.

We were outscored 34-14 in the final period and made only four of 20 shots from the field.

The Nets began picking us up with a full-court press. That caused some turnovers, and the play got very physical. Just about that time, the referees stopped blowing their whistles, which was no help, either. But the major cause of our misery then and throughout the series, was having the Doctor in the house.

Rich Jones hit the last shot for the Nets—his first and only basket of the game (he was 1-10)—and there were still three seconds on the clock when the fans came tumbling down. Fistfights broke out, and the game was called. Final score: New York 112, Denver 106.

Our team received $51,000 for coming in second and $30,000 for having the best record in the regular season. It was convenient spending money, but I would have given it all back and more for the title.

Erving was named MVP of the championship series, averaging 37.6 points, 14.2 rebounds, and shooting 60 percent from the field. Julius had been co-MVP of the league the year before, sharing the honor with Indiana Pacer George McGinnis. He finished in the top 10 in seven different statistical categories, and led the league in scoring with a 29.3 average. There was no way to stop that guy.

I finished third in scoring with a 26.0 average and won the ABA's last Rookie of the Year award. World University Games teammate Alvin Adams took home the NBA's freshman honors. When Alvin accepted his award, he said, "I would like to thank David Thompson…for going to the ABA." I still get a chuckle out of that.

I really believe that basketball historians will regard that era as a watershed point in the evolution of the game. It was a season of epochal firsts and lasts. The 1975-76 season was, in fact, the ABA's swan song. I was the first No. 1 NBA draft pick to choose the ABA. McNichols Arena opened in Denver.

And it was the first time I tried cocaine.

It happened in New York during the finals. Sitting in a hotel one night, I mentioned to one of my teammates that I was feeling a bit run down. I'd never played in over 100 games in one season before, and the travel had also gotten to me.

"No problem," he said. Then he offered what looked like white powder and said, "Try this. It will give you just the lift you're looking for."

I won't deny that I got a lift, all right. Of course, what I didn't realize then, in my All-Star naiveté, was that I was taking my first steps down a path that would ruin my career, my reputation and life. The lift you get from cocaine, high as it is, is nothing next to the slam dunk that comes afterwards.

CHAPTER 14

CRASHING THE PARTY

A t the end of the 1975-76 season, two important mergers took place in my life: one was personal and the other was professional.

Cathy arrived in Denver late in my rookie year, and we were together at last. Oh, the ABA/NBA merger was coming, too, but this was the partnership that I knew would have the most positive impact on my life. Cathy would become my personal MVP.

She and a friend had made the 1,700-mile trek to the great Rocky Mountains from North Carolina. They roomed together, and Cathy took a job at Peaches Records just to tide her over. I'd go see her and convince her to let me have some of those wooden crates that we used to store our record albums.

Monte and I were still living together, but we moved out of our condo just after the season ended. I bought an $85,000 home in Denver's posh Cherry Hill subdivision. The house had a flat roof, stone chimney and an elevated sun porch with blue umbrellas on the deck. There was standard 1970s wood paneling on the inside, complete with a sauna—a nice refuge against the chilly Colorado weather—and a Jacuzzi on the lower level. We were really starting to feel at home.

While my personal and professional lives were bouncing along just fine, my financial life began to show signs of low air pressure.

Ted Shay, my financial advisor, had helped me form a company called D.O.T. Enterprises. Though the company name bore my initials, I was not that involved with its operations. I was only 21 years old and focusing on basketball, and the financial world was not something that I knew much about. I left it totally in the hands of Ted Shay, which was a bigger mistake than giving Dr. J the lane.

The company's investments ranged from real estate in Atlanta and Africa's Ivory Coast to tax shelter programs and high-yield stocks. Though I was (and remain) a low-risk, conservative kind of guy when it comes to money matters, it appeared to some that these were high-risk ventures. In reality, the Ivory Coast real estate was a hotel owned in part by a limited partnership my agent, Larry Fleischer, had put together with other NBA stars such as John Havlicek and Earl Monroe. Though it didn't do too well, it seemed like a solid business deal to me.

The "high-yield" stocks were actually some good certificates of deposit, and I did well with those and had similar luck with the commercial rental properties in Atlanta.

It was the tax shelters that slam dunked me and others who participated. The problem was that while I thought those investments—3:1 government-sponsored tax shelters that were exploratory in nature for oil and gas—would actually provide a safe haven from the IRS, they were eventually disallowed years later by a change in government rules and left me with an almost insurmountable tax bill.

It wasn't until approximately 1982 or 1983 that I was notified of the problem, and by then I had lost my initial investment, plus all of the tax credits. Basically, I walked away with nothing from that program but a plethora of headaches. I should have been more involved and kept a closer eye on the whole operation.

I think now it was all part of God's plan to bring me back closer to Him. When I was at the top of my career, the more successful I became, the further away I was from the Lord. Sure, there were some dishonest people. You trust people and then once they get around your money, they change. They seem sincere in wanting to be your friend, but really only want to get as close as your wallet.

I was changing, too.

The summer brought more summer basketball games with my teammates, more celebrity, more parties, and more temptations. I wasn't using coke every day, but the drug was available at most of the big parties I attended.

As has been documented many times before, there were a lot of NBA players using cocaine in the late 1970s and 1980s. So I joined right in, never considering the potential damage I was doing to myself or to those who loved and depended on me.

I was a recreational user and cocaine didn't affect my play or, to my knowledge, my personality. It seemed so harmless, but in that way it's similar to carbon monoxide poisoning—it's a slow and seemingly painless death.

The world of the professional athlete is a collegial and private existence. Therefore, primarily because of word of mouth among the players, most of us knew who was using drugs. I'm sure my teammates knew, and I'm almost positive that my coaches figured it out over time.

Something else I was getting exposure to was a form of covert racism. There were very few black people in Denver at that time, and the blacks were even outnumbered by the Hispanics.

Sometimes Cathy and I ran into problems. Some of the nightclubs we went to would find ways to keep black people out without posting a neon Jim Crow sign proclaiming "Whites Only!" For example, they'd enforce a dress code at the door that never seemed to apply to white patrons. At least in the South, the bigots were up front about it. In Denver, it was always a guessing game. The situation did get better over the years, however, as I developed a strong relationship with the community.

The most pivotal change was the much-anticipated merger of the ABA and the NBA. Actually, it wasn't a merger at all.

After much negotiation, the NBA agreed to admit four franchises in the summer of 1976—the New York Nets, San Antonio Spurs, Indiana Pacers and my Denver Nuggets—for a sum of $3.2 million each to be paid to the NBA by September 15 of that year. The quartet of clubs agreed not to share in any television revenue for three years—a very tough pill to swallow for the clubs trying to remain solvent and competitive relative to signing top talent. The 1979-80 season seemed like a long way off.

The four refugee teams also could not participate in the 1976-77 ABA dispersal draft or the upcoming college draft for NBA teams. They would also be referred to as "expansion teams," and ended up with no votes pertaining to the distribution of gate receipts or the alignment of divisions for two years.

In essence, then, the ABA teams *bought* their way into the NBA, and that is not a merger. The ABA was tired of constant financial losses over nine years and having to consistently be creative just to survive, and the NBA was tired of star players jumping leagues, the resulting astronomical competition-driven salaries, and of college players they once depended on to fill their rosters leaving school early and signing with the ABA.

The joining of the two leagues was purely and completely born out of basic economics. Both sides felt it was time to end the madness.

Dave DeBusschere, who was hired as commissioner of the ABA primarily because of his strong ties to the NBA, was instrumental in getting the deal done with NBA boss Larry O'Brien—and a bright young lawyer named David Stern.

The NBA had grown into a 22-team league.

Since there were three remaining ABA teams that were dissolved, there was a "dispersal draft" for their players, but ABA teams could not participate.

When the basketball version of musical chairs was over, Moses Malone ended up in Houston, Artis Gilmore in Chicago, Maurice Lucas in Portland, Marvin Barnes in Detroit, Ron Boone in Kansas City, and Louie Dampier landed in San Antonio.

The infusion of ABA teams and players may have actually saved the NBA, which had recently lost such legends as Wilt Chamberlain, Jerry West, Elgin Baylor, Willis Reed and Oscar Robertson. In came Julius "Dr. J" Erving, George "The Iceman" Gervin, Billy Knight, Dan Issel, Artis Gilmore, and myself. A lot of young talent had signed with the ABA in the early 1970s, and the NBA felt a void.

Erving was actually sold to the Philadelphia 76ers by Nets owner Roy Boe because Boe had to not only come up with the $3.2 million entry fee for the NBA, but also had to pay a $4.8 million indemnification fee to the New York Knicks for playing in the Knicks' territory. The Nets had finally made the NBA, but it was bittersweet as they had to sell their franchise's—and the league's—best and most exciting player to get there.

Gilmore turned Chicago into an instant title contender, and they might have won it all had they not run into a scalding hot Portland Trailblazer team that featured not only fellow ABA alum Maurice Lucas, but also my old nemesis from UCLA, Mr. Bill Walton.

Bill and I seemed to always cross paths. We met in Portland in one of our first exhibition games in early October, and it was important to me that the Nuggets serve notice right off the bat to our new league that we were a force to be reckoned with.

On one play in the second half, Walton drove hard and attempted to dunk the ball. I was right there at the apex of his jump and stuffed him cleanly. On another play, I threw down a slam so hard I shattered the backboard. They stopped the game and it took almost as long for our trainer to get all of the glass out of my Afro as it did for them to replace the busted backboard.

This was prime time, baby, and we had officially "crashed" the NBA party.

We won that game 114-96, a strong 18-point victory over a team that would win the title that very year. Though we would lose to Portland two days later, 121-101, we were still quite optimistic about our chances in the new league. We even thumped the defending champion Celtics on October 12, 108-104, with 10,079 Nuggets fans in attendance.

Every single ABA alumnus played with one thought in mind that season—to show that they belonged in the NBA and to prove that the ABA had not been a refuge for the lame, the halt and the blind.

We went 4-4 during our maiden NBA preseason, winning all three of our games at home, but losing four of five on the road. I led the team with a 17.6 points-per-game average and had a high game of 28.

On the eve of the regular season, the team made some moves that changed the entire complexion of our club. Ralph Simpson was sent packing to his hometown of Detroit, and Paul Silas was brought in from Boston fresh off an NBA title. The thought was that Silas would provide the same sixth-man magic that he gave the Celtics and also some much needed rebounding and bulk up front.

With Simpson gone, Coach Larry Brown could now use me almost exclusively at guard. What started as hard worked out to everyone's satisfaction. It was a challenge for me, because I had not had any time to prepare for the guard position since Ralph was with us right up until the last preseason game. Additionally, I sprained an ankle in one of the final exhibition games and was still not fit three weeks into the regular season. But I tried not to let it slow me down. "People don't realize that David shouldn't be playing," said Coach Brown, who knew the score. "But he's got it in his mind to show every NBA city that he is among the best ever, and he isn't going to let anything stop him."

The transition to guard wasn't too tough for me. I knew that sometime in my career it would have to occur. Playing forward, I had to go against guys who were three or four inches taller and 20-30 pounds heavier, and I felt it after a game. I wasn't as tired after a game playing guard. I was bigger and heavier than the other guards and still quick enough to keep up with them.

We opened with as fearsome a front line as there was in basketball. Dan Issel was the starting center over Marvin Webster. Marvin was healthy, but had not performed well enough in the preseason to earn a starting position.

Bobby Jones retained his position at one forward spot, and Gus Gerard played himself into a starting forward. That very well may have been the last all-white starting front line in the history of professional basketball, but I'm not entirely sure of that. What I am sure of is the incredible amount of talent those guys possessed. And with Silas and Webster coming off the bench, we felt we measured up to anybody.

It's not well known, but the Nuggets had a plan in place that would have made our front line maybe one of the best ever. We were going to sign UCLA star and eventual 1977 National Player of the Year Marques Johnson, a 6'6", 215-pound forward. He was going to come out one year early to join us, but when the merger was finalized, the NBA told us to keep our hands off of him. Looking back, I can't even begin to imagine the damage we would have done had we had Johnson on our team that year.

Joining me in the backcourt was a tough "quarterback," as *Sports Illustrated* once called Ted McClain. Nicknamed "Hound Dog" because of the way he hounded and dogged players defensively, Ted once led the ABA in steals.

Monte was still with us, providing excellent guard play when called upon. We had also picked up a former great ABA player, 6'6" 210-pound forward Willie Wise. Willie was a great guy who would come out to the house once in a while and share his profound basketball wisdom with Monte and me.

Roland "Fatty" Taylor, a 6'0", 180-pound guard from LaSalle, was back on our team after a one-year hiatus in Virginia. Guard Chuck Williams started out with us, but was traded to Buffalo (along with Gus Gerard following a late-season injury) during the year for guard Jim Price.

This would be Byron Beck's final season in a Denver uniform, and that's worth mentioning because Byron was the only player in the history of the ABA to play for the same team all nine years. Now that's what I call team loyalty.

We shot out of the gate like Seattle Slew, winning our first seven games. Using at least 10 men per game in the lineup, we utilized a running and passing offense that was generating a lot of points. On the other end of the floor, we used a pressing, jump-switching defense that confounded our opponents. This was not the traditional, patterned attack that other Midwestern teams were employing. Coach Brown was an absolute master of both offensive and defensive schemes, and we were using them all to our advantage.

On November 15, we made the cover of *Sports Illustrated*. The picture showed me soaring toward the rim and the headline read, "Rising to the Occasion—David Thompson and the Nuggets Dazzle the NBA." It was thoroughly satisfying and exciting to have such an esteemed sports authority exalt our play in the league. The title of the article itself was, "They Came To Play," and that's what we appreciated most. Our opponents were dazzled, too.

After a win against the New York Knicks, future Hall of Fame guard Earl "The Pearl" Monroe said, "My, my…it would be hard for this young man to look bad. This team seems to have everything. The dudes are rolling as long as they keep that donut on the ledger." I had 24 points in that one, including a couple of high-wire acts that brought the hometown fans to their feet.

The Pearl was one of those guys I really looked up to and looked forward to playing against. Growing up, I idolized Earl, as did most kids from North Carolina. Nicknamed "Black Jesus," Monroe played college ball at Winston-Salem State. We used to take the bus from my high school in Shelby to see him play against Apollo College—an all-black school with a very small gym.

Earl wouldn't warm up with the rest of the players; he'd just lie there on a towel watching everyone else work up a sweat. Then he'd go out and get 40 points or more every single time. The crowds were loud and crazy, the bands would be playing, and it was a basketball carnival.

Chicago Bulls guard and legendary defensive ace Norm Van Lier said after our first encounter, "Thompson gets so high in the air on his jump shot that it's impossible to stop, and he's quick enough so that you can't really get in good position."

On November 19, we rolled into Boston Garden to take on the champion Celtics. It was my first-ever appearance there, and I wanted to have a strong outing. Unfortunately, my eye was scratched badly in the first quarter and I had to come out briefly. I was pretty scared and my eye was inflamed, but determined to show the Boston faithful what I was made of, I came off the bench and finished the evening with 25 points. I spent most of that night in a Boston hospital undergoing eye examinations, and I still didn't feel right when I left.

The very next night, November 20, we were playing in New York against the Knicks. Madison Square Garden and my still impaired vision notwithstanding, I was determined to show the crowd that I belonged there. Watery eye and all, I hit for 35 points, and a Gotham newspaper reported the next day on my final basket that I "soared to the third level of the Garden, retrieved a missed shot, and floated down to execute a perfect slam dunk."

As the new year began, we were at 23-10 and in first place. I was shooting 51 percent from the field through the end of December, which was really something if I do say so myself, considering more of my shots were launched from longer distances due to my new position, which forced me to play farther away from the basket.

We were playing a game at the Omni in Atlanta in early January when something funny occurred. As we were warming up, I called Monte over and said, "Monte, remember that dude Tommy Barker who was supposed to be our center at NC State our senior year, but then went AWOL on us?"

Of course he remembered, so I directed his attention to the Hawks players warming up at the other end of the court, where the phantom himself, all 6'11" of him, materialized right before our eyes. It was a stunning sight after all these years, and we looked around to see if Amelia Earhart, Judge Crater and Jimmy Hoffa were also in the house.

Everybody wanted to see the fast-paced, high-scoring Denver Nuggets' show. Only one team drew better than us on the road in 1976-77, and that was the Julius Erving-led 76ers.

Another interesting tidbit of forgotten hoops history is that although it took the NBA years to adopt other ABA tenets such as the three-pointer, the league embraced the slam dunk contest immediately.

The contest was taped in various parts of the country throughout the season for broadcast over CBS-TV. It had its share of problems, such as when Julius Erving informed the CBS brass that he did not wish to participate when the network crew showed up in Philadelphia to film his segment.

Early in the season, CBS sent a crew out to Denver to film part of the contest at halftime of a Nuggets game. I went up against another fine young player from the Phoenix Suns, rookie guard Ron Lee. McNichols

Arena was full, and I was well ahead. On my last attempt, I missed a windmill dunk, and Lee advanced to the next round of competition. The three judges—longtime Boston Celtics backcourt star Sam Jones, NBA referee Mendy Rudolph and sportswriter Larry Borstein—were almost lynched on the spot for their decision in favor of Lee. The boos that cascaded out of the stands were so loud, you would have thought I had been traded or something.

In the final, which took place during halftime of the deciding sixth game of the championship series between the 76ers and the Blazers, Darnell "Dr. Dunk" Hillman of the Indiana Pacers beat out nondescript journeyman Larry McNeill. McNeill was not even playing for an NBA team at that point and wore a *New York Post* shirt that was given to him by an opportunistic sportswriter from the newspaper.

And the NBA thought we did weird things in the ABA?

At the All-Star break I was still our team's number-one scoring threat by dint of having been the leading pointsman for the Nuggets 22 times in the first 53 games.

In the All-Star Game balloting, I garnered the most votes ever by any player to that time—*319,047*. It created quite a buzz that a former ABA player led the NBA in fan voting in his first opportunity, and the accomplishment lent additional credibility to the corps of players imported from the defunct league.

Interestingly, I was voted in as a forward, my old position, and played there in the All-Star Game. I had started the first 46 games of the season at guard, although I did play some forward here and there. The rest of the season I played both positions, so maybe nobody knew exactly where to pigeonhole me.

The annual classic was played on Sunday, February 13, 1976, at the Arena in Milwaukee, Wisconsin, before 10,938 fans. Julius Erving's first NBA season thus far had been less than spectacular, but he made up for it on this All-Star day. Though his East team lost to our West team, 125-124, Dr. J won the game's MVP award—something he had not done in five ABA All-Star Games. The Doctor scored 30 points and grabbed 12 rebounds in a stellar performance.

My teammates Dan Issel and Bobby Jones were also voted into the West's starting lineup by the fans. Issel got the nod as the West's starting center over a much more deserving Kareem Abdul-Jabbar because the Denver fans stuffed the ballot box in voting. Gotta love those Nugget fans!

Coach Brown directed the West team, so it almost felt like a Nuggets game. Bobby and Dan only played 14 and 10 minutes respectively, but I was fortunate to spend 29 minutes on the floor in my first NBA All-Star Game.

I played well, getting 18 points on seven-for-nine shooting, and contributed seven rebounds and three assists. Phoenix Suns guard Paul Westphal made two key baskets down the stretch, and when the East went for the win with only seconds left, Paul stole the ball from Pete Maravich to seal the victory.

When the Jim Price trade with Buffalo was made late in the year, a lot of people thought we could have secured Price straight up for Chuck Williams without including the valuable, albeit injured, Gus Gerard. Carl Scheer thought we needed a bona fide shooting guard to take the pressure off of me, but Price had never really fully recovered from a knee injury he had suffered two years earlier. Jim never really panned out for us, and he was gone by the middle of the following season.

It really hurt to see Gus go. He was a friend to me and a lot of guys on the team. Athletically, he was a clone of Bobby Jones and maybe even a little better at the offensive end. Gus could run like a deer and jump out of the gym and was a lot younger than Jim Price. When Gus told us that he was going to Buffalo, that was like hearing that somebody was being sent to Siberia. Nobody's career continued after a stop in Buffalo. It was like the elephant graveyard of the NBA.

We finished the year 50-32 and won the Midwest division by six games over Detroit and Chicago, which finished with identical 44-38 records. Our first-place finish earned us a first-round playoff bye, so we awaited the winner of the Portland/Chicago series.

Portland beat the Bulls two games to one, and I was once again face to face with Mr. Bill Walton. We felt good heading into that series, because while they had to play three games, we were refreshed from the break. We also had the home-court advantage.

But the Blazers were the league's hottest second-half team and were peaking at just the right time. The guy we had to really contain was Maurice Lucas, who'd just scored 67 points against Chicago in three games. The Denver papers speculated that Coach Brown might juggle our lineup in an effort to neutralize Lucas, and when his game plan was unveiled it featured Paul Silas, normally our sixth man, in a starting role opposite Lucas.

We should've equipped him with a net when the series opened in Denver on April 20 because Lucas collected 23 points, hauled in 13 rebounds, and scored what might have been his biggest bucket all year when he nailed a turnaround jumper over Issel with 11 seconds left to give Portland a 101-100 win. I had been fouled on the previous play by Lionel Hollins and made both free throws to give us a one-point lead. We had a chance to score at the buzzer, but turned it over instead.

We redeemed ourselves two days later by pounding the Trailblazers 121-110, but Lucas came up big again with 29 points for Portland. Dan led the way for us with 36 points as he took advantage of Walton's absence when Bill fouled out with 7:36 remaining.

We had achieved a split at home and headed to the Pacific Northwest for Game 3. On April 24, we lost another hard-fought contest 110-106. Two days later Portland handled us again, 105-96, and we were facing elimination. Late in the game, I scored four points and McClain added another two to pull us within one, 107-106, with 21 seconds left, but Blazer guard Herm Gilliam made a foul shot and scored on a breakaway after Walton intercepted a McClain pass.

I scored 40 points in that game, but Maurice Lucas continued his torrid scoring with 27, and Walton added 26 to counteract everything I accomplished. Portland's Bobby Gross had an unusually easy time with Bobby Jones, scoring 25 points, pulling in seven rebounds, handing out six assists and making four steals. Also, the Portland bench played huge in that game.

I not only felt bad for myself, my teammates, and the city of Denver, but especially for Coach Brown. He always managed to achieve great things in the regular season, only to get bounced from the playoffs.

Down three games to one, back home in Denver, we let it all hang out. It was the first day of May, and the contest went into overtime. The Trailblazers came from 12 down in the third quarter to knot the game at 101 at the end of regulation. Blazer guard Hollins scored eight of his team's last nine points in the fourth quarter, and it was his steal and driving layup that forced the overtime.

However, Issel scored nine of his 23 points in the extra period, and I had two of my game-high 31 as we pulled away for a 114-105 victory.

The Trailblazers faced a dilemma as they headed back to Portland for Game 6. Starting guard Dave Twardzik badly sprained an ankle during the third quarter of Game 5, and Blazer coach Jack Ramsey had to replace him. After much thought and consultation with Walton and assistant coach Jack McKinney, Ramsey decided to start Johnny Davis, who had not seen much floor time in the playoffs up to that point.

All Davis did in Game 6 was lift his team to victory, 108-92, by scoring a game-high 25 points, hitting 10 of 14 shots from the field. They didn't call Jack Ramsey a genius for nothing.

Portland went on to sweep the Los Angeles Lakers in the Western Conference Finals 4-0, and then secured their place in basketball history by winning their first NBA championship over the Philadelphia 76ers, 4-2.

Most experts predicted that the 76ers, a team loaded with individual stars such as Julius Erving, George McGinnis, Doug Collins, Lloyd "World B." Free and Darryl Dawkins, would beat Portland handily in the Finals. But as was regularly the case in the 1970s, a club with a true team concept finished in the chips. The Knicks, Bucks, Lakers, Celtics, Warriors, Bullets and Sonics all won the title with an unselfish style of play. The Trailblazers did, too.

It also just went to prove again that you can spend $6 million on the planet's number-one star forward, but the title still goes to the team that controls the middle.

As for us, once again we had finished first in our division only to be extinguished in the playoffs. We went 36-5 at home (second best behind the Lakers' 37-4) but only went 14-32 away from McNichols.

Though we were all highly disappointed in how the year ended, there were some individual accomplishments to be proud of. I was named to the first team All-League squad at forward and was the only ex-ABA player chosen, beating out Julius Erving and George McGinnis. Elvin Hayes joined me on the first team along with Pete Maravich—the league scoring champion—and Paul Westphal. Kareem Abdul-Jabbar was the center.

I finished fourth in scoring with a 25.9 points-per-game average while Issel was tenth with 22.3. Bobby Jones was third in field goal percentage at .570 and was also first-team All-Defensive.

Issel and I were the top scoring tandem in 1976-77 at 48.2 points per game, while Indiana's Billy Knight and John Williamson were next at 47.4.

I also led the Nuggets in assists (337) and contributed 53 blocked shots while starting 46 games at guard.

Something else to be proud of was the performance of all the ex-ABA players. Of the top 20 scorers in 1976-77, nine were former ABA players. There were four in the top 10 (Indiana's Billy Knight, Dan Issel and myself, and San Antonio's George Gervin). Six of the top 10 rebounders were former ABA guys, and even Don Buse of the Indiana Pacers—who led the league in assists (8.5 per game) and steals (3.47 per game)—was originally a red, white and blue alumnus.

Five of the 10 starters in the NBA finals were from the ABA, 10 of the 24 league All-Stars hailed from the ABA, and the Denver Nuggets took first place in the Midwest division. No "expansion" team had ever done that before, and none has done it since.

But even with that kind of success, the Denver Nuggets organization continued to tinker with the machinery. Whoever said "the only thing constant is change," must've been a Nuggets fan—or maybe even running the outfit.

By the beginning of the 1977-78 season, we had a whole new look.

CHAPTER 15

73, $4 MILLION, AND ZERO RINGS

The esprit de corps that was always so evident in our play had deserted us by the end of the 1976-77 season.

"The spirit isn't here any more," noted Bobby Jones as we were going down in playoff defeat to the Portland Trailblazers in May of 1977. Coach Brown was overheard saying, "After this thing is over, I'm backing the truck up." The coach felt it was time to shake things up once again, and he did so with gusto.

The 1977 college draft marked the first time that former ABA teams could participate, and we took full advantage of the situation. We owned the ninth pick, obtained from Kansas City in the Brian Taylor trade, and we selected 6'10", 220-pound center Tom LaGarde from North Carolina.

As a senior, LaGarde had averaged 15.1 points over 20 games for Dean Smith's crew, but two operations on his knee caused him to sit out the national championship game against Marquette—a key factor in the Warriors' victory over the Tar Heels that spring.

We also chose high-scoring Anthony Roberts from Oral Roberts University, a 6'5" small forward who was a classic swingman. Anthony had averaged over 34 points per game in his second year at ORU and had high games of 66 and 65 as a senior.

In the third round, the Nuggets took Robert Smith from the University of Nevada-Las Vegas. Robert was a 5'11" guard who could handle the ball well and had played high school ball with the Bucks' Marques Johnson. He was cut early in the season, but rejoined us later in the year. We also landed 6'9" rookie forward Bo Ellis of the national champion

Marquette Warriors in a trade with the Washington Bullets right before the season started. I had last seen Bo as a freshman when we competed in the NCAA championship game in 1974.

They were all decent players, but we needed some big bodies up front, and with that in mind a person might wonder, like that old gal in the Wendy's hamburger commercial, "Where's the beef?"

There were plenty of changes when management backed up that truck Coach Brown mentioned. In a blockbuster deal, we traded our center of the future, Marvin Webster, to Seattle along with forwards Paul Silas and Willie Wise. In return we received 6'8" forward Bobby Wilkerson—a defensive specialist who had won a national championship under Bobby Knight at Indiana—and my old friend, 7'4" center Tom Burleson. I didn't even get the cake ordered for our reunion, however, before Tom was dealt right to the Kansas City Kings for the player Coach Brown coveted more than any other—guard Brian Taylor.

The 6'3" Taylor had impressed Coach Brown as far back as the 1976 ABA finals, when Brian was a standout guard for the Nets. We needed someone to quarterback the team, and Brian had the credentials for the job. Brian was second in the NBA in steals the year before and had averaged 17 points per game and handed out 320 assists. We had almost secured Taylor as a free agent in 1976-77, but New Jersey Nets owner Roy Boe backed out at the last minute. Instead, he sent Taylor to Kansas City in return for Nate Archibald. After one year with the Kings, Taylor wanted out.

A couple of former Nuggets would rejoin the fold in 1977-78. Mack Calvin actually rejoined us late in the 1976-77 season. Always a favorite of Coach Brown's, he was rescued from San Antonio and brought home to Denver.

Ralph Simpson would also come home to Denver from Detroit in a late-season trade for Jim Price, but he was woefully out of shape after doing little but collecting splinters for the Pistons.

Sending Webster and Silas to Seattle would come back to haunt us at playoff time. Never underestimate the will and motivation of professional athletes who want to prove they still have some gas in their tank.

There were two other noteworthy personnel changes before we began training camp. Byron Beck, the all-time Denver fan favorite and native son, retired to devote the majority of his time to the Muscular Dystrophy organization. I hated to see Byron leave as much as anyone, but what really tore my heart out was when the organization decided it could do without my best friend and housemate, Monte Towe.

To demonstrate our fervor for the upcoming season—and maybe as a form of penance for losing in the last playoffs to Portland—Monte and I decided to bike to training camp, 60 miles from Denver to the U.S. Air Force Academy in Colorado Springs. We didn't know it at the time, but it was like Butch and Sundance's last adventure together. We enjoyed some laughs chugging up and down the mountainous terrain, and when we could take no more we stopped and called Cathy to pick us up. We had pedaled all of 30 miles—but before you laugh too hard, you'd better try riding your bike in that altitude (approximately 6,000 feet above sea level) and see how far you can make it before you start looking around for a Greyhound Bus.

The end of our ride as teammates came just before the exhibition season got underway. The team was loaded with outstanding guards, and Monte was the odd man out. I think I was probably more crushed than Monte when he was cut. For four years of college and my first two years as a professional ballplayer, he was at my side literally and figuratively—a teammate and friend whose diminutive frame belied the heart of a giant. He remains the most special of friends and is as fine a person as you will find.

I always knew, as many people did, that Monte would one day become a coach. It's in his blood. Monte helped recruit many great players for NC State, including my cousin Derrick Whittenburg, who played a key role on the 1983 national championship team. Monte then followed Norm Sloan to the University of Florida as an assistant coach from 1980-89, where he recruited future NBA players Vernon Maxwell and Dwayne Schintzius. He then spent time coaching in the Global Basketball Association, the Professional Basketball League of Venezuela, the Continental Basketball Association, and Chipola Junior College in Marianna, Florida. Monte then assisted head coach Eddie Biedenbach—the man who recruited me at NC State—at UNC-Asheville from 1996-99.

On March 29, 2001, Monte was named head coach at the University of New Orleans, and as proud as I'm sure he was that day, no one was prouder than me. Though a Privateer now, we will be Wolfpack brothers to the very end.

Professional basketball is first and foremost a business. Now it was time to see if all these new pieces were answers to our championship puzzle.

I knew we would score, but could we defend and control the middle—the two necessary components to winning it all?

I started the season at guard with Brian Taylor on the other side. Dan Issel was again our man in the middle, and the forwards were Bobby Jones and Bobby Wilkerson. Coach Brown just loved Wilkerson's size and his ability to play guard, and it wasn't long before he couldn't resist trying Bobby out at that position.

I had become more comfortable and skilled at the guard position myself. I thought I had gotten the hang of it, especially in the last part of the 1976-77 season. Not only was I scoring, but I was also averaging four or five assists each game. In the last 24 regular-season games, I averaged 29.6 points and 4.7 assists. My lowest scoring game was 21, and there were five games where I scored at least 30 and dished out five assists. In one game I poured in 44 points and gave out seven assists. I also benefited from the reduced wear and tear on my body not having to go up against the larger players every night.

I was only 23 as I began my third year in the pros. Therefore it was a surprise when Coach Brown—for the first time since he was named Denver's head coach in 1974—named Issel and myself team co-captains. Respect is a consideration when choosing a captain, and he felt that Dan and I had earned the trust of the team. Though I wasn't much of a vocal leader, I tried to open up more because I knew what the younger guys were going through.

Experience played a big part in my development and growth as a player. Coach Brown felt that, before, I could play spectacularly when needed, but, on a regular basis, not necessarily great. That's a term used in the NBA when you can practically drag a team to victory almost by yourself. Now Coach Brown saw greatness in me, and he wasn't the only one. The last two years had boosted my self-confidence. I was now prepared to lead by achieving my God-given potential as a basketball player.

We were picked once again to finish first in the Midwest division, and our fans were firm believers. We set a new franchise record for season tickets sold—more than 11,000.

We opened the regular season on October 19 with a home win against the Bucks. I scored 36 and added four assists. But it was in the final period when I really gave Coach Brown what he was looking for. The Bucks had snuck ahead, but then I scored 12 points, mainly from the outside, to help us regain the lead, and we won the game in convincing fashion, 133-115.

Even with four rookies playing regularly, we posted a strong 18-8 record through the first third of the season.

But in December our focus and performance suddenly lapsed, and we dropped five straight games—the longest such string in Coach Brown's Denver career. It was a bad stretch for me individually, too, as I suffered through three sub-20-point games. I can't say exactly when it happened, but it was during this time that I was moved back to forward on offense. On defense, Coach Brown would still try to match me with a guard because of my height, but Larry's vaunted "David Thompson, guard" experiment had pretty much run its course.

I couldn't argue with the results. We won our next 10 games in a row, starting with a 127-108 victory over the Phoenix Suns at home. We would not lose again until January 19, 1978, when the Bucks dropped us 114-109 in Milwaukee.

But a critical, crushing blow befell the Nuggets as we were riding high. On January 16, Brian Taylor left the Nuggets over a contract dispute. Coach Brown was livid and made it clear that he did not want Taylor back under any circumstances. Brian was the first legitimate point guard we'd had in a while, and we had played extremely well with him. He possessed excellent speed, had good height, could really shoot, and was as good a defender at the guard position as there was in the league. But now it was sayonara.

The player merry-go-round didn't stop there; in fact it was only the beginning. On January 30, we gave a 1979 second-round draft choice and cash to the New Jersey Nets for forward Darnell Hillman. (Robert Smith was also waived at this time, only to return in early February when NBA commissioner O'Brien allowed us some roster relief in the face of Brian Taylor's defection.)

Hillman was the king of the layup line. He didn't get much actual playing time but was the star of the pregame show. He and a few other guys, myself included, were always trying to top each other's dunks. The pregame slam-fest was always a big hit with the fans.

After Jim Price was dealt off for Ralph Simpson, I was really wondering what was going on. Why make so many changes when we were playing so well? This was as good a team as I had played on in the pros, and yet management couldn't or wouldn't stop tinkering. Apparently nobody in the Nuggets' front office had ever heard the saying, "If it ain't broke, don't fix it."

The All-Star Game was played on February 5, and once again Bobby Jones and I represented the Nuggets. I thought it was pretty cool that President Jimmy Carter's lovely mother, Miss Lillian, opened the game by tossing the ball in. A dunk was probably out of the question.

Our West team had the lead at the half, 66-57, but we were over-shadowed by the eventual MVP of the game—super-quick guard Randy Smith of the Buffalo Braves. Smith went 11-14 from the field and made 30-foot and 40-foot bombs at the end of the first and second quarters, respectively. In the fourth quarter, he scored eight straight points.

Smith's East team prevailed, 133-125. I led the West with 22 points on 10-16 shooting, but, as usual, it didn't mean much if a good personal day was attached to a loss.

Overall I was having an effective year. Through our first 55 games, I was the only top 10 scorer in the league who had not had a game in which he scored less than 15 points. Then I had only 12 in a loss to the Cavaliers on February 16, but the next day I tossed in 30 big ones in a win over the Trailblazers.

Just days earlier, we were the first team to beat Portland in Memorial Coliseum in 45 games. Since it was the Blazers who'd knocked us out of the playoffs the year before, we took particular pleasure in ending their home-court winning streak. The game was on national TV, and I remember the announcers expressing shock at the outcome. I hit a couple of jump shots in the fourth quarter to clinch the win.

Speaking of national TV, I was the "Player of the Game" that season on three different telecasts. It was special to me because the alma mater of each player so designated received $1,000 in his name. Any time the Wolfpack could benefit from my play, I was a happy camper.

We clinched the Midwest division championship for the second year in a row on April 3, whipping the Braves in Buffalo, 104-95. Then we closed out the home portion of our schedule with a 129-121 victory over the New Jersey Nets. A crowd of 16,422 boosted our total attendance for the year to 657,673. Our average attendance of 16,041 topped the NBA for the second straight year. Eleven of our home games that year were sellouts.

There was only one game left before the playoffs. It would be the last game the Detroit Pistons would ever play in Cobo Arena, as the club would begin using the new and spacious Pontiac Silverdome the follow-ing season. But the unsentimental Detroit fans were in no mood to send the fourth-place Pistons off with a fond farewell in the building that had been their home since 1961.

On a cool Sunday afternoon, April 9, 1978, those 3,482 fans more than got their money's worth.

I had been locked in a scoring duel with George Gervin of the Spurs for much of the year. Only 14 points separated us at the top of the league scoring chart heading into our last games that Sunday.

"Do you want to go for it today?" Coach Brown asked me before the game. Whether we won or lost, we were still headed for the playoffs. So the coach was willing to let me shoot to my heart's content to win the NBA scoring title. If I put up astronomical numbers, then Gervin, playing in New Orleans that evening, would be chasing me.

The truth of the matter was that I didn't much care. I wasn't ever about individual accomplishments. From my high school coach, Ed Peeler, to my college coach, Norman Sloan, and then my professional coach, Larry Brown, I had consistently been taught a team concept. Lead, but leave the one-man-band stuff to *The Gong Show*.

So I told Coach Brown that I just wanted to play, and whatever happened was up to the fates.

There were no camera crews at Cobo that afternoon for two primary reasons. First, our game was truly meaningless as far as both teams were concerned. Second, the network saw bigger ratings in John Havlicek's farewell game at Boston Garden, the Celtics versus the Buffalo Braves. No argument there. The individual scoring title really wasn't that big a deal, to me or the media. Later on, I confess, it did occur to me that the outcome could affect my immediate future with the Nuggets.

During the 1976-77 season, when Pete Maravich of the New Orleans Jazz racked up 68 points against the New York Knicks, Pete was in the midst of contract negotiations. I remember thinking then that timing was everything. While I had no plans to attempt something so grand as the regular season was coming to a close, the fact was that I was in the same position as the Pistol. My contract was up due to the "convenience clause" that allowed me the chance to become a free agent at the end of my third year if I so desired. So subconsciously, who knows?

Detroit started M. L. Carr and John Shumate at forward, rookie Ben Poquette at center, and Chris Ford and Eric Money at guard. Robert Kauffman was at the helm for the Pistons. The Motor City was about to witness NBA history.

I hit the first eight shots I took, mainly medium-range jumpers from 15 to 18 feet. As the quarter wore on, I also got a few dunks on alley-oops.

The 6'9" Poquette stuffed me cleanly on one dunk attempt, but I connected on my last five shots of the first quarter, and we took a six-point lead into the second stanza, 42-36.

Not realizing what had just occurred—it all happened so fast—I was amazed to learn later that I had set an NBA record for most points in a quarter with 32. That beat Wilt Chamberlain's 1962 mark by one, set in that historic game where Wilt scored 100 points. Equally stunning was my accuracy in that first quarter. I went 13-14 from the field (Poquette's block being the only shot I missed) and 6-6 from the foul line.

My 13 field goals were also a new NBA record, and it still stands to this day.

I was definitely in the zone; I felt like Superman on steroids. There wasn't a shot I put up that I didn't think, as soon as it left my hands, would go anywhere but in the hoop.

The feeling continued in the second quarter. The first seven balls that I sent toward the rim went in, and the Pistons were starting to look a little nervous. I completed the second frame with 21 points, giving me 53 points in the first half. You could see it on the Detroit players' faces—something like, "There's no way we can let this guy get 100 on us." A hundred points? Heck, I was just a 6'4" guard with a hot hand. I nailed the first 20 of 21 shots I had taken and was 20-23 at the half. I'd caught fire before, but never anything like this. We were also keeping the Pistons at bay and held a dominant 14-point advantage at the half, 83-69.

By now word had found its way out, and the camera crews and TV reporters were pouring into Cobo Arena. Brent Musberger was anchoring the CBS *Game of the Week*, and he cut into the scheduled telecast to report what I had done in the first half in Detroit.

The Pistons came out determined to shut me down in the third quarter, and Chris Ford, Eric Money, M. L. Carr, and Al Skinner all took turns double, triple, and sometimes quadruple-teaming me. I felt like a caged rat, but still somehow managed six third-quarter points. It wasn't a lot, but there wasn't much I could do. Even worse, the Pistons had closed the gap to 106-104. It wasn't about me any more; it was about trying to win the game.

The Pistons scored 10 straight points in the fourth quarter to take a commanding 121-112 lead, and then they held off a late Nuggets surge to win the game, 139-137. I scored on a three-point play in the final minute, but it wasn't enough.

I finished with 73 points—the third highest total ever, the most ever by a guard, and the second most in a non-overtime game. The Big Dipper—Chamberlain—scored the 100 in 1962, of course, then amassed 78 in a 1961 triple overtime contest and hit for 73 twice in 1962. Of course, Wilt was also 7'1" tall. I was a mere mortal at 6'4". My final line for the game: 28-38 from the field, 17-20 from the free throw line, seven rebounds, and I played 43 out of 48 minutes. When I came out for those five minutes, my teammates treated me like the way baseball players treat pitchers throwing a no-hitter late in the game—they wouldn't talk to me. They wouldn't even sit near me, fearing some sort of basketball voodoo jinx.

Here's some food for thought: It has been speculated that had I had the benefit of today's three-point line, my total would have been in the high 80s.

A crowd of 300 people showed up at Denver's Stapleton International Airport that Sunday night. Bob King, executive VP of the Nuggets, was the first to greet me and Coach Brown as we exited the plane. Carl Scheer was there, too. As I was walked down the runway, microphones and tape recorders were thrust in my face. "I just feel great being associated with a player like Wilt Chamberlain," I said, signing autographs on all sides.

When I finally made it home, I scanned the dial on the radio and attempted to pick up the San Antonio versus New Orleans broadcast. If it had been any player other than "The Iceman," I wouldn't have even bothered. But George was ultra-competitive, and he already knew what I had done earlier in the day. He needed 58 points to win the scoring title, and I knew that was not far from his reach. George could fill up the bucket so fast you would swear it was raining basketballs.

I caught the game early into the second quarter, and by halftime Gervin had fired in 53 points. I knew then that my 73 had been in vain. George scored 63 points on 23 of 49 shots from the floor and ended up winning the scoring title in the closest race in NBA history, 27.22 to 27.15.

George's 63 points that night in New Orleans meant that I had only held the scoring lead for about seven hours. Gervin's Spurs lost, 152-132, but George had already broken my mark for most points in a quarter with

33 in the second frame. That has to be a record in itself. It took me 16 years to break Wilt's mark, but it only took Gervin seven hours to break mine.

Did I feel bad? Maybe for a moment or two. But Monte put things in their proper perspective when he told me that night, "You have nothing to be ashamed of, David. Let's face it, 73 points in one game is quite an accomplishment. Not too many people will ever score 73 points in a game." Of course he was right. Since that night in 1978, no one has.

As all this was going down, Carl Scheer got wind that some of my people were talking to the Knicks about acquiring me once my contract was up. The rumor—and I never did find out where it came from—was that Ted Shay, my financial advisor, was seen talking to the New York club's management. The Knicks still coveted my services greatly.

Scheer had already spoken to Shay and my agent, Larry Fleisher, a few days before the 73-point outburst. Carl felt that if he could get me locked up before a bidding war ensued with New York, then all the better. The problem was available funds. Denver was not yet sharing in the league's TV revenue, and wouldn't until the 1979-80 season. Scheer and his partners concluded that the team could go down without me, so they might as well sign me and take their chances that the club might not survive *with* me. Carl basically mortgaged the Nuggets' future on me. He would try and cut corners wherever he could, but this was a deal he felt he had to do for the sake of the long-term future of the franchise. It was an enormous gamble.

There were rumors that the Knicks might go as high as $1 million per year for me, and Fleisher knew it. At that time, the highest salaries in the league were in the $500,000-$600,000 range. Pete Maravich had the richest contract in the league at the time—$615,000 a year.

Scheer struck the deal with Fleisher on the eve of our opening playoff game against the Milwaukee Bucks on April 18. The announcement of the terms of my new contract sent the NBA owners, players and fans into a state of shock. The agreement was for $4 million over five years, or $800,000 per season. I had shattered the payroll ceiling. But Scheer felt that compared to what the Knicks were most likely going to offer, the deal was palatable.

The Nuggets were already operating under a load of debt with the First National Bank of Denver, so they went far out on a limb to secure my services. And only $50,000 of that annual salary was deferred, meaning $750,000 was to be paid in cold, hard cash.

Given the substantial financial strain my new contract put on the Nuggets, I was determined that the organization would look at it as a bargain by delivering everything a franchise player is supposed to contribute—starting that night against the Bucks.

Coach Brown likes to tell the story that the first shot I put up in that game sailed right over the backboard like it was filled with helium, but I don't remember that. According to Larry, my nerves were so jangled by announcement of my contract that I hardly knew which basket to shoot at. It actually wasn't that bad, but I was feeling some pressure, most of it self-imposed. Becoming the richest player in pro basketball with the stroke of a pen will do that to you.

Milwaukee head coach Don Nelson was handed the reins to his team early in the season, taking over for Larry Costello. The young Bucks surprised everyone by finishing right behind us in the Midwest with a 44-38 record, and then they knocked off the heavily favored Phoenix Suns in the first round of the playoffs, 2-0. And though we won that first playoff game in Denver, 119-103, they let us know that we weren't in for a cakewalk.

Sure enough, we battled neck and neck the whole series, notching it up at three games apiece. It was back to Denver for Game 7, and to hear our own coach talk, we were toast.

"I wouldn't bet on Denver in a million years," Larry was quoted as saying. I'm sure he said it to fire us up, but I also have to believe it came from years of frustration caused by Denver's traditional ineptitude in the playoffs.

Frankly, I wasn't sure Coach Brown wasn't right. And a lot of the blame belonged on the shoulders of the team's $4 Million Man.

Larry Brown and Donnie Walsh took me upstairs to talk. We spoke of many things—the contract's effect on me, the team's general play, ridding ourselves of the "choke" tag—and the need for me to come up big. When we finished, I quietly ducked out the back while Larry addressed members of the media in the Nuggets' offices.

"I do know this," he told the reporters, "every big game [Thompson has] ever been involved in, he was ready to play." I was ready that night. On May 3, we finished off the Bucks, 116-110, and I led the way with 37 points, six rebounds, six assists and five blocked shots. "Nuggets Gag but Don't Choke," read the headline in the next day's *Denver Post*.

We were absolutely spent after such a difficult and physically draining series. And up next were the Seattle Supersonics, who had dispatched the Bill Walton-less defending champion Portland Trailblazers in six games and had a little more time to recuperate than we did.

The Sonics were quite the story that year after Lenny Wilkens supplanted Bob Hopkins as head coach 22 games into the season. The club had been floundering at 5-17, but with Wilkens in charge the Sonics took off, posting the best regular-season record from that point forward, 42-18. Wilkens had shuffled the entire starting lineup, except for center Marvin Webster. When he was finished, there were four new faces on the floor surrounding Webster.

Wilkens inserted rookie Jack Sikma and castoff John Johnson at forward and an unknown—23-year-old Dennis Johnson—and another free agent, Gus Williams, at the guard slots. Forwards Bruce Seals and Paul Silas went to the bench, along with guards Slick Watts and Fred Brown. The changes made the Sonics dangerous, because now they had youth, speed, and hungry talent in their starting rotation. The bench also brought toughness and firepower with the rebounding Silas and shot-happy Brown.

As I mentioned earlier, a big key to this matchup was the anger that burned deep within Webster and Silas at Denver for trading them before the season started. They felt like they had something to prove. Still, some of the biggest games I had that season—including a few with over 40 points—were against Seattle. So, exhausted or not, we thought we could beat them, even though they had just overcome an excellent Portland team.

It came out later that the Sonics had done a lot of scouting on us prior to this series. Their staff had pored over countless hours of film looking for weaknesses that they could exploit. Seattle knew we were not an overly physical team. We relied more on finesse, and so the Sonics decided to go right after us, roughing us up as much as possible. In the playoffs, the refs tend to lay off their whistles anyway.

The series opened on May 5, and we thumped the Sonics 116-107 at home. But there was something strange going on. The Sonics had done their homework well. Many times I would start making my moves, only to be matched step for step by defender Dennis "DJ" Johnson.

Once I figured out what DJ was doing—holding and bumping some—I tried to mix up my repertoire to keep all the Seattle defenders honest. It didn't work in Game 2, and on May 7 we lost the home court advantage (once again) and the game, 121-111. The fans in McNichols Arena had seen this act played out too many times before, and they let us know it.

Offensively, when I did get past DJ, the other Sonics players did a good job of forcing me into the middle, where I had to contend with Webster—no easy task, either. It added up to a not-so-dominant David Thompson.

The statistics tell the story. In the first two games in Denver, we outscored the Sonics by 17 field goals, but Seattle was awarded 111 free throws and converted 82. We were given only 58 foul shots and made 47. Larry Brown vented heavily on the refs, but it didn't seem to have any effect.

We headed to Seattle on May 10 for Game 3. The Sonics continued to keep me bottled up, and an increasingly frustrated Coach Brown picked up his third technical of the series. Webster was killing Issel on the boards, 16-7, and blocked three shots. I was averaging six points a game less than I had during the regular season and connected on only six of 19 shots in Game 3. The Sonics coasted to a 105-91 victory.

On May 12, Seattle won their third straight after our lone, series-opening win. Webster racked up more blocks (he had 19 through the first four games), I missed 17 of 27 shots, and DJ scored a game- and career-high 31 points. We were ahead 78-74 early in the fourth quarter, but then "Downtown" Freddy Brown was released from the bench and accounted for 17 Seattle points on four buckets, three foul shots, and three assists—including seven straight in the final four minutes to give the Sonics a 100-94 win. Freddy scored 37 points in the final periods of each of Seattle's three victories.

Two days later, May 14, was Mother's Day. We were back home and were feeling very confident as the noon tipoff approached. I made a vow to just go out and play my game, put up some big numbers and get us back on track. I busted out of my shooting slump and recorded 35 points, while Issel "ran Webster into the floorboards," as *Sports Illustrated* put it and scored 27 himself. Webster did block seven of our shots, but not enough. We led by 19 in the second half as my teammates set some tremendous screens for me.

A late Sonics rally cut our lead to 113-108. After a Seattle timeout, Coach Brown called a play for me and I came through with a double-pumping, high-arcing shot from the key that got us out of the danger zone.

But on May 17, it all came crashing down on us. The Sonics had won 19 consecutive games in the Coliseum, and in Game 6 we were never in contention to snap their streak. The Sonics trounced us 123-108 and went on to lose a thrilling seven-game championship series to the Washington Bullets.

Our loss was a hard kick in the teeth. I have always said that was the best chance we ever had to win the title. But once again we failed to even make it to the finals.

I was chosen first team All-NBA for the second consecutive year, scored in double figures in all 80 games I played in, and was third in voting for the MVP award (Bill Walton won it), *Sport Magazine* named me their "Performer of the Year" in pro basketball, but all of that didn't change the way I felt about losing to the Sonics. I felt I had let the team down.

My first three years in Denver were the happiest. The next four would bring more change, more trouble, and more heartache. I never thought at this point in my young life that things could go so sour, so quickly.

CHAPTER 16

FADE AWAY

There seemed to be a heavy-duty Masterlock on the door to the NBA championship, and the Nuggets just couldn't find the right combination to open it.

We had outstanding teams for three straight years and won our division each time—only to falter in the playoffs. It was difficult on all of us, and our front office continued to shuffle players like a deck of cards, hoping to come up with a royal flush. But 1978-79 would not be that year.

In fact, my remaining four years in a Nuggets uniform would not only leave me without a championship ring, but would also mark the starting erosion of a career once so promising. When I look back, it's hard to believe things could unravel so quickly.

We lacked two things in Denver for my entire seven years there—a true center (Dan Issel was more suited as a power forward) and a genuine point guard. We thought we had the center in Marvin Webster, but we may have given up on him too early. We thought we had an elite point guard in Brian Taylor, but we couldn't keep him happy financially. In the end, I wound up with the lion's share of the money and the implied responsibility of carrying the team on my back. Both facts added to the stress and pressure of trying to achieve the impossible—one man taking his team to the pinnacle of his professional sport. It just doesn't happen that way in team sports.

In August of 1978, Bobby Jones and Ralph Simpson were traded to Philadelphia for 6'8" All-Star power forward George McGinnis. We had already acquired guard Charlie Scott (yes, my boyhood idol) in late June in a three-way trade with the Lakers and the Kings, and though it appeared on paper that we had improved our team with these additions, the fact was that other teams in our division were making substantive improvements that enhanced their chemistry instead of monkeying with it. For example, guard Phil Ford had an immediate impact in Kansas City though just a rookie, and he and second-year backcourt mate Otis Birdsong gave the Kings a formidable pair of top-flight players.

The problem with our new high-profile additions, McGinnis and Scott, was their highly verbose natures. Our new Dynamic Duo was so outspoken that it dramatically changed the whole personality of the team. They were so opinionated that it sometimes rubbed some of the other guys the wrong way. Both newcomers were excitable, and that would cost George the following season. He was downright volatile. In a game in Atlanta, George had actually gone after a fan who had been riding him pretty good throughout the game. It cost McGinnis $500, but he didn't seem to mind.

George wasn't much for practicing, either, which put him on a straight collision course right off the bat with Coach Brown, a strict disciplinarian.

On the very first day of practice for the new season, George ducked into the back of the line when it came his turn to run wind sprints. Seeing that, another player did the same thing. Talk about poisoning the well—Coach Brown wasn't about to put up with that stuff…not from anybody. Even though Larry stood just 5'9" and tipped the scales at 160 pounds, he had the heart of a lion and backed down from no one. He went right to McGinnis, who stood about a foot taller and had a good 75 pounds on him, and barked, "If that's how you approach practice, we're going to have a problem."

McGinnis's ego was too swollen for him to accept even implied criticism, which Larry's wasn't.

"Then think about trading me," George snapped back.

"You got it," Larry said grimly.

Eighteen months later, McGinnis was traded to Indiana for Alex English and a draft choice.

With that kind of commotion a new staple of my basketball life, thank God I had some stability on the home front, provided by my girlfriend Cathy. We had been seriously dating for three years and the time was coming for me to pop the question. But it would still be a few months until a certain special occasion that I had in mind arrived.

While growing dissension and clashing egos were making things more difficult on the court, I did my best to get along with everyone. Of course I had my favorites, and I particularly liked to hang out with Scott, McGinnis and Anthony Roberts. The four of us and Dan Issel were the starters who opened the 1978-79 Nugget season. Bobby Wilkerson would have started in Roberts's place, but he was injured at the time. Still, we did well in the preseason for only having one home game, and the new-look Nuggets finished 5-3.

After an encouraging 9-4 regular season start, we went into a tailspin that became the longest losing streak in the history of the Nuggets. We dropped six straight games between November 11 and November 22. Coach Brown—who wasn't nuts about our team to begin with—was in a panic over the situation. Though we beat Seattle on their home court, 103-100, to snap the dry spell on November 24, we then promptly lost three more in row.

We were a true Jekyll-and-Hyde team that year. After finishing the first quarter of the season 10-13, we immediately reeled off five victories in a row, and won seven of our next nine games. Just as it looked like we had it all figured out, we then lost four of our next five. But then we won eight of our next nine. Go figure.

The weirdness wasn't just limited to the court. In mid-December we played back-to-back games against the Portland Trailblazers. In Denver on Friday, December 15, the Trailblazers beat us, 116-113. I had at least six dunks at one point and we were killing them—but Portland came back to eke out the win. The rematch was two days later in Portland. The Trailblazers won again, 123-110, and I didn't even play in that one because I got TKOed earlier outside the Coliseum by some guy who'd just gotten out of a mental hospital. I was standing there with McGinnis, Tom Boswell and Jeff Compton, when the guy, who appeared to be in his 20s, approached me and asked, "Which one is David Thompson?" Figuring he was an autograph seeker or wanted to shake my hand, I fessed right up—whereupon the guy lunged forward and punched me right in the mouth. He might have been nuts, but he could whack, and I lost a tooth right there.

I don't know what that guy's diagnosis was, but anybody following the Nuggets could only conclude that we suffered from full-blown schizophrenia, the way we'd look unbeatable one night and like a rec-league team the next.

Maybe it was worry about ending up in a straitjacket himself from trying to deal with so many enlarged egos and attitudes that caused Coach Brown to finally call it quits on February 1, 1979. With Denver sporting a 28-25 record, the Nuggets said goodbye to the only coach the team had ever known.

My feeling still is that Coach Brown had just had enough of the veterans' behavior. He was a guy who liked to teach younger players the finer points of the game. Coach Brown also had a history of blowing into town, taking over a franchise that needed fixing, working his magic, and leaving once his job was complete. To this day, he has always left a franchise in much better shape than he found it. Coach Brown resurfaced soon thereafter as head coach at UCLA.

Coach Brown left Denver with a 186-115 record—a stellar 61.8 winning percentage. I never averaged fewer than 24 points per game under Larry, and only wish I could have brought him a championship. Nobody deserved it more.

One last comment on Larry Brown: the man was *loyal*. Many Nuggets fans could not believe it when Bobby Jones was sent to Philadelphia for George McGinnis. Though McGinnis was an excellent player, Jones was a blue-collar, hard-working, team-oriented, outstanding player at both ends of the court. But what most didn't realize was that Bobby took medication for epilepsy and suffered from asthma that was exacerbated by the thin Colorado air. Every game was a struggle for him. Bobby just couldn't breathe well in Denver. So Coach Brown went out of his way to help him, even to the detriment of the team, by getting him someplace where he could be 100 percent again. That was typical of Larry Brown.

Taking over the reins of the team was Donnie Walsh, one of Larry's assistant coaches who had played college ball with Brown at North Carolina, and earned a law degree there in 1965. Though he had opportunities in the legal profession after graduation, Walsh instead chose to become an assistant coach at his alma mater. He went on to serve for 12 years as an assistant under legendary South Carolina head coach Frank McGuire, before deciding in 1977 to belatedly make use of his law degree.

Walsh had just passed the South Carolina bar exam preparatory to hanging out a shingle when, on a hot August day, the scales were tipped back in favor of basketball by a call from his friend Larry Brown offering the assistant coaching job with the Nuggets.

Donnie's coaching style was calmer than Coach Brown's, and though his approach took a few games to get accustomed to, positive results soon followed. But first came the All-Star Game, played February 4 in Detroit, Michigan, at the Pontiac Silverdome.

Cathy and I flew to Las Vegas and married on January 31, and spent a few days there to relax before we hopped on a plane for Detroit. I arrived in plenty of time for the game, and in superlative spirits. My proposal had come as a surprise to Cathy, but it shouldn't have. I loved her very much, and what better time to sign her to a lifelong contract than right before the All-Star Game.

The 1979 NBA All-Star Game had a distinct ABA flavor. Once again, I had led the fan voting, and five out of the 10 starters were former ABA guys. Even George McGinnis, my Denver teammate, was voted a starter. Only three players had over 20 points that afternoon—me (25), Julius Erving (29), and George Gervin (26). Since my West team beat Erving's and Gervin's East team, 134-129, and on the strength of my first-half play (including a number of highlight-reel dunks) that helped us to a commanding 80-58 lead, I was named the MVP of the game. That was quite special, making me the only player ever to be named MVP of both the ABA All-Star Game (1976) and the NBA classic.

Cathy always kids me that the reason I had such a great game and was voted MVP was because we were newlyweds. If you think I'm going to disagree, you're a braver husband than I am. But that was one great weekend. I also signed a new shoe deal and unveiled my new Pony sneakers for the first time during the All-Star Game. The positive vibes continued as we prepared for the stretch drive toward the playoffs.Coach Walsh led us to a 19-10 mark after his promotion, but we had to win 10 of 12 at the end to see postseason action. We made the playoffs, but failed to capture the Midwest division title for the first time since we joined the NBA. On the last day of the regular season, we were tied with the Kansas City Kings with identical 47-34 records. We lost a heartbreaker to the 76ers in Philadelphia, 112-111, as I scored 44 points—including 20 of our last 23.

But the Kings won their game against the Indiana Pacers 107-101, and the division crown was shuttled east to Kansas City. To his credit, Kings head coach Cotton Fitzsimmons did a heck of a job with his young team.

We were dealt another serious blow when McGinnis went down with a severe ankle injury in one of the last games of the regular season, and we lost Big George for the playoffs. That would prove detrimental as we prepared for the Los Angeles Lakers and their All-League center, Kareem Abdul-Jabbar, in the first round, three-game series.

Still, we should've taken them. Our regular-season records were identical, and we had home court advantage. We'd gone 29-12 in Denver during the season and made the Lakers number 30 in the opening playoff game. Issel took Kareem outside and burned him for 30 points and 10 rebounds. We'd all drive the lane and then kick it out to Dan because we knew that Kareem wouldn't go out that far. But it was a different story for Game 2 in L.A. We never did get going and lost 121-109.

Game 3 was played on Easter Sunday in Denver, and it was close the whole way. I hit two free throws with under 20 seconds to play to give us a 111-110 advantage. The Lakers then went to their money man—Jabbar. With 12 seconds left, he converted one of his patented skyhooks to put the Lakers up by one. We had the ball for the last possession, and as precious time dwindled down I drove straight down the lane, determined to win the game and the series.

Just as I went up, the Lakers' Ron Boone bumped me and my shot went off the mark. Down low in the post, the refs don't have a good line of sight, so there was no whistle. The ball came off the rim, and I jumped as high as I could to tap in the rebound. But Kareem swooped in first and knocked the ball away. Game over.

I felt like that skier who tumbled off the course in the ABC *Wide World of Sports* montage. David Thompson had become the NBA's poster child for "The Agony of Defeat." Like that skier, I had tasted "the agony of defeat." And it was pure agony. This was the fourth straight year I thought we could go all the way, only to end up watching the title go to somebody else. It was a very empty feeling.

I did finish sixth in the league in scoring that year with a 24.0 average and also surpassed 8,000 points for my pro career. But that wasn't enough for many people. They could only see that the "Four Million Dollar Man" had scored less than previous seasons and that the Nuggets experienced their earliest playoff exit in four years. What they failed to realize was that we were not a team like the Lakers, Spurs or Jazz, which respectively had Jabbar, Gervin and Maravich as their main source of point production. We also had McGinnis, Issel, Scott and others who could really put up numbers. There was no way I was going to hog the ball just to prove I was worth $800,000 per year. My game was still a team game.

Speaking of team, Cathy and I added a new member to our roster at home with the birth of our first daughter, Erika, on July 20, 1979. My dunks on the courts didn't hold a candle to the joyful leap I did in the hospital when Erika came into this world. In fact, we enjoyed having a daughter so much, we welcomed our second daughter, Brooke, into our lives on July 13, 1981.

As the 1979-80 season approached, Carl Scheer came up with what he considered an inspired idea to have us hit the ground running—literally. Our problem wasn't chemistry after all, Carl decided, but rather conditioning. Or lack of it. Carl himself was a devoted runner and decided that what was good for him would be great for us. So in the preseason we were out on the track a lot, running 10Ks. I don't know what it did for our cardiovascular systems, but thanks to all that running, I developed a condition known as plantar fasciitis, more commonly known as bone spurs on the heel. The more you run, the worse the pain becomes. And the pain was excruciating.

I wasn't the only one having trouble. McGinnis came in out of shape because of his ankle injury, and everybody was grumbling and moaning about all the running. Were we training to play basketball or for the Boston Marathon?

Donnie Walsh had signed a new contract to stay on as head coach of the team. At South Carolina, Donnie had helped develop star guard John Roche. Roche was now working toward his law degree, but Walsh—himself a product of Larry Brown's raid on the legal profession—coaxed him back out onto the court to practice draining three-pointers. The three-point shot was finally being allowed in the NBA that season. I remember one game during the year in which John nailed *eight* three-point bombs. That was amazing after being away from the game for three years. John played in all 82 games that year, scored 11.4 points per game, and led the team in assists with 405—a 4.9 average. He was also ninth in the league in free throw shooting. Beat that, Matlock!

But the season was a flat-out bust for the Nuggets. We emerged from the preseason with a woeful 2-6 record and then proceeded to lose the first seven games of the regular season. Our opening-game loss to the Bucks, 125-96—at home, no less—set the tone for one very long year. We didn't win our first game until October 27 and went on to post a franchise-worst record of 30 wins against 52 losses, including losing a record 15 straight games on the road. In our last game that season, the Bucks put an exclamation point on our misery and frustration by administering the most lopsided defeat in Nuggets history, 143-95. We finished tied with Chicago for third place in the Midwest division. This time we didn't even earn a bid to the playoffs.

There was trouble everywhere that depressing year. In a December 16 matchup with the Seattle Supersonics, George McGinnis collided with referee Jess Kersey. Kersey thought George did it on purpose and tossed him out of the game. Commissioner Larry O'Brien then handed down a 10-game suspension without pay for McGinnis. George insisted the contact with Kersey was purely unintentional and demanded a hearing in O'Brien's office. O'Brien eventually whittled down George's suspension to three games. The very night that George returned to action, January 2, 1980, against Detroit in Denver, he was thrown out of the game after picking up two technical fouls. Even Coach Walsh said it was a good call.

One year to the day from when Coach Brown resigned—February 1—one of the most one-sided trades in the history of the NBA took place. The Nuggets dealt McGinnis, who was suffering from a confidence crisis, and a first-round draft choice to the Indiana Pacers. George would only play two years in his native state before retiring. In return, the Nuggets received the player who eventually became their all-time leading scorer. Six-foot-seven, 190-pound Alex English came out of South Carolina with a feathery touch but absolutely no advance warning that he was an assassin in shorts. But he proclaimed that in his Nuggets debut, scoring 29 points and yanking down 13 boards as we stomped the Chicago Bulls, 122-111 at home.

McGinnis averaged 13.2 points and four rebounds for the remainder of the season with the Pacers, and Alex put up All-Star numbers: 21.3 points per game and 9.4 rebounds. Who would you say got the best of that deal?

If I appear to be bending over backwards to divert attention from my own performance that season, the reason is that there isn't much to talk about. I played in just 39 games.

The heel spurs I'd developed worsened with every game, and by December I was in serious, constant pain. I had to sit out in late December and came back on January 9 against the Bullets in Denver. Though I scored 31 points in the 121-90 victory, I stressed the ligament that runs from the heel to the ball of the foot so badly that it was decided to put my foot in a plaster cast. Thus began some of the darkest days of my life. Cathy and I had been married almost a year, we had our first daughter, Erika, and I was making more money than I ever dreamed of. One would think that I had the world by the tail. To the contrary, though, something had *me* by the tail, and it was cocaine.

My use of the drug had increased steadily the past few years, and now I was thoroughly addicted. I never would have acknowledged it then, of course, but I think that in the back of my mind, I knew it. Cathy knew it, too, and probably a lot of other people close to me. I disappeared from the team for long stretches, causing everyone anguish. Here I was one of the team's premier leaders, and I was running away to be with my mistress drug.

Inevitably, my drug usage began to affect even my play. I resigned my team co-captaincy in early December because it was hard to be a leader when I was frequently late to practice and missing team flights. My behavior was unacceptable, especially for someone who had always held others to a high standard. That was pointed out to me, but I was far too gone to care. There isn't a day that I don't regret what I put the people closest to me through back then.

My personality had undergone a metamorphosis, many teammates and friends noticed. I had a bit more of an edge and was quick to anger. When cocaine sinks its hooks into you, these are just outer symptoms. Throw in a dependency on alcohol, to boot, and what you get is somebody not known and admired for his congeniality.

For all that, I managed to maintain my involvement in the Denver community. It was almost as if I led two very different lives. I performed a lot of work for muscular dystrophy, participated in bike-a-thons and read-a-thons with children. I even donated my time to make a television commercial with four TV sportscasters promoting Denver's annual "Symphony Run"—a charity event to raise money for the civic orchestra. But dearest to my heart was a connection arranged by the Make-A-Wish Foundation, the wonderful organization that helps the dreams of terminally ill youngsters come true.

The team had been contacted by the Make-A-Wish people regarding a 17-year-old named Mark Lyons of Schenectady, New York, who wanted to meet me. Mark had been battling cancer for five years. His left leg had been amputated, and things were looking grim. We had just finished a game in Boston on a Friday night, and I flew into Albany the next morning. When I arrived at the Lyonses' house, Mark's mother told me, "He just got himself so psyched up about this. This morning he told me, 'David Thompson is coming to see me because he loves me.'"

Until the onset of his illness, Mark had been an excellent athlete, as evidenced by multiple basketball and hockey trophies displayed on top of the family television. To see them and then see the boy who'd earned them so sick that he couldn't get out of bed jolted me more than any basketball score ever would again.

Mark had invited some friends to share our visit, and we spent a couple of hours discussing basketball. Before I left to catch a plane for Washington, D.C., where we were playing the Bullets the next day, I asked Mark if he would sign one of his high school pictures for me. Who wouldn't like an autographed photo of a genuine hero?

That evening, Mark Lyons quietly passed away. I carried a heavy heart for months after hearing the news; I also carried his picture everywhere I went. Mark's quiet dignity and enormous courage touched me in a very special way, and I will never forget him.

The summer after the 1979-80 season ended, Cathy, Erika and I took a vacation to Myrtle Beach, South Carolina, so I could clear my head and start over. I just wanted to run on the beach and spend time with my family. Cathy had arranged for our hotel accommodations over the phone, using a credit card. But when we arrived, the hotel clerk—an elderly lady— announced that there wasn't a single room available for occupancy. Our reservation? There was no record of it. Some things were harder to lose— like racial prejudice. It was pretty obvious from the clerk's manner that she didn't want her establishment sullied by an interracial family. Such things were still an abomination in Old Dixie, even in the year 1980. After reporting the incident to my agent and the Better Business Bureau, we moved on to another hotel and had no trouble registering.

As the new hoops season approached, the Nuggets were experiencing deep financial pain. This would be the first year they would qualify for a share of the CBS television revenues, but in the meantime the well was running dry. The organization asked me to do two things: take a deferment on my salary to help out, and write a personal letter to be sent to all Nugget season ticket holders. The letter would express how personally sorry I was for the team's and my own performance the previous season and vow that we were totally committed to turning things around. I gladly did both, and even put the letter on my own personal stationary. I daresay that such a thing wouldn't happen today.

The Nuggets weren't the only ones in a growing fiscal bind. I was racking up some big losses of my own. Ted Shay had resigned his position at North Wilkesboro Bank to manage my financial affairs full-time. D.O.T.,

Inc. had more than enough assets to require a full-time manager, so Ted became that man. He put me on a $1,500 per month spending budget, and I trusted him completely, to the point of even signing my power of attorney over to him. With that one act, I basically handed over the keys to my entire financial empire to one man—a fatal mistake.

Ted kept me insulated from a lot of things. He never failed to give me good news when it came to my finances. It was the bad news, however, that Ted was reluctant to share.

But Ted couldn't keep me insulated from the letters I began receiving from my bank informing me about concerns regarding some of the suspicious transactions he was making.

I thought I had a lot of money saved up, but in fact Ted had made a lot of bad investments on my behalf. What hurt the most was when he sold our Cherry Hill home and pocketed about $134,000 in cash. Unbeknownst to me, Ted had developed a serious gambling problem, and the $134,000 went up in smoke.

After I fired Ted, I took him to court and a judge awarded me the deed to Ted's home. But Ted's wife and kids were there in the courtroom, and I knew I couldn't toss them out on the street. So I let it go, basically.

My finances went from bad to worse after Ted left, and I got involved in some other risky ventures. I became involved with the Red Robin restaurant chain through a partnership with Mark Oiness, president of MRD, Inc. of Denver. The arrangement was made by my new financial manager, Ron Gollehon. Oiness purchased the territorial rights to northern Colorado and southeastern Wyoming. This was 1980, and the 12-year-old Seattle-based firm specialized in gourmet hamburgers, but also offered steaks, seafood, salads, and various desserts. I thought it was a good investment because the original Red Robin grossed $1.65 million in 1979. My up-front investment was around $650,000 for two franchises. The plan was for me to make special appearances when the restaurants opened and then stop in from time to time just to see how things were going. Never in a million years did I think this potential cash cow would yield only sour milk.

I also invested heavily in exploratory tax shelters for oil and gas, which were later disallowed by the government. These particular investments would ultimately lead to a knock on the door from the IRS and become my financial downfall.

Another constant drain on my finances were my friends, who thought nothing of sponging off their buddy, the "Four Million Dollar Man." I owned a condo on a golf course at Perry Park, which I leased out as an investment. I brought a few people out to Denver around my third year in the league, gave them the keys to the place and paid the mortgage every month. Some got jobs, some came to me for handouts, and some just up and disappeared after a stint of non-stop partying at my expense. It was a constant headache, and if you want to lose your faith in your fellow man real fast, give that arrangement a shot sometime.

The good news was that when I showed up at my summer basketball camp in Golden, Colorado, I was running like the Skywalker of old. My feet weren't aching, and I was throwing down violent dunks like a college senior. Too violent, I guess. It was during a dunking routine that I suffered a bruised shoulder, which curtailed my play for a while. "It's nothing to worry about," I told the press. "It resulted from my being so happy to be able to do the things I've always done on the basketball floor. I guess I went a little overboard."

I had an excellent year in 1980-81, averaging 25.5 points per game and finishing second to Bernard King of the Golden State Warriors in the "Comeback Player of the Year" voting. My scoring average was good for fifth in the league, but we still finished with a losing record, 37-45, a meager seven-game improvement over the year before. We did become the first team since the 1971-72 Warriors to post a trio of 20-point-a-game scorers. Alex English was tenth in the league at 23.8, and Issel finished with 21.9 per game. In fact, that season the Nuggets began a five-year string in which the team averaged better than 120 points per game. On February 13, the Nuggets set a new single-game scoring franchise record while beating the Portland Trailblazers 162-143. The problem was that while we could score virtually at will (a league-leading 121.8 points scored per game), we couldn't defend to save our lives (a league-worst 122.3 points given up per game).

Losing doesn't get you into any All-Star Games. Though I felt strongly that Alex and I deserved to be in the midseason classic that year, we were shut out. How the fifth leading scorer in the league is excluded from the All-Star Game is something I still haven't figured out yet. There must have been some kind of new math involved.

There was a key addition to the team in 1980-81. As if we didn't already have enough offensive firepower, Carl Scheer went out and picked up 6'8", 220-pound Kiki Vandeweghe from UCLA. Kiki would become a real force the next year.

Thirty-one games into the season, Donnie Walsh was fired and assistant coach Doug Moe was promoted. We were 11-20 when the change was made, and under Moe we went 26-25 for the remainder of the year.

Once a star of the New Orleans Bucs in the ABA, Doug became an assistant coach under Larry Brown with the Carolina Cougars and worked his way up through the ranks. Moe was fired as head coach of the San Antonio Spurs in 1980 after posting a .500 record. That's when Walsh made him his assistant coach.

Doug favored the run-and-gun motion offense, designed to wear down the opposition every time out. He called it "playground style with a little supervision." Doug was a harsh disciplinarian—a tough guy whose vocabulary could make a longshoreman blush. Everybody knew that if you got out of line, Doug wouldn't put up with it. His own behavior could be wildly unpredictable at times.

Here's a true story that illustrates my point. A few years after I left the team, Moe got so disgusted with his players' lack of defensive play in a November 2, 1983, loss to the Portland Trailblazers that, with a minute to go and trailing 146-116, Moe ordered his players to stop playing defense altogether. As a result, Portland blazed up the court for five uncontested layups to end the game. Moe was fined $5,000 and suspended two games for his "strategy."

It all came to a head the next season, 1981-82, my last in Denver. We improved to 46-36 and were back in the playoffs. We became the first team in league history to average more than 100 points per game in all 82 regular-season games. Unfortunately at the same time we were also the first team to *allow* our opponents over 100 points per game. Our average of 126.5 points per game was a new NBA high-water mark; once we even scored 150. We were an offensive juggernaut, but it was no thanks to me.

"Our offense comes to a grinding halt whenever David comes in," Moe told the *Rocky Mountain News*. That was news to me, but I wasn't surprised to learn how Doug felt about me.

I hadn't exactly endeared myself to him when I was 10 minutes late to practice on December 25. In my defense, it was Christmas Day. I was playing with my daughter Erika and had lost track of the time. Besides, who has practice on Christmas but Doug Moe?

As a result of being late, Doug was going to fine me $2,000 when normally a fine for the offense was $150. Clearly, Doug was trying to teach me a lesson.

I thought I'd find a sympathetic ear when I went to Carl Scheer to plead my case, but by then, the front office had decided to suspend me for two games. That cost me about $16,000 in salary. What should have been a $150 fine ended up costing me a whole lot more.

Because of my already strained relationship with Doug Moe, I was replaced in the starting lineup by T. R. Dunn despite the fact that I was still the most talented player on the team and the most beloved by fans. After the suspension, I never got my starting job back.

I couldn't place my finger on why, but Doug, I felt, had it in for me personally, and all my teammates knew it. Let's just say there was no love lost between the two of us at the time.

I missed 20 games in the early part of the season due to a back injury. But there were also incidents caused by my heavy drug and alcohol use.

On February 24, 1982, I missed a team flight from Los Angeles after a game against the Lakers. Three weeks later, on March 16, I missed a mandatory 11 a.m. game-day shootaround.

Of the 61 games I appeared in during my last season in Denver, I started in only five. I averaged 14.9 points per game playing only 20 minutes per game. It's tough to be very productive when you're in the proverbial doghouse.

The scoring leaders for our team that year were English (25.4), old reliable Dan Issel (22.9), and Vandewheghe (21.5). They led us into the playoffs after a two-year absence. We lost our opening series two games to one to the Phoenix Suns. I saw such limited playing time that it was obvious the time had come for me to go. Coach Moe played two 6'0" guards, Billy McKinney and Kenny Higgs, against the Suns' 6'4" Dennis Johnson and 6'6" Walter Davis. A neon sign over my place on the bench saying, "You're through!" might've been less obvious. In the last game, I played maybe 10 minutes. What hurt most was knowing that I could have helped us win.

Because I had a no-trade clause in my contract, the Nuggets couldn't ship me off. In fact, they even offered to resign me at $450,000 per year for five years. However, they didn't need to show me the door because I asked to be traded.

I presented the front office with a list of five teams I'd be interested in playing for, and found a willing taker in the Seattle Supersonics.

Head Coach Lenny Wilkens expressed immediate interest in me when he learned that I might be available.

Lenny and I agreed to fly out to Las Vegas in early June 1982. We took in the Gerry Cooney vs. Larry Holmes heavyweight championship fight and sat down for a long getting-to-know-you chitchat.

Lenny didn't waste much time before bringing up reports that I had a drug problem and was often late to practices or blew them off altogether. I told Lenny that I had used drugs, but that was a thing of the past. An honorable man, he took me at my word and we shook hands.

On June 16, the day before my trade was to be finalized, the *Denver Post* ran a front-page story exposing my problems with cocaine.

Britain and Argentina were at war over the Falkland Islands and there was trouble in Lebanon, but my drug use eclipsed that, at least in the Mile High City.

The *Post's* exposé consisted of seven separate stories and various charts, graphs and photos, none of which would get me elected mayor or voted "Citizen of the Year."

The paper jumped through the legalistic hoop of "alleging" my denudations and noted that I had never been arrested for a drug-related offense. There were no eyewitness accounts of my stumbling out of a cocaine den with white powder all over my face.

But it was reported that the Denver Police Department started its own investigation of me after the Nuggets front office hired three off-duty Denver policemen to keep an eye on my extra-curricular activities. My days as a model Denverite and exemplary professional basketball player were kaput. It was definitely a time for a change of scenery.

As I said earlier, professional sports is a business, and if you think the revelations about me put the kibosh on Seattle's interest in making a trade, I admire (and worry about) your innocence. The Sonics still went for it, only now it didn't cost them so much. In return, Denver accepted 6'7" forward Bill Hanzlik and a first-round draft pick.

I finished my Denver years with 11,992 points—good enough for third on the Nuggets' all-time career scoring list. I also still rank in the top five in nearly every Nuggets scoring category.

I just wish that I would've gone out in a blaze of glory instead of headlines and scandal.

CHAPTER 17

A CHANGE IN SCENERY

A t 28 years old, I was considered an old man in the NBA, with my greatest conquests behind me. "King David" was no longer viewed as basketball royalty, but as an expensive benchwarmer at a crossroads in his career.

"Today, the crown on Thompson's head is cracked and more than a little askew," wrote Kevin Quirk of *The Charlotte Observer*. "Whether he can straighten it this season or next season—or ever—is something far more difficult to visualize than a Monte Towe-to-Thompson alley-oop against UCLA."

I greeted the news of my trade to Seattle as a welcome new chapter in my career—the second chance I needed. But the question that dogged me around the league was: Could I come back or was I on my way out?

Injuries had plagued me the past three seasons, and I was coming off my lowest scoring year as a pro. I averaged 14.9 points a game in 61 games during the 1981-82 season. That still wasn't so bad considering that I came off the bench and averaged about 20 minutes a night, or only about half a game.

I knew my talent was still intact, but it was my head that needed some adjustment. I had a lot to prove, mostly to myself. A change of basketball scenery would recharge my batteries and let me prove to everyone that I still had it on the hardwood. Second chances in the NBA didn't come often, and I was determined to make the best of my situation in Seattle.

Founded in 1869, the City of Seattle is located on Puget Sound, 113 miles from the U.S.-Canada border. Today, Seattle is a commercial, cultural and advanced-technology hub in the Pacific Northwest and a major port city for trans-Pacific and European trade.

Surrounded by majestic mountains and water, the greater Seattle area features picture-perfect views of Mother Nature. It was also a great place to raise our kids.

Cathy and I picked out a four-story, 3,800-square-foot condominium in Kirkland, Washington, overlooking beautiful Lake Washington.

Same as in Denver, I soon fell in love with Seattle. The city excelled in livability with a mild climate, a full range of arts, cultural and sporting events, an abundance of shops and restaurants (with some of the greatest seafood cuisine in the world), and easy access to outdoor recreational activities throughout the year.

Seattle was especially attractive to me because of its mild winters and cool summers. High temperatures in July average about 75 degrees, while lows in winter drop below freezing an average of only 15 days per year. It was a nice contrast to those harsh Rocky Mountain winters.

The basketball climate was equally attractive.

Seattle was awarded an NBA franchise in December 1966, and the club began play in the 1967-68 season.

Seattle's first NBA season ended at 23-59, second worst in the league to San Diego's rookie 15-67 mark. The Sonics experienced a typical expansion season, but were well received by the community and led the league in attendance from 1979 to 1982.

In the 1978-79 season, the Sonics won the NBA championship.

The Supersonics front office, specifically Lenny Wilkens and Seattle general manager Zollie Volchok, knew they were taking a gamble on me. They didn't seal the trade with Denver until after asking the NBA's security office to investigate rumors of my alleged cocaine abuse.

Weeks before, the Nuggets were being sold to B. J. "Red" McCombs, and the team's assets were tied up in escrow, which forced the Nuggets to miss their payroll.

I was due $350,000, and I brought in Larry Fleischer to get my money. We went to arbitration over the last check, and the Nuggets told me that if I said anything or made waves to the media, they'd bring up the rumors of my drug use.

Luckily for me, everything was cleared and the Sonics took me. I didn't even flinch when asked probing questions by the suspicious press corps.

"I'm denying I ever had a problem with cocaine," I boldly told reporters at my first press conference in Seattle.

Lenny planned to have me in the backcourt with Gus "The Wizard" Williams, one of the game's premier players of that time, averaging 23.4 points and 6.9 assists a game the previous season. We were going to be one of the most potent offensive combinations at the guard position.

"I've always been a big David Thompson fan, and at one time considered him to be among the 10 best players in the league," Wilkens told Kevin Simpson of the *Rocky Mountain News*. "Thompson will give a big dimension to our club."

I couldn't help but admire Lenny Wilkins, a great coach and motivator of people. Lenny is a natural teacher of the sport, and it's no accident he's the most successful coach in the history of the game.

Few people have enjoyed the success at both ends of the bench that Lenny has experienced. As a player, Lenny was both a collegiate headliner and an NBA All-Star playmaker. He led his Providence College teams to back-to-back NIT appearances and took tournament MVP honors in 1960.

By the close of his brilliant 15-year pro career, Lenny racked up 17,772 points and owned the NBA's second highest career assists mark.

As a coach, Lenny has rewritten all the coaching records in total victories, with more than 1,300 to his credit. Lenny joined John Wooden as the second man ever elected to basketball's Naismith Memorial Hall of Fame as both a player and a head coach.

As intense as he was as a player, Lenny was just the opposite as a head coach. Soft-spoken and laid back, Lenny realized he didn't need to scream at players in the pro ranks to motivate them.

Lenny constantly let me know that I had his full confidence and that he would try to take as much pressure off me as he could concerning the press. I couldn't help but be inspired to give the man my all.

I had the opportunity to play for Lenny before I signed on with the Sonics when I was invited by the NBA's Players Association to go on a two-week goodwill tour of China and the Orient.

Also along were Kareem Abdul-Jabbar, Artis Gilmore, George Johnson, "Downtown" Freddie Brown, Maurice Lucas, Marvin Webster, Alex English and John Havlicek.

We played teams from China, and the trip was a blast from day one. In China the fans didn't know our names, but they sure knew our numbers and all our moves on the court.

I wore jersey number 13 on that tour and was astounded when people constantly called out my number and asked me to dunk.

"You're number 13," one enthusiastic fan said after stopping me on the street. Then he pantomimed a two-handed dunk. Basketball is truly an international language.

The locals notwithstanding, I wasn't the most amazing sight in China. We went to Bejing, Shanghai, Hangzhou and Tiananmen Square, the infamous site where a military assault by the Chinese government would take place on pro-democracy demonstrators in and around Tiananmen Square in June 1989.

We also visited the Great Wall, the Forbidden City and the Ming Tombs, and the Mao Zedong Memorial Hall. Chairman Mao, of course, was the founder of the People's Republic of China in 1949 and one of the founders of the Chinese Communist Party. I learned that Mao was recognized as one of the most prominent Communist theoreticians and a great poet.

With red Sichuan granite at its base and trees around the hall, the facility is designed on principles of symmetry and "centrality." Sculptures north and south supplement the artistic rendering of national struggle presented on the Monument to the People's Heroes.

The first floor is open to the public. Behind the white marble statues of Chairman Mao is an immense tapestry of China's mountains and rivers.

In the Hall of Mourning, the heart of the mausoleum, lies Mao himself in his usual gray suit, draped with the red flag of the Communist Party, in a crystal casket.

Dead since 1976, the chairman nevertheless continued to draw crowds, although looking quite a bit worse for the wear.

After China, we found time to visit Hong Kong and Japan, but China to me was special.

Not only was it a great cultural experience, but it was an excellent way to get in shape for the upcoming season. I also had the opportunity to show my coach what I could do, and he was very pleased with the results.

I was also pleased with the Sonics' prospects of winning another NBA title. The team finished the 1981-82 season with a 52-30 record (.634) in the Pacific Division, second only to the Los Angeles Lakers.

Lenny boldly predicted that 1983 would be the year the Sonics would overtake the Lakers with a youthful, exuberant bunch of achievers. At the very least, we were ready to take responsibility for knocking Los Angeles off the cakewalk to its third NBA title in the last four years.

With me, Gus Williams, Jack Sikma, Lonnie Shelton, and guards Freddie Brown and Phil Smith coming off the bench, we had six players who had been NBA All-Stars. The Lakers had five.

The roster also included capable bench players such as 6'9" forward Ray Tolbert, 6'7" forward Gregory Kelser, 6'4" guard Mark Radford, 6'7" forward John Greig, 7'3" center James Donaldson, and 6'7" forward Danny Vranes.

Because number 33 was already taken by Ray Tolbert, I decided on number 44, my old number at NC State, thinking it might bring me good luck. For a time, it did.

My teammates made a concerted effort to make me feel welcome and had a lot of empathy for me and my situation in Denver. They accepted me right away, and I felt comfortable in the locker room despite the fact that I am quiet by nature.

"I was a loner as a player, too," Lenny told reporter Kevin Simpson, "and I have empathy for someone who wants to get back to where he was. When you're quiet, people make assumptions about you."

I preferred letting my play do the talking for me. The Sonics got off to a booming 12-0 start, and I was averaging 21.1 points a game on 52 percent shooting.

All streaks do eventually come to an end. We were dealt two consecutive losses by the New Jersey Nets and a crushing defeat by the Los Angeles Lakers. In those three games, I averaged 8.0 points a game on 27 percent shooting.

Even worse than those three defeats were my two sore knees, the right one from an accumulation of fluid and the left from a collision with the knee of Lonnie Shelton, a strapping 6'8" forward who weighed about 250 pounds.

The right knee began locking up on me, and the team's trainer diagnosed it a case of traumatic arthritis. I was forced to wear a brace on the right knee and had to ice down both knees for 20 minutes after each game.

Finally, I decided to have an arthroscopic examination done on November 29 on the right knee, which put me out of commission for seven games. The results were negative, but the knee remained sore for longer than anticipated. My condition left me depressed, and I took up again with a few "friends"—alcohol and cocaine. Even though I was a virtual stranger in Seattle, it didn't take me long to find a connection to get what I wanted. I had to take medication for the pain in my knee, but it only served to fuel my other addictions—insecurity being the worst of them. A lot of fears and doubts come with injuries, as pro athletes worry if they've lost their spot on the roster.

Freddie Brown, someone I respected, said he noticed I sank into an impenetrable shell after the injury, which affected my whole outlook. He suggested that I go to management and tell them I needed time to heal from the injury.

Upon reflection, I tried to come back way too fast from my injury. I felt that if I wasn't back out on the court, I'd end up knee-deep in the throes of my addiction. Playing hurt was the lesser of two evils.

As things played out, everything on the basketball court was just fine; it was off the court where I obviously had a problem.

We went on to win the next seven out of eight games and posted a 23-7 record going into the new year. I continued to play well, averaging double digits and taking top scoring honors in several games.

Unfortunately, I wasn't at the top of my game for my Denver homecoming on February 9.

It was nice to see old friends and fans, and I received a nice round of applause upon my introduction, but it was strange coming back and staying in a hotel in a city where I still owned a home.

Something else was missing, reporters noted. With seven minutes left in the fourth quarter, I stole the ball at halfcourt and had nothing but the hoop in front of me. But instead of throwing down a backboard-rattling jam, I politely dunked the ball. There was no use tearing up my knee in order to impress the crowd, but the critics tore me apart for not putting on a show.

With the Sonics mounting a last-minute threat, Lenny took me out of the game and replaced me with Freddie Brown. I had 18 points for the night, not bad by any means, but the Nuggets ended up with the victory,

134-125. The pressure of my return to Denver was finally over, but it had the wrong ending.

"The moment was there. The magic was not," wrote Rick Reilly of the *Denver Post*. "The night wasn't spectacular. David Thompson's return wasn't spectacular. But it was Everything-But-David-Thompson night at McNichols."

Columnist John Meyer called me America's highest-paid athlete who faded into the background.

Ouch! I think their comments hurt my pride more than my aching knees hurt me, and they really made it clear that the Mile High City was no longer my home.

I did, however, find a home on the West All-Star team roster when I was selected first team guard for the 33rd annual NBA All-Star Game on February 13, 1983.

"I'm as shocked as you guys," I told reporters upon hearing the news. I was both delighted and honored that fans thought enough of me to vote me onto the team.

I was also delighted to know that teammates Jack Sikma and Gus Williams, elected as reserves, would accompany me to Los Angeles for the All-Star Game.

I pulled out all the stops and flew out my parents and Vellie, Jr., from North Carolina for the weekend festivities.

"I knew you could do it, son," my mother said upon hearing about my selection. "I knew you could do it." Even though my parents lived in North Carolina, they knew all about the negative things that happened in Denver those last few years. This was the first good news they'd heard in a long time regarding my career.

Much to my surprise, the game's program featured me on the cover doing a reverse slam dunk.

Despite the fact that the West All-Stars lost, 132-123, my old rival from the ABA, Julius Erving, won the MVP on a 28-point performance. I managed to score 10 points, dish out two assists and make a steal in 17 minutes. Eight of those points were in the first half, and then Pat Riley, the coach of the team, started giving a lot of other guys (mainly his Laker players) some playing time.

The All-Star Games are usually fast-paced and loose and always a lot of fun. It was a great weekend.

Perhaps the most gratifying moment of that trip took place off the court. I was returning a rental car with my father when we happened to bump into Academy Award-winning actor Sidney Poitier, who happened to be one of my father's personal heroes.

Poitier in the 1960s was like Brando for the black generation. He was about the only actor we identified with and was a man of great dignity.

"You did a fine job raising this young man," Mr. Poitier said to my father, shaking his hand. "He's a good man and a great player." You should have seen the smile on my father's face. It only took about a month for him to stop beaming from ear to ear.

The Sonics, however, didn't have much to smile about. From December 30 to March 9, the team did an about-face and went 10-22, including an eight-game losing streak—the longest in the last 10 years of the franchise.

Things picked up when I returned to the starting lineup on March 9 against the Boston Celtics in the Garden. Williams, Sikma and I combined for 75 points in a 112-106 victory. Then the Sonics really got hot, taking 15 of 17 games during March and April.

On March 30, I went 15-22 from the field and achieved a season-high 38 points against the Detroit Pistons on our home court in a 135-124 victory.

The final 20 games of the season, we went 15-5, including winning streaks of six and eight games.

Despite this personal and team success, I turned once again to cocaine. I'd get high at night and not sleep much. Then I'd get up early and go to practice and repeat the same pattern over again. After a while, it started to wear me down.

By mid-April, Lenny noticed my erratic play. Sometimes I'd be great in practice and have a lousy game. Sometimes I'd have a great game and be lousy in practice. This inconsistency made him wonder, but Lenny had no concrete proof. That's when he placed a call to Doug Moe. Lenny made no mention of drugs or alcohol, but after he talked to Doug he was no longer suspicious. Still, he never said anything to me.

At times, I felt very alone in Seattle. Being in a new environment, and with so much riding on that season, a lot of my fears came to the surface. In an effort to avoid reality, drugs were the route I took. I used cocaine as my escape.

One morning after having indulged deep into the night, I reached my emotional saturation point. There was no particular game and no particular incident that brought me to the brink. I just woke up one morning and felt lousy.

I asked myself, "Why can't I live a normal life like the rest of the guys, like most of the world?"

I was tired of living in isolation, feeling paranoid that someone would eventually find out about my problem. I hid the problem from my teammates, which doesn't nurture healthy relationships. It was like driving a car and continually looking in the rearview mirror to see if anyone was following me. Years of living on the edge were catching up with me, and I wanted to make a clean break.

I had consulted with ex-Nuggets coach Donnie Walsh and Tom Baca, deputy director of Washington House, a treatment center in Denver, to discuss the possibility of getting help. That was a tough prospect, because not only did I have to admit to myself I had a problem, but being a national sports figure, I would have to admit it to the entire country.

I was also concerned about going into treatment at the end of my contract. Despite the fact that I had a 15.9 point-per-game average, shot 48.1 percent from the floor and was a starter on the All-Star team, I found little or no interest from other teams in the league.

The league had not exactly entered the age of enlightenment concerning addiction. Spencer Haywood claimed that when he approached Lakers head coach Paul Westhead about his problem, he was not only kicked off the team, but was blackballed from the league for a year.

"My confession was the leverage he needed to get me off the team," Haywood recounted in his autobiography, *Spencer Haywood: The Rise, The Fall, The Recovery*. Haywood was probably the only guy in the NBA to be tossed out of the league without ever getting drug tested or given any warning of his fate. The former Olympic hero was exiled to Italy for a year. Haywood did come back to the NBA for two more seasons, but his career was never the same and his name was besmirched for many years.

The NBA and the Players' Association were months away from establishing a landmark program in sports to battle drug abuse, provide treatment and rehabilitation. That meant I had to pay for treatment out of my own pocket, which wasn't cheap.

Today, the NBA teaches players how to recognize patterns of drug abuse in their teammates, how to react, how to intervene, and how to assist a person in getting help.

But back in the early 1980s, confession of a drug problem was an iffy proposition at best, with the Haywood case fresh in everyone's consciousness. Once you get that stigma attached to your name, it's a long row to hoe.

Donnie and Tom convinced me that going into a treatment center would help my position, but ultimately it worked against me.

With three games left in the regular season, on April 13, Cathy and I went to Lenny with the admission that I had a chemical dependency problem. That was a humbling experience, given that I had told Lenny to his face that all the long-standing drug rumors of my drug abuse were a thing of the past. Because of that, Lenny had pushed hard for my acquisition and stood fast in my corner when criticism of the deal mounted following reports detailing my possible involvement with cocaine.

It helped to have Dr. Ulysses Whitehead, a Seattle psychiatrist with close ties to the Sonics, with me when I told Lenny. Now I had to admit I had a real problem, and it was one of the hardest things I've ever had to do in my life. Naturally, Lenny was unhappy about being lied to before, but he was a complete gentleman and showed he cared about me as a human being.

"The way I see it, there's only one way to do this," Lenny said. "Complete rehabilitation, or don't come back to the team." No one had ever really put it to me in those terms before, but I respected the fact that Lenny was both tough and fair.

Everyone agreed the best course of action was for me to enter rehabilitation after the playoffs.

Meanwhile, I was placed on a medication to stop the cravings for drugs, but it didn't offer much help to me in my personal or professional life.

The Sonics lost their last three games of the year and placed third in the Pacific Division with a 48-34 record (.585). We drew the Portland Trailblazers in the Western Conference first round and knew we were in for a good, old-fashioned fight.

The Blazers were led by the balanced offensive attack of Jim Paxson, Calvin Natt, Mychal Thompson, Darnell Valentine, Kenny Carr, Wayne Cooper and Fat Lever. Defensively, the team got in our shorts and made us work for every shot down the floor.

The series started in Seattle on April 20, but the home-court advantage didn't matter much that night because we lost, 108-97.

Whenever a team loses a first game in a short series, the pressure to win the second game becomes even greater. Worse yet, we had to travel to Portland to try to even things up. That would be no easy feat, given the Blazers' toughness plus the ferocity and loyalty of their fans.

Two days later on April 22, we stayed with the Blazers for most of the second game, but then they pulled it out, 105-96.

For the most part, our effort against Portland was lackadaisical; we basically phoned in our performances. Gus Williams was the only Sonic player who showed up ready to play, averaging 32.5 points per game in the series. The rest of us just shot poorly, with Sikma going 40 percent from the field. I shot just 36 percent while the usually reliable Fred Brown shot 22 percent.

The only upside to the loss was that it cleared the way for me to get immediate treatment in a 28-day program.

On May 4, I entered the Washington House in Denver. For a young man accustomed to Marriots and Hiltons, it was a rude awakening.

The first hurdle I had to clear was the shock of getting out of bed at the painfully early hour of seven o'clock in the morning. Shoot, when I was out carousing and getting high, that's the time I usually went to bed.

The daily regimen was strict, and everything on our schedule was mandatory. No ifs, ands or buts. Breakfast was at 7:30, and then the real fun began. Housecleaning was never my thing, but everyone was required to make their beds, vacuum the floors and clean the bathrooms. Inspection was three times a week, followed by a meeting called, "Client Community." That meant if anyone missed a hair in the sink or left dust on the doorsill, they were called on the mat by inspectors.

The first week was tough, but eventually I became comfortable with the routine. I learned that a daily schedule was even helpful in keeping my mind occupied while my body detoxified itself.

Part of the therapy at Washington House involved writing an autobiography in which I had to recount everything about my addiction, with no lurid detail left out. I had thought that would remain a private matter between a counselor and myself, but much to my uncomfortable surprise, I had to share it with a group of other addicts in the program.

Emotionally, I was a tough nut to crack because I'm a very private and shy person. But when I heard the revelations of other addicts, I realized the sessions were designed to serve as a catharsis for all of us.

When it was my turn to pour my heart out, I was surprised at the weight that was lifted off of my shoulders. It was such a release.

For years, I had been hiding the details of my addiction. So many things I was afraid to tell other people and didn't even want to have to deal with myself. All the guilty feelings I associated with my character defects were buried deeply in the pit of my stomach.

The rehabilitation process, I came to discover, was like releasing pressure at intervals—much like letting the air out of a tire little by little. It started with the pressure of the world finding out about my addiction. When that fell to the wayside after I sought treatment, then came new pressure in facing other anxieties such as dealing with fear and anger.

I had a lot of hostility built up over the years, combined with resentment towards certain people. Because I don't vent my frustrations as often as I should, that triggered my addictions and made it harder to break free.

Rehabilitation offered another unexpected sort of release, involving a reunion of sorts. Part of treatment encourages belief in a higher power—albeit not necessarily one with religious overtones—as a means of dealing with addiction. For me, my relationship with God had been a foundation of my youth when life was much simpler.

I came to the realization that I could no longer take on my addiction alone, and by reestablishing my relationship with God, I could put things in His hands to take the pressure off of me.

Looking back, the pressure I felt at Washington House was nothing compared to the pressure waiting when I got out. Facing all the worldly temptations on my own was, I discovered, when the problems really began.

One of the first things I concentrated on when I got out was starting the process of making amends to people I harmed through my addiction. Two people loomed large on that end: my wife Cathy, and my coach, Lenny Wilkins.

Cathy was there for me; that I knew and could count on. Lenny, however, wasn't a sure bet. I felt horrible about letting him down after he went out on a limb for me in public.

A formal apology to Lenny from me was a sure thing, and when he came to visit me one day at the Washington House, it was the first thing I did. Lenny, as gracious as ever, accepted my apology without so much as blinking an eye. He also told me he still needed me on the team. I needed to hear that.

While my friendship and trust with Lenny was secure, I couldn't say the same for the Sonics' front office.

You see, my $800,000 contract with the Sonics had expired after the playoffs, and they weren't so sure they wanted me back on the team.

I had no bargaining chip I could cash in. Everybody was waiting to see if I would play it straight, or go straight downhill. It was all my choice.

One thing was for sure: my days as one of the league's top-salaried players were over. Larry Fleisher was very upfront and told me to expect less money and more stipulations. If the Sonics, or any other team in the league, was willing to take a chance on me, he said, they would demand a clause stating that if I ever used drugs again my career would be over in the snap of a finger.

Sonics owner Sam Schulman had been very upset by the team's sudden implosion during the playoffs. I'm not sure if Schulman took into consideration that we had a lot of key injuries throughout the year, affecting Jack Sikma, Gus Williams, Danny Vranes, Freddie Brown and myself. Schulman was equally put out when he found out through a reporter that I was entering a treatment center. As far as my future with the Sonics was concerned, Schulman was not about to tip his hand as to what course of action he intended to take.

"The proof of the pudding is with him," Schulman told reporter Kevin Simpson of the *Rocky Mountain News*. "He has to prove himself. I've seen a lot of so-called rehabilitation cases. Some succeed, some don't."

While the Sonics pondered their options, I stayed busy working on myself. I also stayed in shape by playing lots of basketball, hosting clinics for underprivileged youth, visiting children's hospitals, and getting reacquainted with my family. I hung around with the people I loved—people who naturally made me feel good so I wouldn't have to look for approbation in a bottle or a glass pipe.

And, for a while, it seemed to work.

CHAPTER 18

WOUNDED KNEE

T here's only one fate worse for a professional basketball player than sitting on the bench—not knowing if you're going to suit up at all.

That's the reality I faced going into the 1983-84 season with the Seattle Supersonics.

But I wasn't the only one in the organization facing a possible change. Sam Schulman and his partner, Eugene Klein, who owned the Sonics for the first 16 years of their existence, were selling the team to Ackerley Communications, a Seattle-based communications firm owned and operated by Barry Ackerley.

Ackerley was a hands-on owner who announced right up front that he intended to hold the coaches and general manager, as well as the players, accountable for any failure. The rainy Northwest metropolis of Seattle had gotten used to being a winner in pro basketball and now had little patience for anything less.

The new ownership regime and Team Thompson (Larry Fleisher and I) started all from ground zero, mapping out my future with the Sonics.

The 1983-84 squad saw the sad departures of several teammates. Veteran guard Phil Smith (5.7 ppg, 1.6 rebounds, 2.7 assists) was given an unconditional release from the team and decided to retire. Power forward Lonnie Shelton (12.4 ppg, 6.0 rebounds, 2.0 assists) fell into disfavor with the coach and was virtually given to the Cleveland Cavaliers for a second-round draft choice and some cash. We also lost backup center James Donaldson (11.8 ppg, 7.9 rebounds, 1.9 assists), who signed a four-year deal with the organization and then was promptly traded to San Diego.

Shelton and Donaldson had taken a lot of the rebounding and physical pressure off Jack Sikma, who would now be required to carry most of the workload down in the trenches.

The team featured several new faces acquired through a series of trades and draft picks: 6'6" guard-forward Al Wood, 6'9" forward-center Steve Hawes, 6'6" forward Reggie King, 6'4" guard Clay Johnson, 6'10" forward-center Tom Chambers, 6'2" guard Jon Sundvold, 6'9" forward Scooter McCray, and 6'8" guard-forward Craig Dykema.

Returning to the team were veterans Sikma, Gus Williams, Freddie Brown, John Grieg and Danny Vranes.

In August 1983, Lenny Wilkins took 12 players on an exhibition tour of Europe. The swing took the team through West Germany, Italy, and Switzerland. It was a great way for the ball club to jell before the upcoming exhibition season.

Unfortunately, I didn't make the trip because I was still a contractual holdout.

I stayed clean of drugs for several months, but alcohol was another story. My drinking had become daily at that point, but I still had to remain drug-free, because at any point Larry could have struck a deal with the club. I had to be ready to submit to a drug test at a moment's notice.

In September, the Sonics' training camp opened in Bellevue with 10 veterans and eight rookies in attendance. I was the only veteran player unsigned, and the team forged ahead into the exhibition season.

I'm sure Lenny Wilkens was disappointed I couldn't come to some sort of agreement with the front office, but Larry's word was law when it came to business.

The team went 4-4 in the exhibition season, and everyone in the organization felt they had the makings for a possible championship year. However, most basketball experts didn't feel the same way and picked the Sonics to finish no better than third in the Pacific Division. In this case, the experts happened to be right on the mark.

On paper, the pieces of the puzzle all looked very nice, but for some reason we just didn't seem to fit together as a team. Too many changes on the roster shook up the team's chemistry, which led to a sluggish start.

On October 28, the Golden State Warriors spoiled the Sonics' home opener 110-109 in the Kingdome.

While the team inched along with an 8-7 record in November, my situation with the team inched closer toward some sort of reconciliation. Arbitrator Arthur Stark ruled that Seattle management could sign me at a preset salary figure without affecting the Sonics' salary cap. By December, things took a downward turn as the Sonics took a nose dive, posting a 4-8 mark for the month.

The Sonics ended 1983 with a crucial victory, defeating the Philadelphia 76ers in a 97-93 overtime game in Seattle. The win ended a string of three consecutive defeats in the Kingdome, the longest home losing streak of the year. Still the team was nothing more than a .500 ball club (17-17) when I came back in mid-January.

The reason the contract took six months to negotiate was that my agent, Larry Fleisher, insisted on a guaranteed contract, something the team brass did not want to go along with. The front office felt I was too fragile and my play too erratic to warrant such a deal. Luckily for me, Larry was a skilled negotiator whose tenacity landed me a one-year contract for $500,000. To make room for me on the roster, the Sonics placed Clay Johnson, who suffered from chronic tendonitis of the left knee, on the injured list.

The amount of the contract was for less than my previous $800,000-a-year deal, but still well above the league average. Let's just say I wasn't complaining and was more than glad to get back in a uniform and lend a helping hand to the team.

The Sonics were in third place behind the Los Angeles Lakers and the Portland Trailblazers when I suited up on January 18. The matchup against the Dallas Mavericks was the first regular-season game to be played in the new Tacoma Dome, which opened in April 1983.

The game was also memorable because our 114-107 win gave Lenny Wilkens his 500th coaching victory and the Sonics six straight wins.

On January 26, we reached the midway point of the season with a 22-19 record. I was splitting time with Al Wood on the floor. Al was having a very good year, posting an average of 14.3 points a game. As the sixth man, I was averaging 12.3 points a game and shooting 46.8 percent from the floor, even sparking a two-game winning streak.

On January 31, I injured the abductor muscle in my right leg on the last play in regulation in a 98-94 loss to the Utah Jazz. I was forced to sit out the next six games.

In mid-February, the team steadily improved and nailed its 11th straight Kingdome victory—the longest streak of the year—when we trounced the Washington Bullets, 116-99.

I also bounced back from my injury, and I had one of my best games of the year against the Los Angeles Lakers on February 21. The 102-91 victory in the Forum was one of our team's high points of the year. My 19-point outburst was especially satisfying to me as it came opposite Michael Cooper, one of the best defensive players in the history of the game. Michael was gracious in defeat, telling reporter Kevin Simpson, "David Thompson is an All-Star and is on his way back. I'm quite sure he's here to stay."

I wish he'd been a better fortune teller.

The Seattle Supersonics flew to the Liberty City to take on defending world champion Philadelphia on March 9.

The 76ers, led by Julius Erving and Moses Malone, handed us our fourth straight defeat, 92-84.

After the game, several of us decided to take our minds off our losing streak with an impromptu field trip.

Danny Vranes, Tom Chambers, Jack Sikma, Jon Sundvold and I decided to rent a limousine to take us to the Big Apple and Studio 54, the famous New York City nightclub that gave disco a face.

We arrived at the club around 2:00 a.m. and were instantly made at home. A bouncer let us through the throng of people waiting behind the velvet rope that stretched across the entrance, hoping to get a chance to party with the stars.

About an hour and a half after our arrival, I had already downed a few a drinks and was feeling no pain. That would soon change and I would be left with a hangover that would last for years.

One of the few things I remember about that night is asking Tom Chambers for directions to the men's room. He pointed toward a room at the top of a flight of stairs. I left our small group and headed in that direction.

Upon my ascent of the stairs, a man I came to know as Martin Santiago, a club employee, approached me.

Santiago was furious about something, but with the music blaring, it was hard to understand what he was yapping at me about. All I knew was that the man was giving off some bad vibrations, and he was right in my face.

I had my back to the staircase when Santiago suddenly pushed me. I fell back and instinctively grabbed his shirt. Together we tumbled down the stairs, just like in the movies. I felt my knee pop on the way down, and it started to swell up instantly. As we hit the bottom, I couldn't get up and Santiago popped me a couple of times in the jaw before another bouncer appeared out of nowhere and applied a full nelson on me. My teammates couldn't believe what they were seeing, and rushed over to peel the two employees off me. Our entire group was asked to leave the club, which was all well and good except for the fact that I needed an ambulance. The agony from the knee injury was unbearable, worse than any injury I had ever experienced before.

When Santiago found out I was a professional basketball player and not just some John Travolta-wannabe, he went into panic mode and invented a version of what occurred that had as much in common with the truth as disco has with gospel singing.

According to the official Studio 54 version, kindly provided to the press by club manager Neil Wilson, I was flirting with a hat-check girl and started coming on too strong. At which point, Santiago, being the Good Samaritan that he was, intervened. Wilson said I grabbed Santiago, ripping his shirt and tearing a gold chain off his neck. It was only then that Santiago was forced to defend himself and shoved me down the flight of stairs.

The only part that was accurate was that Santiago had shoved me down the stairs.

The fact is, though, that even the truth didn't exactly put me in a positive light. Getting hurt on the court and off the court are vastly different. It's easily justifiable for a player to get hurt on the court, but in a nightclub on a Saturday night at the world's most famous disco? It's not exactly falling on your face in church on Sunday morning.

On top of that, the news on my knee was devastating.

When I got to the hospital, the Sonics' orthopedic consultant was waiting to examine me. The knee had swelled to three times its normal size and was filled with pus and blood. The doctor knew there was extensive torn ligament damage, and he didn't make me wait for his prognosis.

"Your career is over," the doctor said. "You might as well retire."

The effect of his words was worse than the pain I felt in my knee at that moment. My heart just dropped. Basketball was my whole life—my entire identity. I wasn't David Thompson, who happened to play basketball. I was David Thompson the basketball player. That's certainly the wrong way to think, but for a long time basketball was my god. It was something I had done for most of my life, and all of a sudden, it was over. Just gone. Vanished.

Of course, Cathy wasn't happy about the incident either, which caused headlines in all the major sports pages across the country. In fact, she was both devastated and humiliated.

I had to keep the faith that everything would turn out okay, which is why I got a second opinion from Dr. Robert Loeffler, a well-respected surgeon from Denver.

"Your career doesn't necessarily have to be over," said Loeffler. "We've got some good techniques that will get you back out on the floor again." I must admit I liked his opinion much better.

On April 12, 1984, I underwent surgery at Denver's Presbyterian Hospital. The four-hour operation was to reconstruct the posterior cruciate ligament—which stabilizes the front and back knee—with tissue from a kneecap tendon. Loeffler also repaired a torn medial collateral ligament, the knee's inside stabilizer.

I left the hospital three days and 20 stitches later in a thigh-to-ankle cast that remained on for six agonizing weeks and subsequently was in an immobilizer for two more weeks.

Fortunately, I was able to watch the Sonics in the first round of the Western Conference playoffs. Unfortunately, they got dropped by the Dallas Mavericks 3-2 and went home early.

Next came the first weak efforts at rehabilitation, which were as frustrating as they were painful.

For some reason, I thought that as soon as the cast came off, I'd be walking in no time. But all I felt was severe pain for a long time, and my legs were weak and unmanageable, like I had polio. I was forced to use crutches to get around.

Only after several weeks of intense therapy did I finally see some improvement, and with that my hopes began to soar again. I targeted January 1985 for my return to the Sonics' lineup. Dr. Loeffler did not dismiss that prospect entirely, though he felt that might be a bit too optimistic.

I felt that even if I got back to the point where I was 75 percent, that was still better than a lot of players in the league.

The next few months my knee felt wobbly, and the eight-inch scar was a constant reminder to take it slow. But because of my reputation as a tough ballplayer, I tried to push myself harder than ever to show everyone I could still play.

My contract ran out in June, and major changes were again taking place within the Sonics organization that year. This led to much uncertainty about my future and left me wondering if I was ever coming back to the team.

This was also the season when the idea of a salary cap made a comeback in the NBA. The salary cap was not a new idea, and one was actually instituted in the inaugural 1946-47 season. The cap then was $55,000 per team, with most players earning between $4,000 and $5,000 per year. By 1984, that amount had swelled to $3.6 million per team, and the average NBA salary was $333,000.

The salary cap was instituted both to help maintain a competitive balance in the league and to quell skyrocketing salaries.

The former was necessary, salary cap proponents said, because teams with deeper pockets could simply outspend other teams for the better free agents. The basic idea was that a team can only sign a free agent if the total payroll for the team did not exceed the salary cap. So a team with deep pockets is playing on a level field with every other team.

Ackerley had signed 28-year-old Jack Sikma to a five-year, $7.5 million contract in June. Sikma, who led the team in scoring with a 19.1 ppg average on 49.9 percent of his shots, also led all NBA centers and power forwards with 4.0 assists a game and a personal best of 327 total.

Sikma's rebounding total of 11.1 a game ranked him sixth in the league, and he was the only member of the Sonics to play all 82 games in the 1983-84 season.

While Sikma was certainly worth every penny of his contract, his signing left the rest of the players wondering what their exact worth was and what their roles on the team would be for the upcoming season.

With a new NBA salary cap in place, it was apparent that Ackerley was building the team's future around Sikma, who would be in a Sonics uniform until at least 1990. We instinctively knew that meant other key players on the team would have to find a new home.

The Sikma contract virtually forced the Sonics front office to unload Gus Williams and his hefty $725,000 annual salary. Rumors had it that the Sonics' front office didn't relish the thought of having to deal with Gus's agent, skilled negotiator Howard Slusher. It was Slusher who advised Gus to sit out the entire 1980-81 season, which resulted in the Sonics missing the playoffs that year. That didn't endear Gus or Slusher to the Sonics' front office at all.

Gus was sent to the Washington Bullets for 6'3" veteran power guard Ricky Sobers and 6'11" rookie Tim McCormick as part of a three-way transaction in which Cleveland forward Cliff Robinson wound up in Washington and rookie Mel Turpin went to Cleveland.

McCormick, who hailed from the University of Michigan, was voted the MVP of the NIT the previous March. He was expected to play backup to Sikma.

I felt it was a trade that did the Sonics as much harm as good. Gus was an extremely talented All-Star guard who led the team to an NBA championship and was the heart and soul of the Sonics. Williams, in the words of Blazer coach Jack Ramsay, was "the best open-court player in the league."

Gus was second in team scoring (18.6), led the team in assists (8.4) and steals (2.36), and was a major box-office draw.

And sadly enough, 13-year veteran "Downtown" Freddie Brown, who was a free agent and legend in Seattle, didn't survive the cut.

My own future with the ball club still hung in the balance.

Larry Fleisher was busily negotiating a one-year $250,000 guaranteed contract for me, even though my playing status was a big mystery. To be honest, I didn't even know if I could play yet. When I played in pickup games during the summer, it was obvious that my jump had no spring or explosion to it. In professional basketball, a player needs that extra edge over his opponent because the level of talent is so great. A quick first step or a few extra inches on the vertical leap can make all the difference in the world. Once your body is out of synch, your whole game is off.

My knee's strength was also in question. Whenever I went in for a layup, my knee buckled. I even wore a knee brace full-time, but that didn't guarantee any stability.

Lenny Wilkens, who was my biggest supporter the past two seasons, spoke guardedly to reporters during training camp on the subject of my possible return to active duty. He himself refused to broach the subject at all and tried to deflect those who did by discussing the team on the practice floor.

"I'm really into this team right now," Wilkens said to reporter Kevin Simpson. "You're taking me down an avenue I don't need to be in. I wish him well and hope he gets back to where he can play. But we haven't had David since he was hurt. And we started building our backcourt. It's a good backcourt, we're confident in it. And as the year goes on, it's going to get better."

That wasn't exactly a ringing endorsement, and a pessimist could take it as a sign that my future in Seattle was as gray as one of the city's trademark overcast days. Like Lenny's answer, it appeared as if the question of my return might be best left unanswered. For the first time in my basketball career, it appeared as if there was a frightening ring of finality concerning my future.

One evening in October 1984, as the Sonics were leaving for an exhibition game in Vancouver, I wanted to show my support and bid them a fond farewell.

As I waved goodbye to my teammates on the special chartered bus, I had a sinking feeling in the pit of my stomach that I was on the outside looking in.

A week later, the Sonics waived back.

It was decided by the front office to place me on waivers because of my injury. By waiving me, the Sonics still had to pay me, but the contract wouldn't be counted against the team's salary cap. The Sonics gambled that while on waivers (a 48-hour process) no team would pick up the contract of a severely injured player with a troubled reputation.

This move allowed the organization to acquire guard Gerald Henderson from the Boston Celtics for $325,000. And if the organization wanted, they could wait for me to recuperate from my knee injury and add me back to their roster. Under terms of the collective bargaining agreement, Seattle would not have to sign me to an additional contract but merely resume the current deal, and consequently only a prorated portion of my salary would end up counting against the salary cap.

Had the Sonics kept me on the injured reserve list, my entire $250,000 salary would have counted toward the team's cap. That meant I was still too good a deal to cut loose just yet.

The Sonics were having a rough go of it in the 1984-85 season, and their status in the Pacific Division had dramatically dipped. They were tied for second to last place with the Los Angeles Clippers, the perennial doormat of the NBA.

Lenny wanted to activate me again, but Dr. Loeffler put his foot down and told me no. For the first time in my career, I listened to doctor's orders and didn't try to rush back out onto the court. My ultimate goal was to build up the strength in my knee and get back into the starting lineup. I didn't want to put an end to my career because I didn't have the patience to ride out the storm.

I guess it was just as well. The Sonics' record was a disappointing 31-51 (.351), and the team had no chance at making the playoffs. It was the first time since 1981 that the team didn't make a postseason appearance.

Rarely do athletes recover sufficiently from the sort of ligament damage I did to my leg and successfully resume their careers. However, I felt having the entire season off gave me sufficient time to make a full recovery.

I was still under contract to the Sonics for the summer, which meant that I was still regularly being drug tested. But that was okay by me; I just stuck to alcohol.

After the season, I spent a lot of time in Shelby playing one-on-one with my old teammate, Jerry Hunt, who gave me some really good workouts.

I was doing well by the time I joined the Sonics' pro summer league, a team comprised mostly of rookies and free agents who were looking for a spot on the roster. My comeback was miraculous considering that I was out of commission for so long.

Despite the fact that I played well in the summer league, the Sonics opted not to renew my contract and gave me an unconditional release. That meant I was a free agent and that the Sonics did not want compensation if another team signed me to an offer.

The Studio 54 incident had branded me with basketball's version of the scarlet letter, and the Sonics quietly waited out for my contract to expire before telling me they no longer required my services. Actually, I found out through a reporter that I was no longer with the team, and he knew a few days before I did. His pipeline to the management was obviously much better than mine.

The NBA could be a cold and harsh business. I compare the experience to being a new car. When a car is available on the market for the first time, everyone wants to be the first to test-drive it and show it off to the world. But after so many miles and expensive tune-ups, that same car is no longer able to perform like it used to, nor maintain its value. Inevitably, it gets traded in for a newer car. Some cars are a great deal, others…not so great.

I really couldn't tell what the owners thought of me or what kind of deal I was. Was I a used-up lemon that cost too much money for upkeep? Or did they view me as a classic Corvette with considerable miles but the potential to still tear it up every now and then?

The jury was still out on that one, but one thing I knew for sure: I was a player whose future was running on fumes with no garage in sight.

It was the first time in my life that I was a man without a basketball team. And I must say, I felt quite lonely without a uniform on my back, an arena full of fans to cheer me on, and a fat paycheck in my pocket.

CHAPTER 19

THE SLIDE

I was looking for a cure to get my basketball career and life back on track. In my particular case, a "geographical cure" was just what the doctor ordered.

In 12-step programs, a geographical cure means literally moving away from your problems. The idea behind a geographical cure is that by changing your playgrounds and playmates, life will somehow get better. Unfortunately, I found out the hard way that my surroundings might change, but my addictions did not.

Case in point: I had been given yet another shot at playing professional basketball, and I literally drank it away.

Donnie Walsh had taken over for George Irvine as the head coach of the Indiana Pacers, a relatively young team when they entered the 1985-86 season. Walsh, who went to bat for me in Seattle, was now taking up my cause with the owners of the team in Indianapolis.

By now, my name and public image had been severely tarnished, but Donnie, God bless his soul, felt for me and put his own neck on the line once again.

Walsh said he needed a proven veteran to help his young team get off the ground and that I was just the man for the job.

The Pacers had the makings of a playoff contender with the draft picks and trades they made their previous two seasons, although the team had taken a couple of hard shots.

In 1983, the Pacers lost a coin toss to the Houston Rockets for the rights to Ralph Sampson, a much-heralded 7'4" center from the University of Virginia. Sampson, whose career ultimately short-circuited in the pros, might have contributed greatly to the franchise. Instead, the Pacers had to settle for 7'0" center Steve Stipanovich from Missouri, who averaged 13.2 points a game over five seasons before injuries killed his promising career.

Perhaps even more heartbreaking than the Sampson coin toss was the missed opportunity to land 7'0", 240-pound center Patrick Ewing from Georgetown. Ewing had led the Hoyas to a national championship and was the most celebrated center in the NBA in years. Once again, the man flipping the coin for the Pacers called the wrong side, and the Pacers instead got 6'9" Wayman Tisdale, a scoring sensation from Oklahoma. Tisdale, a three-time All-American and one of the greatest players ever to come out of the Midwest, didn't quite mature into the prime-time player the Indiana front office had hoped for. Then again, the same was being said about me those days.

The Pacer 1985-86 roster included: Vern Flemming, a 6'5" guard out of Georgia who averaged 14.1 points a game his rookie year; Chuck Person, a 6'8" rookie forward from Auburn, who ended up averaging 18.8 points his rookie season; Steve Stipanovich; Wayman Tisdale; Clark Kellog, a 6'7" forward from Ohio State who contributed 18.6 ppg in his last season; Herb Williams, a 6'11" forward who averaged 19.9 points a game the previous season; and my old friend Quinn Buckner, a 6'3" 205-pound guard.

The Pacers finished in last place with a 26-56 record in the 1984-85 season, so the only place they could go was up. The same could be said for me, and the Pacers obviously felt the same as the team prepared to offer me a one-year $300,000 contract.

I had played extremely well in camp, got my hops back, mastered all the drills, and shot the ball well. I wasn't in the best of shape, but I was lighting it up in scrimmage games.

And because the team wasn't stockpiled with superstars, I honestly believed I had a real shot at the starting lineup once I got my wind back.

But as my confidence returned, so did my urge to celebrate. It was time to kick my feet up and toast my return to the NBA. In my book, the only thing that equaled the taste of success was the taste of a crisp, cool beer in a bottle.

The day before I was to sign my contract, I found a quaint little bar not too far from the practice facility. I was having a beer when a few basketball fans spotted me sitting there by myself. They asked to join me, and being that I was in a particularly good mood that day, I didn't object. People from the Midwest are quite friendly, and with some beer in me, I was at ease with these Hoosiers who lived and breathed basketball—my kind of people!

I asked the waitress for my bill before I excused myself to go the bathroom. When I got back, my new friends were gone. But they had left me a present. What should have been a $10 tab was now about $50. They had stuck me with the tab. I didn't mind their company, but I sure didn't want to pay for it. The waitress told me that after I went to the bathroom my "basketball buddies" told her I would pick up the tab. When I insisted that I had said no such thing, she got the manager, and he wasn't sympathetic at all.

"Pay the bill or I call the cops," he told me in no uncertain terms. I should have just paid the tab and been done with it, but you know how it is when you have liquid courage in your system: you're bound to put your foot in your mouth.

"Go ahead and call the police," I said "I'm not going to be black-mailed into paying this bill."

Within minutes, uniformed police officers arrived on the scene. The manager greeted them at the door and had a chance to make his case before I had the chance to tell my version of the story. Basically, the owner told them I hadn't paid my tab, which wasn't exactly true. I was just disputing the charges.

Not only did the police make me pay the entire amount, for good measure they hauled me off to jail for public intoxication. It took more than two beers to get me drunk, but the cops weren't in a listening mood. As a matter of fact, they were in more of a chatty mood, and once they caught wind of the fact that I was a professional basketball player, they called the media.

My arrest not only hit the local media, but burned up the sports wires across the nation. Not surprisingly, the owners of the Pacers no longer wanted me because of my self-destructive tendencies, and neither did any other team in the league.

Larry Fleisher had worked wonders for me over the years, but this time, even he lacked the magic to get an owner or coach to hire me. After nine years in the NBA, my basketball career was kaput.

Like a comet, I had blazed across the horizon and then burned out. The worst part was, I had no one else to blame.

I was so accustomed to a six-figure income for so long that it didn't really sink in how far I had fallen until the bills started to pour in and I had no means to pay for them. I was entitled to about $60,000 a year in disability pay from the NBA, but that was still a big drop in income. I had a large monthly nut that included a nice townhouse in Kirkland, Washington, a home in Denver, a wife and two kids to support, and a fleet of expensive cars.

I also experienced a precipitous drop in popularity. Friends who came by all the time stopped coming around. It was as if they had a sudden attack of amnesia and forgot how to find my home or dial my phone number. Guys in the league no longer called, either. Nobody wanted to be associated with me because of the stigma attached to my name. I can't say I really blamed them. Association brings assimilation, and in the NBA a whisper is as loud as a scream. So they all stayed away.

There was a former teammate of mine from Seattle, John Greig, who tried to be a good friend to me. John, a man of Christian faith, told me I needed to make more of an effort to get involved in the church.

"Quite often, if you pray, anything can be answered," John said. Other than John and my family, I had no real support system in Seattle.

Another part of my past was catching up with me as well. The Internal Revenue Service, in its infinite wisdom, disallowed a government-sponsored tax shelter that was part of an investment I made in Derringer Oil. Once they had been perfectly legal, but a few years later they were disallowed. Now the bad news: they presented me with a back-tax bill for $812,461 for 1978, 1981, 1982 and 1984. When Uncle Sam wants his money from Joe Citizen, he wants it now, and I was no exception. Well, I take that back; I was an exception because the amount in question was much higher than the Joneses down the street.

The IRS seized my $250,000 Kirkland home and two vehicles, a Mercedes 450 SL and a Ford Bronco.

Luckily for me, I managed to sell the home in Denver and cleared about $180,000. However, that money just went into the pocket of the attorney I had to hire to fend off the IRS, which was also slapping me for penalties and interest. All that brought my debt to a whopping total of approximately $1 million.

Even though I was once the highest-paid player in basketball with a $4 million contract, now I didn't have enough in the bank to write the IRS a check and wipe the slate clean.

When a $1 million debt is staring you in the face, the number becomes unreal, and then it becomes overwhelming. There's simply no way to pay it back, especially when you have no career any more. After some serious soul searching, I had to file for Chapter 11 bankruptcy, citing $2.2 million in debts.

I played all those years in the NBA only to find myself $2.2 million in the hole. I was wallowing in self-pity. I isolated myself and not only got deeper in debt, but deeper into the throes of addiction. At that point, I had no reason to stay clean. I was no longer being drug tested and was free to do as I pleased. The problem was, it didn't please anybody who loved me.

I was in serious pain and wanted to numb myself. I was looking for anything that would take me out of reality and give me a momentary emotional lift. I'd go through periods where I'd alternate addictions, first drinking heavily, then switching to freebasing cocaine. Then right back to my old reliable friend alcohol. It was a vicious cycle that had me in a vise-like grip, and I didn't know how to break free.

Finally I admitted myself to a treatment center in Seattle in January 1986.

The center followed the same principles of the Washington House, and both worked the 12-step program. I had become familiar with the steps, but I didn't take it seriously and just went through the motions.

Because my NBA insurance had run out, I had to pay for the treatment out of my own pocket. It turned out it was a big waste of my money and time because I simply wasn't ready to get clean and sober.

I ended up pinning all my hopes on a $10 million lawsuit pending against Cobhurn Enterprises, Inc., owner of Studio 54. I felt that if somehow I won the money, I could pay off the IRS and dance my way out of debt. But, I was to discover, I wasn't the only one suing the famous disco—there was a long line of claims filed against them to the tune of $20 million.

One of the lawsuits involved Mark Gastineau, a former New York Jets defensive lineman who was quite popular in the 1980s as a member of the infamous "Sack Exchange." Apparently Gastineau had challenged a handsome bartender to an arm wrestling match at the club and lost. Patrons were stunned and Gastineau was embarrassed, and he ended up punching the bartender in the face. The bartender ended up suing his employer instead of Gastineau.

Another story that made the rounds was that a jury awarded $50,000 to a patron who was kept outside of the club and sued for mental anguish. Turned out his fiancée broke up with him because he didn't have the clout to get inside.

Insurance companies recognized that as soon as they heard the words "Studio 54," juries immediately found for the plaintiff.

The new asking price for an insurance policy on the nightclub was $1 million, and as a cost-cutting measure the nightclub ended up dropping its policy. So much for hopes of a nice settlement.

So I turned to my two old pals, alcohol and cocaine, who always seemed to lift my spirits when I was down.

I was under the influence of both alcohol and freebase cocaine when I committed one of the worst mistakes of my life. Some of the symptoms of drug abuse are paranoia and the loss of the ability to control your emotions. You begin to think that everyone is watching you and that they're against you. Unfortunately, the people who are closest to you usually bear the brunt of it. You become short, testy and angry—just like the night when Cathy and I got into an argument.

Cathy made it known that she was tired of my behavior—the feeling sorry for myself, the odd hours I kept, getting drunk and high with alarming frequency. She had had it. We usually both gave as good as we got, but on this night, I gave her a little bit more than usual—I shoved Cathy, and she became quite afraid of me. I can't say I blame her for calling the police, because I crossed the line. It's something that still shames me to this day, but it's also something I can never take back. If I could take back one night of my life, it would be that one. Even though I've apologized to her many times over, and she's definitely forgiven me, it's an act I will always deeply regret.

I was charged with assault. I spent the night in jail and had plenty of time to ponder my actions. In Seattle, even though a spouse might decide not to press charges, the courts will pursue it regardless. The case goes through the system with or without the consent of the parties involved. Cathy didn't want to press charges, but it didn't matter, and I ended up having to hire an attorney and face the music.

Former teammate John Greig arranged for his wife, an attorney, to represent me. She plea-bargained a sweetheart of a deal whereby I would get counseling in an intervention program in exchange for having the assault charge dropped with no jail time. It was a deal I readily agreed to, although ultimately I didn't live up to my end of the bargain.

I arranged for marriage counseling with Ken Hutcherson, a former professional football player for the Seattle Seahawks and Dallas Cowboys. "Hutch" was, and still is, the pastor of the Antioch Bible Church in Kirkland. In addition to being a former athlete, Hutch was an all-around good guy and a very strong Christian.

So strong, in fact, that when Ken wrecked his knee in 1977 and ended his pro career, he reportedly reacted with a huge smile.

"I'm excited to see what God has in store for me," Hutch supposedly told his teammates. Now *that's* a man of faith!

Unfortunately for me, at that time in my life I didn't have the same outlook.

I attended counseling a few times with Hutch, but didn't attend the agreed-upon number of sessions. The bottom line was that I was embarrassed about the whole situation. My ego kept getting in the way and I didn't want to deal with it. When it came time for a follow-up with the judge, Hutch had no choice but to tell him the truth—that I hadn't fulfilled my commitment to the court. The judge then issued a bench warrant for my arrest.

A few months later, I was pulled over by a police officer for a minor traffic infraction, and when he ran my driver's license through the system, the outstanding warrant turned up. I was taken to the Kings County Jail and languished there for about five days. Cathy refused to bail me out, and so I got three hots and a cot. It was another low point.

But I believe that's exactly the state in which God wanted me, because He sent a man to witness and minister to me.

I met pastor Doug Murren a few weeks before I was sent to jail on April 28. Doug is the author of nine books, but is perhaps best known for the pace-setting church he pioneered, the Eastside Foursquare Church in Kirkland. He started his ministry with 10 people in his living room and grew the church to 8,300 families, registering 17,000 decisions for Christ through its ministries. Doug also conducts training events, leads evangelistic outreaches, hosts a radio show and advises churches that target baby boomers through his ministry. I met Doug exactly at the right time in my life.

In the early part of April 1987, I attended an Easter Sunday sunrise service with my family. Doug had made it a point to welcome our family, and I liked him immediately.

Unbeknownst to me, Doug kept a prayer list of people in the Seattle area. I landed on the top of that prayer list when Doug heard of my problems through the newspapers, even though he had never met me before. Then, lo and behold, I ended up coming to his church with my family. Doug felt as if the Lord had delivered me to his doorstep. After all, what are the chances of a professional athlete showing up at 6:00 a.m. at a Sunday church service? Doug seized the opportunity to offer Cathy and me counseling, and we readily agreed. Doug came over to the house a few times, and we built a nice friendship. It was shortly after that that I was pulled over and arrested.

When Doug heard I was in jail, he became a stalwart friend and a brother in Christ during my time of need. When he wasn't looking out after me, he watched over Cathy and the kids to make sure all their needs were met.

Doug called my probation officer and asked him to make arrangements to have me relocated to North Rehabilitation Facilities in nearby Shoreline. He also went to bat for me in front of the judge, which had great influence.

Founded in 1981, the 291-bed special detention and treatment center had an innovative approach to jailing people with drug or alcohol problems. They did so by providing addiction and anger-management counseling, therapy, high school diplomas and job placement for low-level offenders who are nearing their release date.

The place sounded much better than being locked up with dangerous criminals for the next six months, which is what my sentence was. Where do I sign?

I ended up staying at North Rehabilitation Center for the next two months. While there I attended a lot of group counseling where we discussed substance abuse, but we really didn't scratch the surface of addiction. Then again, this wasn't the Hazelden Clinic and I wasn't paying $20,000 a week, either. In addition to counseling, I worked in the kitchen preparing food and cleaning dishes, something I didn't even do at home. It was a way to pass the time, but it was also a pretty humbling experience.

Even more humbling was when I watched a televised basketball game with a group of about 30 guys on April 17, 1987. As it turned out, it was

Julius Erving's last game and retirement ceremony in front of an appreciative Philadelphia crowd.

During halftime, Julius was brought out at halfcourt for a major presentation. The network showed a highlight reel of spectacular plays the Doc made during his career, followed by the usual presentation of awards and the time-honored tradition of having the jersey being raised to the rafters. The announcer then asked Julius who were some of the toughest people he had faced during his career. My name was the first one out of his mouth, and all of the guys in the joint gave me a standing ovation. But instead of feeling proud and worthy, I was deeply ashamed and felt totally empty inside. The weight of the situation hit me all at once. There was Dr. J, a talented player whose career path paralleled mine in many ways, being revered in his community for his accomplishments, and here I was in a jail because I couldn't control my addictions. It was a mirror reflection of how far my life had gone downhill. For a man who played so far above the basket, the fall was quick.

It was time for some serious self-evaluation and a radical change in my life. I was sick and tired of being sick and tired.

At that crossroad in my life, the funding ran out for my stay at North and I was sent back to Issoquah City Jail, a small 10-cell facility where I would finish out the remainder of my sentence. In no time I became a trustee, serving breakfast to the inmates.

Doug made sure to drop by daily so we could fellowship and pray. On one of those visits to Issoquah, Doug brought with him an imposing figure—a guy by the name of Ron Rearick.

Ron, I came to discover, was a former Mafia enforcer known as the "Iceman." His resume included several petty and major crimes, including an attempt to extort $2 million dollars from United Airlines by threatening to blow up one of their flights. Ron got 25 years for that in the federal prison on McNeil Island, Washington.

While in prison, an older convict walked up to him and said, "Rearick, you can learn a lot of things in here. You can learn counterfeiting. You can learn safecracking. Or you can get smart." With that, the older con shoved a Bible into Ron's gut.

Ron, who had never been to church, never prayed, and never read the Bible, couldn't get the old con's words out of his head. Two nights later Ron knelt in his cell, prayed and was born again. After he was released, he became a full-time evangelist.

A pastor and a former mob enforcer, both of them on fire for the Lord, came to witness to me and became my good friends. The Lord does indeed work in mysterious ways.

Every day for an hour for the duration of my incarceration, the three of us read the Bible together and had great fellowship.

Doug, Ron and I studied the book of Romans, which talks about the fall of man, his rejection of God, and how Christ became our bridge back to God through His grace.

Growing up in a Christian household, I knew the difference between right and wrong when I ventured off on my own in college. Little by little, inch by inch, I strayed from God's word and His way of life as it was intended for me, to the point where I was off on my own little island. Over time, I grew ashamed of the things I had done and the person I had become. I didn't believe I was worthy of God's grace, but Doug insisted I was wrong.

"God will accept you the way you are and the person you are today," Doug said.

I thought upon those words, and tears filled my eyes. I hadn't cried for a long time, but like an apple that's ready to fall from the tree, I was ready to accept Jesus Christ back into my life as my Lord and Savior.

"Right now, at this very moment, do you confess with your mouth and your heart that Jesus Christ is Lord?" Doug asked.

"I do," I replied. We huddled together, holding each other's hands, and I felt a rush come over me, and then a calm quickly took its place. I felt this great sense of serenity I had never felt before, an inner peace I had been searching for my entire life. It was as if I had finally become at ease with who I was. My tears of sadness had been replaced with tears of joy, and I felt that the mess that had become my life was finally going to work itself out.

Doug arranged for my early release, and he baptized me in water at the church the day I got out. My life finally had some hope, and I had something to live for.

That didn't mean, however, that God was going to perform miracle after miracle and pave the way for me. He would show me the way, but I would have to be the one to pave it. And there was lots of paving to be done in my life, starting with my marriage.

Before I entered jail, Cathy was fed up with me and my erratic behavior, and we separated. Our situation had become intolerable to Cathy, who deeply resented my addiction and how it affected our family. After the IRS repossession of our home, Cathy rented a place with the girls, while I stayed with Doug in a home on the church property.

Thank God for Doug, who helped get me back on my feet after I was released on August 25, 1987. Doug provided me with a place to stay while encouraging Cathy to stay in the Word and work on her personal happiness.

But room and board weren't free. I ended up swapping a basketball for a broom handle and became the custodian at the church during the day, while studying the Bible at night. That's when I started to learn more about the Bible and not think so much about myself.

The church was also very active in the public school system in drug prevention, and Doug arranged for me to visit schools and give my testimony. I talked to kids about the dangers of substance abuse, because you have to get the message to the right audience at the right age.

The message I was giving to the kids was both helpful to them and healing to me. At that point, addiction to drugs no longer had a hold on me. The stranglehold, the chain, the bondage was breaking, and I was free from its grip. However, I couldn't say the same thing for alcohol, which, for me, was a harder addiction to kick.

One night, a friend cabbed out to my place and we cracked open a few beers. He pulled out some cocaine and asked if I wanted to do a line. It was my first real test, and, thank the Lord, I passed. My friend decided to leave the cocaine in case I wanted it later on. With the beer in my system, I contemplated it for a long time. Thankfully, Doug was tipped off by someone at the church and immediately rushed over.

"David, I know you're a Christian, and you're dealing with your problems the right way, but addiction doesn't go away overnight," Doug said. "We've got to get you where you're not around this stuff for awhile." He suggested I check into a 28-day substance abuse program at Monroe Hospital in Monroe, Washington, approximately 30 miles from Seattle.

Cathy's insurance through work paid for the program, and it was a good way to stay away from temptation. The more days of sobriety you have under your belt, the clearer your thinking and perspective become.

But what about when I returned to Seattle? I needed to get on with my life. The question was, doing what? I couldn't land a job with the Supersonics, much less any other team in the NBA. At the time, the NBA's attitude was a lot less forgiving than it is today, given that their drug policy was in its infancy and had a tendency to blackball players for their involvement with drugs rather than get them any sort of help.

Doug was also worried that my friends and former drug dealers would lure me away from sobriety, and when family members from Shelby called offering support, Doug felt that was the place I needed to be.

Separated from Cathy and the kids, with no job prospects on the immediate horizon, I decided to move back to North Carolina. I needed to bask in my family's love and support, and, hopefully, heal my heart.

Having been on top, and now having to return to the place where I was born to live with my parents, was humiliating for me. It was also hard on my parents, because in small towns everybody knows your business, and they talk. My return to Shelby had tongues wagging all over the place, like a convention of dogs at the Purina factory.

Mostly I stayed inside my parents' home, reading the Bible, and spending time with my mother, dad, and siblings. I also regularly attended church services.

For a long time I was in a state of depression. Then my dad sat me down for a little talk.

"David, you've still got a lot of potential," he said. "You've still got your name, and you can go out into the world and still do a lot of positive things. You've got to pick yourself up by your bootstraps and help yourself." Good ol' dad, always looking at the bright side of life. And he was right on target. Not long after his pep talk, I began to feel a sense of purpose again. Armed with newfound courage, I placed a call to my old friend Carl Scheer. It was a phone call that changed my life.

Scheer had taken a job with the Charlotte Hornets as their vice president and general manager in June 1987.

Charlotte was the first of two teams (the Miami Heat was the other) in 1988 to be awarded a new NBA franchise. The Hornets were the first major league sports franchise in Charlotte and the community welcomed them with open arms for the 1988-89 basketball season.

Carl and I met for lunch, and after a cordial conversation he promised to talk to Hornets' principal owner George Shinn about a possible job for me.

A few weeks later, Carl invited me to the Charlotte Coliseum to watch an Olympic team taking on a group of NBA All-Stars. I was reluctant to go because it would be the first time I was in a North Carolina basketball venue since my playing days. I didn't know how I would be received by the public. Would I be ridiculed? Chastised? Would I garner strange looks and stares?

As it turned out, none of those things happened. In fact, my appearance generated a lot of excitement, and I had a line of 50 people wanting my autograph. The old and young alike gathered for my signature, which was not only a confidence builder for me but also left a lasting impression on Shinn.

Shinn, I later found out, had been initially very skeptical about the idea of even meeting with me.

But Shinn was a risk taker by nature. A poor kid from Kannapolis, North Carolina, as a young man Shinn worked in a textile mill, washed cars and was a janitor in a school he would later run—the Rutledge Education System. Shinn began to grow the chain of business schools, which was the building block to his fortune. Shinn expanded his empire to include real estate investment, auto dealerships, publishing (he's the author of five books), and a traffic reporting company.

Shinn helped define the 1980s as the decade of prosperity in this country, and by the end of the decade he was worth millions. Already a high-profile businessman in the Charlotte area, he was ready to take it to another level when, in 1987, he and business partners Rick Hendrick and Felix Sabates paid the NBA $32.5 million for the rights to bring professional basketball to the Queen City.

A week later after we met, Shinn told me that he was interested in hiring someone to speak to young people and encourage them to stay in school and away from drugs. I told him I thought I was his man.

"David, if I knew that you would never use drugs again, ever, even though I've never heard you speak, I would hire you today," Shinn said.

"I know this is my last chance," I said, shaking his hand. "I won't let you down."

He then hired me as the organization's director of community relations. It was nice to finally be wanted, especially in the NBA. More important, the opportunity showed me that despite my personal problems, the people in North Carolina still loved David Thompson.

But what about the people David Thompson loved most? Finding a career was great, but it meant nothing without my wife and children to share it with.

CHAPTER 20

REBOUND

---

elling your spouse you're clean and sober is one thing; proving it is a whole different story.

In North Carolina I stayed clean for a few months, but it wasn't long enough to convince Cathy to uproot the kids and move back with me. No sir. Cathy had been through the wars with me over a period of several years, and she wasn't about to come running just because I said I had gotten my act together. How many times before had she heard that?

Cathy's skepticism was entirely justified. I was a babe in my sobriety, and the best thing I could do was to not drink. Cathy was smart and level headed. She wanted to see some stability in my life before even contemplating a reconciliation.

I lived in my parents' home in Shelby for about a year before I moved to Charlotte, an hour's drive away. It was close enough so I could still have my support system at hand, but also have some independence. Both were crucial at that point in my life.

The Charlotte Hornets arranged a press conference to announce my job with the organization, and to say it was a hot topic in the press corps is a major understatement.

"Hiring Thompson was the gutsiest move the Hornets have made," wrote *The Charlotte Observer*. "And it could be one of their best."

I knew the press was going to ask about my checkered past and that I had to face the tough questions head on. No ducking, fudging or artful pretense. I answered all questions truthfully and talked about my newfound faith and how I had finally found peace.

"I've gone through a period of total adjustment in my life," I told reporters. "I've hit bottom, and I've totally brought myself back."

I was also honest about my tenuous sobriety and admitted I was not out of the woods by any stretch of the imagination. I explained that I had to take it one day at a time. The media didn't harangue me the way I feared. It was refreshing to learn that honesty truly is the best policy.

I was laying the groundwork for a new life, and the Hornets really helped in that regard. The timing of everything just fell into place, and it was a great partnership. The Hornets needed someone who was a name in the community, and I needed a hand up.

Through my job I was able to go out into the community to promote the Hornets and do a lot of positive work at the same time. I spent the majority of my time at schools talking about the dangers of drugs and how they had a devastating effect on my life.

When I wasn't speaking, I was behind the scenes on game nights, doing little things here and there to help out the organization. My responsibilities included interacting with special guests and groups who came to Hornets games. I remember entertaining the likes of the Rev. Jesse Jackson, two-sport athlete Deion Sanders, and Atlanta Braves players Steve Avery and Sid Bream.

I'd also lend a hand whenever the coach, Gene Littles, asked me to work with a player. I remember Gene asking me to work with guard Rex Chapman on certain aspects of his game.

My new career also required me to attend a lot of parties and social functions, and with that came those temptations I wrestled with on a daily basis. Alcohol was abundant at these functions, and it just about killed me to watch others enjoy their spirits while I abstained.

Pressure also came from the strains of being separated from my wife and two daughters, and the hectic pace of my job. After a while I could no longer resist and suffered a relapse.

It all started when I began drinking at home after work. I rationalized that having a beer every now and then was no big deal because I was working extremely hard. I often made seven appearances a week, and felt I earned the right. But of course alcoholism is a disease, and it is progressive and terminal. That meant every time I had a relapse, my drinking would only get worse.

I had a very close call on October 1, 1988, when I was involved in an early morning incident while visiting old friends in Shelby. When alcohol is involved, it's not hard to find trouble, or for trouble to find you. While I was talking with a few buddies, a stranger approached me from behind and hit me with a stick on the side of my left eye.

It happened at 3:15 a.m., and while I wasn't arrested, the incident did make the news.

Alcoholism is tricky and baffling and will slowly rob you of everything you love. It almost cost me my job with the Hornets.

The final straw was when I canceled a speaking engagement before a youth group at Charlotte's Longhorn Restaurant.

The Hornets employee who handled my speaking schedule assured me she would pass on my regrets to the group and reschedule my appearance for a future date.

But she forgot, and a room full of kids, anxious to hear my life story, were left hanging for a long time. The group's irate leader called the Hornets to complain that I was a no-show, and when someone was dispatched to my house to see what the problem was, there I was with a buddy and a couple of beers.

But rather than fire me on the spot, the Hornets' front office spoke to someone in a 12-step program who told them I had no business drinking at all. It was strongly suggested that I take the first plane to California and check into the ASAP Rehabilitation Center in Van Nuys. The implication was that if I didn't follow their orders, I could kiss the Hornets goodbye. And if I lost my job, I also lost another chance with Cathy and the kids. I couldn't risk all that, so I went along with the plan. As it turned out, it was the best thing that ever happened to me.

While on the plane to California, I left a huge mess for the Hornets to clean up. They canceled all of my scheduled appointments for the next few months and fielded phone calls from the media. It didn't take them long to find out I had relapsed.

I arrived at the facility on December 15, 1988, and I spent the next four months of my life there. Rehab is not how I'd recommend spending the holidays and ringing in the New Year.

To my surprise, I discovered I wasn't the only famous face in the place. I met lots of famous celebrities, including movie stars, rock stars, doctors and lawyers. I wasn't even the only NBA player in the facility. In fact, we probably could have suited up a team.

It was the most intense four months of my life. For first time I didn't fake going through the motions, but actually lived, breathed and worked a 12-step program.

The center had several homes in the compound, and I lived with five other people. Each of us was assigned daily tasks, and the routine was a good structure for all of us whose lives sorely lacked discipline.

Living with strangers in such an intimate setting was hard, but it taught all of us how to co-exist peacefully together. In rehab, if you don't interact with others, you've got real problems, because of the mandatory group sessions. In my case, when I drank or got high, I had a tendency to isolate myself from others. The open forum forced me to let it all hang out, something I hadn't done for a long time.

I was encouraged to talk about myself in the meetings, something I was quite uncomfortable with at first. Deep down I'm a very private individual and would rather talk about someone other than myself. I especially didn't want to discuss my personal problems. But in rehab no one gets off the hook, and they didn't hesitate to knock the high and mighty off their perch.

I learned that once addiction begins to take control of a family unit, one of the first things to go by the wayside is honesty. The alcoholic constantly lies to cover up for how much he or she really drinks—to camouflage the addiction. Yet the vicious cycle of denial can be broken through honesty.

In these meetings I had to identify that I had a problem. If I wanted to get better, I had to admit I was powerless over alcohol and cocaine and that my life had become totally unmanageable. That's an incredibly hard step for anyone who's so used to being in control of his mind and body. Ego was a defense mechanism for me in the pros because it was as a weapon against my opponents, and was also what kept me on top. Ego gives you that extra push to be great, and it's a hard habit to drop once it's ingrained. To admit I was powerless over anything was quite foreign to me, and in my case there was a fine line between self-belief and self-delusion. I thought for the longest time I had a handle on drinking and drugs, but the truth of the matter was, they had a handle on me.

As a consolation, I learned that while I was powerless over alcohol and drugs, I did control my immediate actions. That, I discovered, was the cornerstone of recovery.

For example, if I walk into a room and a group of guys is drinking a few beers and doing a few lines, I have an immediate choice: I can stay, or walk out of the room. However, if I stay and have a drink or snort up a line, then the addiction grabs hold of me and I'm powerless. If I really wanted to stay sober, I'd have to take control of my immediate actions. And if I didn't take control, I knew exactly where that road would lead me.

Addiction was an uncontrollable obsession that caused me to drink even when I didn't want to. Since the obsession was uncontrollable, I could not predict when I would start drinking.

Coupled with the obsession to drink was an allergy of the body. This meant I possessed the knowledge that once I started drinking or drugging, I could not predict when I would stop. That was a scary proposition. After years of denial, my recovery started with one simple admission. I was powerless over alcohol and cocaine. Today, I regard it as an invaluable tool to my continuing sobriety.

Now that I had admitted I had a problem, the second and third steps were a little easier for me to digest. I had to let go of my life and turn everything over to my higher power so that he could help restore some form of sanity. It helped that I had rededicated my life to Christ so he could help the healing process begin. It's amazing to find out that as soon as we give our lives over to God, He begins to take care of us in miraculous ways.

But giving my life over to God didn't mean He was going to instantly take care of all my problems. We can make lots of decisions sitting down in a chair, but it doesn't mean we'll do anything about it later. It is the course of action we take as a result of making that decision that gets us up and out of that chair. People who have addictions *must* decide on recovery. More importantly, we must choose not to continue our addictive behavior. That meant I had to turn my will and life over to the care of God. A decision that is not followed by action doesn't do any good, and this is the key to understanding the function of the first few steps.

The fourth step is to take a fearless and moral inventory of ourselves. It's the first of the external action steps and forces us to take a look inward. In no way was that an easy thing to do. In the years in which my addiction took hold, I became a completely different person. Before, I was an amiable, selfless and respectful young man. I was goal-oriented, an overachiever, and wanted the most out of life. But under the influence of alcohol and drugs, I became a shell of my former self. I became sullen, rude, short-tempered, and paranoid, not to mention downright selfish. Everything revolved around me and satisfying my immediate needs. I put my addiction before everything—my wife, my kids, my career, my family and friends—and they all suffered horribly.

Once I was able to take a personal inventory of my behavior, warts and all, I felt deeply ashamed and embarrassed. Like the layers of an onion being peeled away, I began to recognize that my addiction affected all of my loved ones, and it hurt them a whole lot more than it hurt me.

With the passage of time, I became more lucid and got a clearer picture of how my behavior affected my life and others around me, which made the fifth step relatively easy: to have the integrity to admit to God that it was wrong. Through a conversation with God in the spirit of prayer, he helped reveal to me the exact nature of my sinful ways. The fifth step provides the change to start "growing up" spiritually and gives those with addictions the opportunity to cleanse their souls of the burdens of the past.

Once the addict is cleansed then they are ready for the sixth step: identifying individual shortcomings.

Only after I admitted my faults was I able to move to the seventh step and ask to have my character defects removed. For me, that was mainly dishonesty about my addiction to loved ones, hiding my problems, holding past resentments, and harboring guilt. All those pent-up feelings had to be released from inside. Once God was able to do that for me, a huge emotional and psychological burden was lifted from my shoulders.

That led me to the eighth and ninth steps, which included making a list of everyone I had harmed along the way and attempting to make amends. At the top of that list was my family, which definitely suffered the most.

Even though I apologized time and time again to Cathy for pushing her when I was under the influence of alcohol and drugs, I needed to make sure she understood I was sincerely sorry for my actions on that day. The whole process of making amends is a humbling, but healthy experience. The payoff, however, was worth every second. Because I was willing to ask Cathy for forgiveness, she was willing to grant it, and a new beginning started to take place.

As others forgive you, so you are forgiven. Those experienced in spiritual matters know that it is almost impossible for us to truly be forgiven without forgiving others and ourselves first.

Keeping spiritual house is the basis for the tenth step, and I did that by continually monitoring myself and my faults. Addicts must monitor themselves because the two biggest dangers we face are guilt and resentment. By promptly facing mistakes and taking responsibility for them, the wrongs are quickly settled rather than weighing on our conscience. It's easier to nip it in the bud quickly rather than let it linger and produce doubt or guilt. Righting a wrong quickly helps keep my mental house in order.

Another danger for addicts is complacency, because we can actually lose ground on our recovery if we don't continue to monitor our behavior.

The purpose of the eleventh step is to discover what plans God has for me and my life, through prayer and meditation. What's the difference between the two? Well, like the old saying goes, "Prayer is talking to God. Meditation is listening."

It was through deep prayer and meditation that God revealed His true purpose for me and my life. I truly believe God wanted me to take my life lessons to kids and warn them of the dangers of alcohol and drugs.

But being armed with all of that knowledge means nothing if you're not willing to impart your wisdom, which is what the twelfth step is all about: service. In service we find redemption.

In order to keep the gift of sobriety, we must give it away. Carrying the message to others by sharing experiences, strength and hope, enables me to keep the gift of sobriety. Without these final works, 12-step programs would simply cease to exist. Once we experience the power of the 12 steps, the focus turns to helping the newcomer, who will hopefully have a spiritual awakening just as we did.

As I racked up more days of sobriety, the stronger I became. Eventually, I was able to find clarity. The timing was uncanny, because I was about to be put to the ultimate test. While in rehab, my sister Pecora called to tell me that our beloved mother had died of a heart attack.

I felt like someone had reached inside of me and pulled my heart out. My continual problems and troubles with alcohol and drugs caused my mother a lot of anguish. The guilt I felt almost overwhelmed me, and I hadn't experienced anguish on that level before and haven't since.

There's a special bond between a mother and her son, and my mother was truly a special woman. I called her my earth-angel because she was truly a saint.

After I talked to my sister I dropped right to my knees. I prayed to the Lord to help give me the strength to get through this crisis. Luckily, I had the friendship of another fellow NBA player who stayed up through the night praying and crying with me.

The facility allowed me a three-day pass to attend my mother's funeral, but it was all a blur. When I returned, I counted my blessings that I had staff members to give me tools to deal with her death.

They had me sit down and write two letters: one to my mother, and one to God. I was encouraged to express the grief I felt in the letters. Somehow, putting all of those feelings down on paper made it a whole lot easier because the impact is so great when you see your words in print. And it's been easier ever since.

I figured if I could make it through that, I could make it through almost anything. I know that my mother's death was not in vain because she gave me a renewed dedication to make my life work and stay sober for myself and my family. Perhaps it was her parting gift to me, as I've never experienced another relapse.

Upon the conclusion of my rehab, the Hornets gave me a little time to get my footing. When I did return to work, it wasn't to the big, plush office that I once occupied. I was stuck in a little cubbyhole as a reminder that I was skating on thin ice.

Slowly but surely, I began to rebuild trust within the organization and the community through my continued sobriety. I shared my story with kids at schools, the YMCA, the Boys & Girls Club, non-profit organizations and city functions.

My desire to stay clean didn't go unnoticed by Cathy, who had made a life for herself and the girls in Seattle. She certainly didn't need me any more, but Brooke and Erika were missing their daddy more and more. We spent the summer together and they were able to meet my family and enjoy their relatives. It was a great visit, and I followed up a few months later with a visit to Seattle.

Cathy, who had stayed in the Word at Eastside Foursquare Church, was open to reconciliation. As newfound Christians, we felt closer than ever and had a common bond. God was the center of our lives.

Marriage is a sacred bond in the eyes of God, and it's forever. Cathy and I had our ups and downs, but we never stopped loving each other. We decided to put our trust in the Lord and give our marriage another go.

Cathy and the girls moved to Charlotte in 1991, and we've been together ever since. Our love just gets stronger as the years go by, and I thank God every day that he gave me a spouse who supports me in everything that I do.

It was that same year that Charlotte hosted the NBA All-Star Game and my father was able to see me play on a national stage one last time in the Legends Game.

It was a blast, and it was nice being the hometown favorite. Even nicer was the fact that my team won, and I was the leading scorer with 11 points.

It was my last hurrah before my father passed on at the age of 78 from prostate cancer. Dad had won a previous bout with cancer, but when my mother passed away I think it devastated him and triggered another onset of the disease. Looking back, her death sapped his will to live, and he wanted to be with her again.

But now it seemed as if every time I suffered a setback, something good would happen to offset the bad. In the summer of 1991, Cathy and I were invited to Hawaii by Magic Johnson to play in his All-Star Slam Jam.

The game was a charity benefit for the Magic Johnson Foundation, but it was also a great way to reconnect with other members of the NBA. It was an eye-opening experience for me, in that so many younger players told me how much I meant to them growing up. Magic, John Salley and Sean Elliot all told me I was their favorite ballplayer growing up. Before this, players in the NBA were afraid to acknowledge my influence on the game, but now they were publicly announcing I had been their childhood idol.

It was as if David Thompson was discovered all over again. I must confess…it was nice.

But those displays of affection were nothing compared to the public relations boost that I got from a fellow athlete from North Carolina. You may have heard his name before: Michael Jordan.

I was still playing for Seattle when I first met Michael, then in college at the University of North Carolina. As Michael tells it, I was the guy he idolized as a kid, and he even rooted for NC State all those years. When we met, my nephew Curtis Brown and a friend, Walter Bell, happened to be with us. Luckily for us, Walter had a camera to snap a picture for posterity.

"You need to take a picture of the two greatest players in the history of the ACC," I said to Walter. Michael and I wrapped our arms around each other, and I immediately liked him. He was not only a talented player, but I could tell he had a good heart.

Michael has been there for me time and time again. Despite his demanding schedule, Michael always found time for me and is very giving of himself. We've spoken at many clinics together, and he always talks me up to the kids, telling them he patterned his game after mine. Let's just say that when he's finished talking, they look at me in a whole different light.

I continued speaking in front of school kids and doing other special engagements, but this time I returned with a real message that spoke directly to them. The reason? I was finally able to speak from the heart.

"Do you know me?" I start off. The kids usually shake their heads no.

"Do you know Michael Jordan?" I ask, and everyone shakes their heads yes. "Well, before I took drugs, I was Michael Jordan's hero."

I tell them that life is about making intelligent choices.

"A lot of your success will depend on your ability to make the right choices," I tell them, "but the most important choice you'll ever make is whether to accept Jesus Christ as your Lord and Savior."

That's when I launch into my story and tell them my background, my highs and lows, about going to jail and finally accepting Jesus into my life and how He turned my life around.

I make sure to tell the kids I care about each and every one of them, and that I want to see them become successful and "SCORE" big in life.

SCORE is an acronym I made up for Sacrifice, Confidence, Organization, Respect and Education. If they follow that recipe in life, they will find all of the happiness and success that eluded me for years.

"I may not have the wealth and fame that I once did in my life, but in a lot of ways, my life is far richer today than it ever was," I tell them.

For a long time, I had everything that a person could want—money, fame, and a great lifestyle—but there was something missing. All those things didn't bring me happiness or peace of mind. There was a void in my life, and that void was the love of Jesus Christ in my heart. For a long time, I didn't have my priorities straight.

Basketball was my god. It was the number-one priority. Everything I felt about myself was built around the bouncing ball, which also happened to be an appropriate metaphor for my life.

Life, I tell people, is a lot like basketball. It has its ups and its downs. But what really matters is where you are in the game at the end of the buzzer. The way I look at it, instead of saving games now, hopefully, by giving my testimony, I'm helping to save the lives of kids.

Now that I'm a Christian, God comes first, then my family. For a long time, it was just the opposite, but I learned that if I don't prioritize my life that way, then my life's going to be off balance and I'll never feel successful.

Once I became a Christian, Jesus Christ removed my compulsion and obsession to use drugs and drink. By God's grace, I'm clean and sober, and that, in and of itself, is a miracle.

"Say no to drugs, and yes to Jesus," is how I end every speech.

The NBA community finally began looking at me in a different light. I was honored when I learned that the Denver Nuggets wanted to retire my jersey—number 33.

As if Carl Scheer hadn't done enough for me over the years, I eventually found out that he was behind the push for my retirement ceremony.

It wasn't that long ago that, from a Washington jail cell, I had watched Julius Erving's retirement ceremony unfold. But now my life was finally coming full circle, and I was ready for such an honor.

On November 7, 1992, the opening night of the season, the Nuggets organization held the ceremony at halftime in a packed McNichols Arena.

Al Albert, the official voice of the Nuggets and brother of broadcaster Marv Albert, was emcee for the presentation. The evening included a highlight reel of my seven years (1975-1982) with the Denver organization, in which I scored 11,992 points in 448 games.

After the highlight reel, I received a few videotaped messages from Julius Erving, Larry Brown and even Doug Moe, with whom I managed to bury the hatchet. To top it off, I received a $10,000 check to put towards my daughters' college educations.

Albert also read a telegram from a very special person, David Stern, then the commissioner of the National Basketball Association. It read:

"What's most important to remember about your career is not just the number of points you put on the board, but the way you scored them. You helped pioneer the high-flying, creative style that is so prevalent in today's game, a style which has forever changed the game. It is only fitting that McNichols Arena should forever display your jersey as a constant reminder of the contributions you made to basketball. Congratulations."

The telegram brought the appreciative Denver crowd to its feet for a rousing standing ovation and brought tears to my eyes.

Next, Albert brought out Bob "Chopper" Travaglini, the Nuggets' longtime trainer, Monte Towe, and Byron Beck, the first Nugget ever to have his jersey retired. My jersey would be hanging up in the rafter alongside Beck's and that of my former teammate and Nugget great, Dan "The Horse" Issel.

Beck held the blue and white banner and released it so that it could be hoisted to the ceiling. Number 33 ascended one last time in McNichols Arena, and the feeling was just awesome.

"You've made a young man from Shelby, North Carolina, a very, very happy man tonight," I told the crowd. "This has been one of the happiest days of my life."

And it was because, in a way, my life in basketball had proper closure. In 1982, I had been enshrined into the North Carolina Sports Hall of Fame, which represented my college career. Now, the Denver Nuggets put another part of my life to rest.

While it was nice to be recognized for my collegiate and professional contributions to basketball, it was equally nice to be recognized for my work in the community. In 1994, the Carolinas' Athlete of the Year Awards Selection Committee honored me with the Joe Mallamo Humanitarian Award. The award annually honors an individual who has freely given to the betterment of sports and the community in the Carolinas.

Two years later, the Colorado Sports Hall of Fame inducted me on February 5, 1996, for my contribution to sports and basketball in the state of Colorado.

It was on that same day that I learned I would be accorded the ultimate honor for a basketball player—I was to be inducted into the Naismith Basketball Hall of Fame in Springfield, Massachusetts.

Can you imagine being inducted into two Halls of Fame in one day? You could say the honor took the Skywalker to new heights.

CHAPTER 21

NEW HEIGHTS

ll the seeds I had been sowing for the past few years were starting to yield harvest. The more awards I won, the more recognition I received, and the more in demand I became.

I had been receiving good press locally for some time, but the announcement that the Naismith Basketball Hall of Fame (BHOF) was going to induct me put an exclamation point on my career and would preserve my legacy.

The BHOF was acknowledging my role as one of the most outstanding players in NCAA and NBA history. That includes being a three-time All-American, leading NC State to the 1974 NCAA championship, being the only player ever to be named MVP in both the ABA and NBA All-Star Games, scoring 73 points against Detroit in 1978, and scoring an overall career average of 22 points per game and 16,305 NBA points.

My career was rich in awards and accomplishments, but unfortunately, it had always been overshadowed by my personal demons. In fact, I had my doubts the BHOF would ever acknowledge my contributions to basketball.

For years, people didn't talk about David Thompson in connection with basketball, even though my innovative style of play and records spoke volumes. I always felt the things I accomplished in college and the pros were worthy to get me into the Hall, but I also worried that my well-documented problems with drugs and alcohol would steer voters away.

It took many years to show people I had finally turned my life around and rightfully earned a place in the Hall. I came a long way, and we're talking from the ground up.

It was a special honor to learn that my good friend and former San Antonio Spurs standout George "Iceman" Gervin would be inducted alongside me.

George was one of basketball's most prolific scorers, racking up more than 2,000 points in six consecutive seasons. He averaged 26 points during 14 seasons with the ABA and NBA, and his 20,708 career points ranked him as the 19th best in history at the time of the induction.

The two of us had some great scoring battles, and the 1978 scoring title that was decided by four points will forever link the two of us. Despite our battles on the hardwood floor, we've always had mutual respect for each other both on and off the court.

Others chosen for induction that year were former UCLA and Los Angeles Lakers star Gail Goodrich, Olympic champion Nancy Lieberman-Cline, former NBA scoring star George "Bird" Yardley and the late Kresimir Cosic of Croatia. The induction ceremonies were set for May 6, 1996 at the BHOF in Springfield, Massachusetts.

I received about 50 phone calls from old friends and well-wishers the day of the announcement, and it was nice to know people still cared.

The real push for my BHOF enshrinement came through Frank Weedon, former sports information director at NC State.

"Just based on your college career alone, you should get in," Frank told me. "We're going to try and make this happen."

Frank asked the BHOF for a nomination packet and then helped me assemble a packet of news clippings, magazine articles and factual data on my life and career. He also had me start a letter-writing campaign to several key figures in the NBA, including Lenny Wilkens, Donnie Walsh and Larry Brown, who, in turn, petitioned the BHOF screening committee on my behalf.

All of the materials were presented to the president/CEO of the BHOF during the period beginning October 1, 1995, and ending January 31, 1996.

The purpose of the screening committee, a 24-member board, is to carefully review a candidate's basketball record and then take a vote. A candidate must have a minimum of 18 votes from the committee, which was a pretty tall order.

The next thing I knew, I was on the ballot for consideration. And much to my delight, I was voted in on the first try. That was a slam dunk even I could appreciate.

Can you say "Amen?" I know I did.

The day of the induction was full of activity and emotion. Everything got under way with a press conference in the morning.

Reporters fired questions at all of us, but mostly at George and me about how our careers paralleled on and off the court.

They noted we both started our careers in the American Basketball Association, excelled after our respective teams merged in the NBA, and engaged in an unforgettable scoring race in the 1977-78 season.

"[Gervin] edged me out in the closest scoring race in the history of basketball," I said, jokingly adding, "Gervin should have let me have that one because he got three more after that."

Of course, we both also overcame substance abuse problems. I can't speak for George, but I know he has overcome that aspect of his life. He is very devoted and gives of his time to youth in the San Antonio community today.

My history is something I will always have to answer for, but the only way to deal with a problem is to confront it head on and turn the negative into a positive.

"Everybody has skeletons in their closet," I told a room filled with reporters. "But when you're a pro athlete, you're in a position where you can have an influence on people's lives, and that's what I'm trying to do now."

I spoke frankly about the long road back, the ups and the downs, financial ruin and treatment programs. Out of all that tragedy came triumph, I emphasized.

"That's when I knew I had to have a personal relationship with Christ," I said. "That was something all the money I made in basketball couldn't buy."

I also told the reporters that it was only through the grace of God that He helped me to overcome adversity in my life, and I've been transformed from the inside out.

In Second Corinthians 5:17, Paul says, "Therefore if any man be in Christ, he is a new creation. Old things have passed away, all things have become new."

My faith and family, I said, are most important to me today. My wife Cathy and daughters Erika and Brooke were by my side, and I could see they were especially proud of me.

Before that, I don't think my daughters had any real clue as to how good a basketball player I was. That was partly due to the fact that they were too young to see me play. I remember one time I tried to show them some of my highlights on video, but they said, "Take that out, Dad, we want to see Penny Hardaway play." Nothing like your kids to keep your feet firmly planted on the ground.

After the press conference, there was an autograph session with each of the inductees, and I signed for about an hour for a very enthusiastic crowd.

As the old saying goes, they saved the best for last, at the induction ceremony later that evening.

Robin Deutsch, the BHOF's director of public relations who introduced me, reminded everyone that it was me, not the University of North Carolina's Michael Jordan, who was considered the greatest player in the history of the Atlantic Coast Conference.

With that, he turned the microphone over to an esteemed guest.

Each inductee must have someone who's already a member of the BHOF officially induct them. I originally chose my former Denver teammate, Dan Issel to induct me, but he already had a commitment on that date.

I then asked Celtic great John Havlicek, who readily agreed to walk me down the red carpet to induct me. "Hondo" is a person I greatly admire both personally and professionally and got to know on an NBA Players Association trip to China in 1983.

We had the opportunity to play against each other for a couple of years before he retired at the age of 37. Even when he was a "Lion in Winter," he was the still king of the jungle in my book.

When it came my turn to speak, I felt overcome with emotion. I guess you could call it closure. Even though I hadn't played professionally in well over a decade, I felt my career had ended on a sour note. I needed that closure in order to move on to the next phase my life. All I know was that it was good for the soul.

As I looked out into the audience, I saw all the basketball greats— players I grew up admiring, like Jerry West, Bob Cousy, Earl "The Pearl" Monroe, John Havlicek, Bill Walton, Gail Goodrich and Connie Hawkins.

I was a little nervous, but also excited to be a part of this exclusive club.

I opened my speech by thanking the fans and all of my coaches and former teammates.

My three coaches in Denver—Larry Brown, Donnie Walsh and Doug Moe—I said, all taught me something different about the complexities of the game.

"Donnie Walsh taught me some offense, while Larry Brown taught me some defense," I said, taking a pause for effect. "And Doug Moe taught me some choice four-letter words."

The hard feelings I had towards Doug had long since passed. Doug was a good coach and he did what he thought was best in order to keep the team together. Once I left Denver, I never had any ill will towards him and let bygones be bygones. Today I consider Doug a friend.

I then moved on to the second part of my career in Seattle and thanked Lenny Wilkens for being a great coach and for taking a chance on me when no one else would. I feel so honored to have played for Lenny and even more honored that he cared for me as a human being when I needed help for substance abuse.

I also thanked my former teammates in Denver and Seattle, who made my job so much easier: Dan Issel, Alex English, Kiki Vandeweghe, "Downtown" Freddie Brown, Gus Williams and Jack Sikma.

I thanked my good friends who were in attendance that night, including a group of people from North Carolina. They were Les Robinson, Herb Sendek and Frank Weedon, all affiliated with NC State. My best friend from Charlotte, Chris Edwards, and his father Billy were there as well as Billy Bryson, my AA sponsor. I also thanked Masako Oishi for 20-plus years of great friendship and Scott Jimison, a fan from Gastonia who came to my jersey retirement in Denver as well as the induction, and Rob Walker and his wife, Jacqui, who have been great friends for 12 years. Robert has helped my career immensely.

Lastly, I thanked my All-Star team at home: Cathy, Erika and Brooke. Cathy made me a better man even though I tested her patience many times, and she never lost faith in me. I thank God every day for giving me a faithful and loving wife like Cathy whose love transcends anything else I have on this earth. I'm certain God had Cathy in mind when he allowed Proverbs 31:10 to be written. It says, "A wife of nobler character who can find? She is worth far more than rubies. Her husband has full confidence and lacks nothing of value. She brings him good, not harm, all the days of her life."

As for my two girls, they give me nothing but pure joy. Their presence in my life brings a whole new dimension I never knew existed. The combination of their inquisitive minds, trusting spirits, wit, innocence and unconditional love causes my own spirits to soar. Their presence in my life surpasses any other high I've ever known. Though they have both left my home in recent years, they will never leave my heart.

Lastly, I thanked my parents. I told audience members how my parents never made more than a $100 a week and somehow were able to raise 11 children in a cinderblock house on a dirt road outside Shelby, North Carolina. I told them we might have been poor monetarily, but were rich in love.

"The only regret I have this evening is that my parents aren't here to witness this event because they were so proud of me," I said. "But I know we're going to be in heaven together and see each other for eternity."

The standing ovation I received when I finished capped off one of the most perfect days of my life.

As if things weren't sweet enough, the Charlotte Hornets honored me a few days after the BHOF induction at a special halftime ceremony. And they gave me more than just a plaque.

Owner George Shinn and GM Bob Bass agreed to cover in-state college tuition for our daughters, Erika and Brooke, who were 16 and 14, respectively. If my daughters decided to attend an out-of-state school, George would pay the equivalent of what a North Carolina school would charge for tuition.

George didn't forget about Cathy and me and presented us with an all-expenses-paid vacation to France.

George was also generous to me in the press, telling reporters, "He's been a tremendous asset to basketball, not only college, but professional. But he's also a darn good human being who's had some tough breaks in his life. I'm fond of him."

And I was especially fond of him.

The Hornets organization was great to me over the years. They were the first NBA team to give me a chance to get my life together, and for that I'm eternally thankful to them.

Sadly, George moved the team to New Orleans in the spring of 2002 after reporting losses of $2 million a month. George endured many battles while in Charlotte his last few years. The capper was a failed bid for taxpayers' help in a public referendum to build a new arena.

George will always remain a good and loyal friend and one of the best human beings I know. I wish him nothing but the best.

Much to my delight, the accolades for me haven't stopped coming. In March 1998, the *Greensboro News Record* selected the 10 players who were standouts during NCAA play over the years in the Greensboro Coliseum.

The paper named me to their first team All-Greensboro NCAA team, highlighting my accomplishments at NC State during the 1974 championship run.

Also on that first team list were my teammate at NC State, Tommy Burleson, Bill Walton of UCLA (who made it on a technicality), and Johnny Hawkins and Christian Laettner of Duke.

Monte Towe made the list on the second team for his floor generalship in the pair of games in Greensboro in 1974. Joining him were Maurice Lucas of Marquette, Eddie Jordan of Rutgers, Will Bynum of Virginia Military Institute and Willie Burton of Minnesota.

A year later, *Sports Illustrated* named me to its All-Century team. They picked the five greatest college basketball players whose contributions stood the test of time. *SI* named Oscar Robertson, Jerry Lucas, Kareem Abdul-Jabaar (aka Lew Alcindor), Bill Bradley and yours truly as their starting five.

"Close your eyes and you can still picture him: gliding over the rim to guide in the follow shot that beat Maryland in that memorable game on Super Bowl Sunday, 1973. Or rising straight into the air, copter-like, to release the most righteous-looking jumper in college hoops history. Or plummeting frighteningly to earth the time he had his feet cut out from under him at the 42-inch vertical leap," *SI* wrote about me.

"The ACC has produced more great players than any other conference, but none of them, even Michael Jordan, was a better collegian than the versatile, all-but-unguardable 6'4" Thompson, who in his first two seasons led the Wolfpack to a 57-1 record and an NCAA championship."

By the start of the new millennium, I had been named one of the top five basketball players in college basketball history and the top ACC player by almost every major newspaper and sports publication in the country, including *The Sporting News, College Sports Magazine, The Charlotte Observer, Raleigh News and Observer, The Virginian-Pilot,* and the *Richmond Times-Dispatch.*

Many basketball historians have hailed me as basketball's original high-wire act, the architect of the high-flying era of above-the-rim basketball that is so common in today's game.

In fact, Rick Clemens, a producer for Los Angeles-based TriMotion Films, is preparing a documentary on my life that is expected to air in 2004.

The documentary, tentatively titled *Skywalker*, will illustrate my impact on the way the game is played above the rim and the ultimate emergence of the NBA as an international influence in culture, music and fashion.

I think part of the reason I'm being pulled back into the public's consciousness is that there's a whole retro movement among basketball fans who pine for the days of old.

In the 1970s, basketball emerged from the Dark Ages into prime time. It was an era that boasted many great superstar athletes who also knew how to play the team game.

A lot of the kids (and some of them literally are) who come into the pros now are so young they really don't know how the game is meant to be played. All of the guys in my day who lived up to all the hype came in with a grasp of the fundamentals.

To be honest, I think what it boils down to is the fact that most players today aren't being taught the fundamental concepts of the game.

You may have noticed that nowadays most fans don't follow teams, but individuals. I think a lot of it has to do with the "me-first" attitude of the pro players.

Recently Dan Issel and Kiki Vandeweghe, who now have front-office jobs with the Denver Nuggets, asked me come to Denver to speak to their team, which was going through a rough patch. The Nuggets were in the throes of a horrible losing streak, and several players had been talking publicly about wanting to be traded.

Dan and Kiki assembled the players in the locker room before a game with the Los Angeles Clippers. Dan put his arm around me and paid me the ultimate compliment.

"Now, no disrespect to Kiki or Alex English, but this young man is the greatest player ever to wear a Nugget uniform," Dan said. You could say I had their undivided attention at that point.

Whenever I speak to players, it is always from the heart. That day was no different, and I wanted to get my message across gently, but firmly.

"Gentleman, there's only one path to winning, and that's to put the team first," I started off.

I told the players that back when I entered the league, it was a universally accepted idea by everyone that basketball was a team sport. I spoke about how team unity and chemistry have to be built from within and how each individual player has to make sacrifices for the team.

"Each player has a role on this team, but it is up to you to find out what your role is and then go out and do it every night to the best of your ability," I said.

But today's players aren't the only ones who should get the blame. A lot of it has to do with the coaching they're receiving, and the fact that the owners are giving players a lot more power than they did in the past.

Coaches today can't bench an unruly player, because the player will just go above his head to the owner.

Owners pay obscene amounts of money to players who please the crowd. Players are basically rewarded for their individual achievements even though they may have no idea what it's like to be on a winning ball club.

Back in my day, they taught fundamentals first, then you built upon your game, instead of doing all this fancy stuff right off the bat. Growing up, I attended a lot of basketball camps and went through good programs with coaches who were excellent teachers and emphasized right things. That's why you see so many pros pay big bucks for basketball camps that teach them the fundamentals, because they're not being taught the fundamentals growing up.

Even though my game was exciting and thrilling to watch, I still had the fundamentals covered. I learned firsthand that once the fundamentals are mastered, you can achieve success on all levels of basketball.

Is it any wonder that fans are pining for the old days? I hate to say it, but pro basketball is more and more out of step with the fans, and that's why fans are flocking to college basketball. The game on that level is still fun to watch because it's played on a much purer level.

College basketball also does a good job when it comes to tipping its hat to the past.

In March 2003, the ACC named its top 50 athletes of all time in conjunction with the league's 50th anniversary.

Dick Vitale, the famed but flamboyant basketball broadcaster, cast me as the early favorite to win top honors.

"My pick for the best player in ACC history is a guy who redefined the small-forward position. I loved watching David Thompson, the skywalker from NC State," Vitale wrote in an article for ESPN.com.

"He was Baryshnikov in shorts, a ballerina of basketball. Along with Dr. J, Thompson set the tone for athleticism at the small-forward slot."

This time I finished second to Michael Jordan when the votes were tallied. When reporter Todd Graff of the *Greensboro News & Record* asked me if I hated losing to Michael, I honestly told him I didn't feel slighted in the least.

"When you're second to a player with the magnitude of Michael Jordan, and what he's done after he left the ACC, what can you say? He's a well-deserving guy. His career after the ACC has been unparalleled," I said.

That outcome notwithstanding, I feel my collegiate accomplishments are second to none in ACC history. I averaged 26.8 ppg, 8.1 rpg, a .553 field goal percentage and .763 from the free-throw line in my three-year varsity career at NC State. I'm still the only unanimous three-time ACC Player of the Year. I was a three-time unanimous first-team All-American, led the Wolfpack to an undefeated season in 1973, led State to the national title in 1974, and was National Player of the Year in 1975.

"Of all the great players who have passed through the ACC, Thompson is regarded as the best ever to have played in the league," wrote Ron Green, Jr., of *The Charlotte Observer.* "Others went on to greater professional careers, but Thompson remains the gold standard in the ACC."

In addition to Michael Jordan and myself on that ACC list were teammate Tommy Burleson and former Maryland star Tom McMillen.

The list also included my niece, Charlotte Smith, who played at the University of North Carolina, as one of the top 10 ACC female athletes.

Charlotte, my late sister Etta's daughter, hit the buzzer-beating three-pointer that won the 1994 title for UNC. She was the 1995 ESPN National Player of the Year and is the only UNC women's basketball player to have had her jersey retired. She gave me credit for the player she eventually became. The two of us spent many afternoons in the YMCA going one-on-one, and let me tell you, she gave this old man all he could handle.

Two players from the same family on such a prestigious list is an amazing feat.

But more amazing is the person that Charlotte has become. She has always been a role model for my two daughters, and now, known as Charlotte Smith-Taylor, she is a role model for the whole community as a small forward for the Charlotte Sting in the WNBA and an assistant coach at UNC.

While it's nice that I'm recognized for my achievements in the past, what I am doing with my life today has far more impact and meaning to me.

Before, I was an exceptional basketball player who made a difference on the court. Today, hopefully, by telling my story, I am making a difference in people's lives.

In the Bible, the book of James says that faith must be accompanied by works, which is why I'm very active in the community, schools and churches. I feel God has called me to speak to youth who are young enough to understand my message about making wise decisions in life. Who better to turn others away from sin than a sinner who has seen the light?

In today's world, kids especially need firm direction. I'm willing to give them my time because I know how much kids identify with NBA success. Sometimes I can reach them before their parents and coaches can, but I'm quick to tell them their parents and coaches love them and are doing the best to guide them on the right road to success in life.

I might not see right away how I affect their lives, but later on down the line I often do. It might be in the form of a letter, a firm handshake or even a hug from a parent.

Not too long ago I spoke to a military group, and afterwards a young man about 25 years old walked up and shook my hand.

"Mr. Thompson, I doubt if you remember me, but I will never forget you," he said, smiling ear to ear. "You came to our school and told us of the dangers of drugs, and about your life. Because you warned us, I never touched drugs in my life."

Those kinds of accolades are far more rewarding than any trophy, plaque, award or amount of money I have ever received.

Speaking of money, since the Hornets left town, I have primarily made my living as a motivational speaker. My business manager since 1991, Robert Walker, president of Charlotte-based U.S. Sports, keeps me busy with about 50 to 60 speaking engagements a year.

I speak at corporate functions, fundraisers, non-profit and youth groups, and autograph signings.

I'm also involved in several basketball fantasy camps where I get paid handsomely to take middle-aged men to the hole and dunk on them.

People still can't believe it.

"How old are you now?" they ask. Well, I'm chasing the half-century mark, and even though my hops aren't what they used to be, I still have some serious ups for an old man.

The fantasy camps are fun because I get to see old friends like Bobby Jones, George Gervin, Artis Gilmore, Jo Jo White, Darryl Dawkins, Scott Wedman, Otis Birdsong, Sidney Moncrief, Ralph Sampson and Spud Webb.

And I also make a lot of new friends. The camps are mainly composed of men ages 30 to 50 and a few women who were hoops junkies growing up. While they may not have been talented enough to make it to the big time in basketball, most made it big time in the business world, which is good because the camps are not cheap. The bottom line is we have great fun and fellowship.

My life continues to be blessed today, and every day I wake up is a gift from God.

My wife Cathy has a great job with Wachovia Bank in Charlotte as a product assistant. We've been married now for more than 25 years, and like that old cliché says, each year gets better and better.

Our children are a constant source of great joy, and we have seen them grow into wonderful young adults. Erika, now 23, recently graduated with a degree in film studies from my alma mater, NC State. It wasn't easy for the daughter of a legend to go to the same school as her old man, but she handled it just fine. When people found out that she was David Thompson's daughter, they naturally assumed she played basketball. She didn't much care for all the attention, but her pride never wavered when she went into the NC State arena and saw her dad's jersey hanging high from the rafters.

Erika has enrolled in a graduate program in film studies at Full Sail University in Orlando, Florida. She eventually wants to become a filmmaker.

Our baby Brooke, now 21, is studying psychology at UNC-Asheville. Brooke holds a 3.9 GPA and has been an academic honors student her entire college career.

Erika and Brooke aren't the only Thompsons enrolled in an institution of higher education. Decades after I left NC State, I went back to school through a direct studies program. I earned my degree in sociology in 2003.

As I close in on the half-century mark, I can't believe the good fortune God has bestowed upon me—a wonderful wife, two great kids, a fantastic job, a college degree, good health and almost 15 years of sobriety.

I still follow the guidelines of the 12-step program and stay out of sticky places and situations. I don't hang out with anyone who does drugs, and most of my friends are respectful around me and don't drink.

I'm still powerless over drugs and alcohol, but to be honest, it's not that big a deal. I no longer crave those things, and I consider that a miracle by itself.

Of course, none of it would be possible without the watchful hand of the Lord.

It took me years to figure out that all the fame and fortune in the world won't make you happy or give you real peace of mind. When Christ came into my life, my priorities got straightened out and everything just fell into place.

I don't dwell on or long for the past because it's not someplace I want to go again. But I don't regret the past, either. What Christ did was to bring me to my knees so that I could look up at Him again.

One of my favorite Bible verses is Romans 10:13, which says, "Whosoever shall call on the name of the Lord shall be saved."

When the ball was bouncing my way, God was way down on my list of priorities. Every now and then, I'd give Him an occasional bounce pass, but He wasn't my go-to guy. Now that I've turned everything around, all of life's plays must go through Him first.

I'm excited about the next half of my life and eagerly anticipate any new challenges that await me. I truly believe God has many good things in store for me. I'm just waiting for it all to unfold.

Like Philippians 4:13 says, "I can do all things through Christ, who strengthens me."

When I wore shorts and gym shoes to work, the sky was the limit for me. Hopefully this time—knock on wood—I'm not coming down. The Skywalker is still soaring—just in a different arena.

STATISTICS & HIGHLIGHTS

Crest High School

Year	G	FGM-FGA	PCT.	REB.	AVG.	PTS.	AVG.
1968-69	21	137-300	.456	198	9.4	379	18.0
1969-70	22	207-402	.515	360	16.4	590	26.8
1970-71	28	328-608	.539	392	13.7	834	29.2

North Carolina State

Year	G	FGM-FGA	PCT.	REB.	AVG.	PTS.	AVG.
1971-72	16	214-386	.554	217	13.6	569	35.6
1972-73	27	267-469	.569	220	8.1	666	24.7
1973-74	31	325-594	.547	245	7.9	805	26.0
1974-75	28	347-635	.546	229	8.2	838	29.9

Denver Nuggets

Year	G	FGM-FGA	PCT.	REB.	AVG.	PTS.	AVG.
1975-76	83	807-1567	.514	525	6.3	2158	26.0
1976-77	82	824-1626	.506	334	4.1	2125	25.9
1977-78	80	826-1584	.521	390	4.9	2172	27.2
1978-79	76	693-1353	.512	274	3.6	1825	24.0
1979-80	39	289-617	.468	174	4.5	839	21.5
1980-81	77	734-1451	.505	287	3.7	1967	25.5
1981-82	61	313-644	.486	148	2.4	906	14.9

Seattle SuperSonics

Year	G	FGM-FGA	PCT.	REB.	AVG.	PTS.	AVG.
1982-83	75	445-925	.481	222	3.6	1190	15.9
1983-84	19	89-165	.539	44	2.3	240	12.6

Crest (NC) High School (1968-71) Highlights:

•Three-year letter winner
•All-State (1970, 1971)
•All-Conference (1969, 1970, 1971)
•North Carolina Player of the Year (1971)
•MVP, East-West All-Star Game
•Crest High School all-time leading scorer
•Jersey retired
•All-American (1970-71)

North Carolina State University (1971-75) Highlights:

•Three-year letter winner (1973-75)
•World University Games MVP (1973)
•*The Sporting News* national Player of the Year (1975)
•Consensus First-Team All-American (1973, 1974, 1975) by AP, UPI, Eastman, Kodak, *The Sporting News*
•AP National Player of the Year (1974, 1975)
•*Sport* magazine College Basketball Player of the Year (1974)
•UPI Player of the Year (1975)
•Eastman Kodak Award (1975)
•Naismith Award (1975)
•Adolph Rupp Award (1975)
•*Coach & Athlete* magazine Player of the Year (1975)
•Helms Foundation Player of the Year (1974, 1975)
•NABC Player of the Year (1975)
•USBWA Player of the Year (1975)
•Dunlop Player of the Year (1975)
•Sullivan Award finalist (1974, 1975)
•Widely considered the greatest ACC player in history and one of the greatest college players ever
•ACC Player of the Year (1973, 1974, 1975)
•ACC Athlete of the Year (1973, 1975)
•All-ACC First Team (1973, 1974, 1975)
•NC State retired his jersey number 44 (1975)
•Led North Carolina State to the 1974 NCAA championship (30-1 record), 76-64 over Marquette

•In national semifinal win over UCLA, scored 28 points
•In championship game, scored 21 points against Marquette
•MVP, NCAA Tournament (1974)
•Led Wolfpack to a 79-7 record, including 57-1 over two seasons (27-0, 30-1), the best in ACC history
•Scored 2,309 points (26.8 ppg) in 86 varsity games; including highs of 57 points as a senior, 41 as a junior and 40 as a sophomore
•Averaged 35.6 ppg, including a 54-point high on the NC State freshman team
•Grabbed 694 rebounds (8.1 rpg) in 86 games
•Most Valuable Player, Honolulu All-Star game (1975)
•Enshrined in North Carolina Sports Hall of Fame (1982)

ABA Denver Nuggets (1975-76), NBA Denver Nuggets (1976-82), NBA Seattle SuperSonics (1982-84) Highlights:

•Atlanta's first pick in the 1975 NBA draft
•Virginia's first pick in the 1975 ABA draft
•*The Sporting News* ABA Rookie of the Year (1976)
•ABA Rookie of the Year (1976)
•Second Team All-ABA (1976)
•MVP, ABA All-Star Game (1976)
•Colorado Professional Athlete of the Year (1977)
•All-NBA First Team (1977, 1978)
•Scored a career-high 73 points against Detroit (April 9, 1978)
•Scored a then-NBA record 32 points in the second quarter against Detroit, a record that was broken by George Gervin (33 against New Orleans on the same day) when Gervin won the 1978 scoring title with a 63-point output
•Four-time NBA All-Star
•MVP, NBA All-Star Game (1979)
•Only player in history named MVP of both the ABA and NBA All-Star Games
•Scored 2,158 points (26.0 ppg) in the ABA
•Scored 11,264 points (22.1 ppg) in the NBA
•Nuggets retired his jersey number 33 (Nov. 2, 1992)
•Inducted into the Naismith Memorial Basketball Hall of Fame (May 6, 1996)
•*Sport Magazine* Performer of the Year Pro Basketball (1978)

Box Score from
David Thompson's 73-point game

Denver at Detroit on April 9, 1978

Denver	FG	FT	Pts	Detroit	FG	FT	Pts
Jones	2	0-0	4	Carr	10	5-6	25
Wilkerson	1	0-0	2	Shumate	8	4-4	20
Issel	6	2-2	14	Poquette	5	1-2	11
Thompson	28	17-20	73	Money	11	1-1	23
Roberts	5	2-2	12	Ford	8	3-4	19
Ellis	2	1-1	5	Bostic	4	2-5	10
LaGarde	2	3-4	7	Skinner	8	11-11	27
Simpson	4	1-1	9	Price	2	0-0	4
Cook	1	0-0	2				
Calvin	3	1-2	7				
Smith	1	0-0	2				
Totals	55	27-32	137	Totals	56	27-33	139

Denver	42	41	23	31	—	137
Detroit	36	33	35	35	—	139

Fouled out—None.

Total Fouls—Denver 24, Detroit 21.

A—3,482.

Celebrate the Heroes of College Athletics
These Other 2003 Releases from Sports Publishing!

Dick Vitale's Living a Dream
by Dick Vitale with Dick Weiss

• 6 x 9 hardcover
• 275 pages
• 16-page color photo insert
• $24.95

Tyrone Willingham: The Meaning of Victory
by Fred Mitchell

• 8.5 x 11 hardcover
• 144 pages
• color photos throughout
• $24.95

Tales from the Iowa Sidelines
by Ron Maly

• 5.5 x 8.25 hardcover
• 200 pages
• 20-25 photos throughout
• $19.95

Tales from the BYU Sidelines
by Brad Rock

• 5.5 x 8.25 hardcover,
• 200 pages
• caricatures throughout
• $19.95

John Laskowski's Tales from the Hoosier Locker Room
by John Laskowski with Stan Sutton

• 5.5 x 8.25 hardcover
• 184 pages
• 34 photos throughout
• $19.95

Tales of the Magical Spartans
by Fred Stabley, Jr. and Tim Staudt

• 5.5 x 8.25 hardcover
• 200 pages
• 25 photos throughout
• $19.95

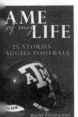

The Game of My Life: 25 Stories of Aggies Football
by Brent Zwerneman

• 6 x 9 hardcover
• 250+ pages
• photos throughout
• $29.95

Paul Keels's Tales from the Buckeyes Championship Season
by Paul Keels

• 5.5 x 8.25 hardcover
• 200+ pages
• 20-25 photos throughout
• $19.95

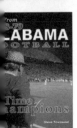

Tales from 1978-79 Alabama Football: A Time of Champions
by Steve Townsend

• 5.5 x 8.25 hardcover
• 200+ pages
• 20-25 photos throughout
• $19.95

Tales from the Maryland Terrapins
by David Ungrady

• 5.5 x 8.25 hardcover,
• 200 pages
• caricatures throughout
• $19.95

To order at any time, please call toll-free **877-424-BOOK (2665)**.
For fast service and quick delivery, order on-line at **www.SportsPublishingLLC.com**.